MILTON STUDIES
55

Laura L. Knoppers
University of Notre Dame
EDITOR

EDITORIAL BOARD

Sharon Achinstein
Johns Hopkins University

Ann Baines Coiro
Rutgers University

Thomas N. Corns
Bangor University, Wales

Mario A. Di Cesare
University of North Carolina, Asheville

Karen L. Edwards
University of Exeter

Stephen M. Fallon
University of Notre Dame

Stanley Fish
Florida International University

Estelle Haan
Queen's University, Belfast

Maggie Kilgour
McGill University

Paul J. Klemp
University of Wisconsin, Oshkosh

Barbara Kiefer Lewalski
Harvard University

David Loewenstein
University of Wisconsin, Madison

Catherine Gimelli Martin
University of Memphis

Stella Revard
Southern Illinois University

John Rogers
Yale University

Jason P. Rosenblatt
Georgetown University

Elizabeth Sauer
Brock University

Nigel Smith
Princeton University

Paul Stevens
University of Toronto

James D. Simmonds
FOUNDING EDITOR, 1967–1991

Albert C. Labriola
EDITOR, 1992–2009

∽ Milton Studies ∽

Volume 55

∽

Edited by Laura L. Knoppers

Duquesne University Press
Pittsburgh, Pennsylvania

Milton Studies is published annually by Duquesne University Press as a forum for Milton scholarship and criticism. Essays submitted for publication may focus on any aspect of John Milton's life and writing, including biography; literary history; Milton's work in its literary, intellectual, political, or cultural contexts; Milton's influence on or relationship to other writers; or the history of critical response to his work.

Manuscripts should conform to *The Chicago Manual of Style* and be approximately 8,000–12,000 words in length. Authors should include a written statement that the manuscript is being submitted exclusively to *Milton Studies*. We encourage electronic submissions in Microsoft Word format, sent to Laura.L.Knoppers.3@nd.edu, followed by one hard copy (printout) of the essay sent by regular mail to Laura L. Knoppers, Editor, *Milton Studies*, Department of English, 356 O'Shaughnessy Hall, University of Notre Dame, Notre Dame, IN 46556.

Milton Studies does not review books.

Within the United States, *Milton Studies* may be ordered from the Duquesne University Press, c/o CUP Services, 750 Cascadilla Street, Box 6525, Ithaca, NY, 14851-6525. Toll free (800) 666-2211.

Copyright © 2014 Duquesne University Press
All rights reserved

Published in the United States of America by
Duquesne University Press
600 Forbes Avenue
Pittsburgh, Pennsylvania 15282

No part of this book may be used or reproduced,
in any manner or form whatsoever,
without written permission from the publisher,
except in the case of short quotations
in critical articles or reviews.

ISSN 0076-8820
ISBN 978-0-8207-0480-7

∞ Printed on acid-free paper

Contents

Preface   vii

Medicine and Science

The Masque and the Matrix: Alice Egerton,
   Richard Napier, and Suffocation of the Mother   3
     BOYD BROGAN

"His Footstep Trace": The Natural Theology
   of *Paradise Lost*   53
     KATHERINE CALLOWAY

Classics for the Contemporary Age

Milton's Tended Garden and the Georgic Fall   89
     SETH LOBIS

Milton's Poetics of Supplication   113
     LEAH WHITTINGTON

Striking a Miltonic Pose: William Jackson's *Lycidas*
   and National Musical Identity   147
     JOHN LUKE RODRIGUE

History, Politics, and Poetics

Satan's Pardon: The Forms of Judicial Mercy
   in *Paradise Lost*   177
     ALISON A. CHAPMAN

Foreign Policy and the Feast Day: Milton's
    Poetic Nativity   207
        ANDREA WALKDEN

"On the New Forcers of Conscience" and Milton's
    Erastianism   237
        MICHAEL KOMOROWSKI

Index   269

Preface

"Poetry makes nothing happen," W. H. Auden famously wrote in his 1939 elegy for William Butler Yeats.[1] This apparent dismissal seems antithetical to Milton's thought and work and perhaps an inauspicious opening to an issue of *Milton Studies* that explores how Milton's poetry engages with medicinal, scientific, political, juridical, and ecclesiastical issues. Yet Auden's pronouncement, in context, reveals a complex view of the relation of art and society that resonates with Milton and with Milton scholarship. The young Auden, newly arrived in America, evaluates the vatic, visionary, politically activist mode that marked not only Yeats's but also his own previous work, qualifying and making more modest claims for what poetry actually can do. The opening stanza of "In Memory of W. B. Yeats" refuses the reassurances of traditional elegy; here is no lamenting nature, no troupe of mourners, not even a grief-stricken speaker. Rather, the poem opens with a clinical, impersonal description of both the frozen city and the absence of the poet: "He disappeared in the dead of winter: / The brooks were frozen, the airports almost deserted, / And snow disfigured the public statues; / The mercury sank in the mouth of the dying day." Far from the pathetic fallacy of nature mourning the death of the poet, the wintry weather seems only a coincidence: "What instruments we have agree / The day of his death was a dark, cold day." The second section addresses Yeats directly. For all of Yeats's activism ("Mad Ireland hurt you into poetry"), nothing much has changed: "Now Ireland has her madness and her weather still." Disenchanted with Yeats's obscure mythologies and flirtation with fascism, Auden critiques as much as lauds his subject.[2] Yet the full force of the stanza moves from seeming negation ("For poetry makes nothing happen") to a new affirmation: "it survives / In the valley of its making...it survives, / A way of happening, a mouth."

Indeed, Auden constructs his anti-elegiac verse by absorbing and reworking earlier elegiac modes and language—including Yeats's own poetry, but also Milton's *Lycidas*.[3] Some of the linguistic revisions are ironic. Milton's day-star that "sinks...in the Ocean bed," has become the "mercury" that "sank in the mouth of the dying day," and his "grim Woolf with privy paw" becomes the "wolves [that] ran on through the evergreen forests," oblivious to the poet's death. But the "Blind mouthes" of *Lycidas* have become a positive way of speaking, poetry as vision. Milton himself, of course, also rejects the natural consolation of the flower-strewn "Laureat Herse" as "false surmise," unable to offer comfort for the unburied Edward King. But while Milton rejects the natural only to move to heavenly apotheosis in pastoral terms—"For *Lycidas* your sorrow is not dead / Sunk though he be beneath the watery floar / So sinks the day-star in the Ocean bed, / And yet anon repairs his drooping head"—Auden does not resurrect the body. If Lycidas has "Sunk low, but mounted high / Through the dear might of him that walk'd the waves," Yeats is and remains dead. But his poetry is alive, remade by his followers, as "the words of a dead man / Are modified in the guts of the living." For Auden, once we recognize poetry as poetry, as text that must be interpreted, it can then take its place in society and in history.

This issue of *Milton Studies* explores how Milton's poetry engages (or is rewritten to engage) precise social, scientific, religious, and political contexts. The contributors also consider and, in some cases, foreground how Milton works out his poetics in history, how Milton's formal, generic, and rhetorical innovations develop in and through his politics. As such, the contributors bring new attention to poetic form and generic innovation, alongside the historicist concerns that have prominently featured in Milton scholarship in recent decades.

Opening our first section, "Medicine and Science," Boyd Brogan considers Milton's *A Maske* in the context of seventeenth century medical understandings of the suffocation of the mother, including the previously unnoticed records of Buckinghamshire physician Richard Napier regarding Alice Egerton, who was being treated for this chastity disease and who would go on to play the role of the Lady. Brogan correlates key features of the Lady's character with suffocation of the mother, reinterpreting Sabrina's ministrations in the context of the "midwife's cure." Katherine Calloway then examines Milton's engagement with seventeenth century science in *Paradise Lost*, arguing that Milton objects to the anthropomorphism of scientific discourse and wants to keep the end of god-knowing in empirical inquiry. In *Paradise Lost*, Adam and Eve's empirical learning is crucially supplemented by divine instruction and includes tracing a divine presence in the natural world.

In our second section, "Classics for the Contemporary Age," Seth Lobis analyzes how Milton engages the georgic mode through the language of "tending," contrasting Adam and Eve's care and stewardship of the garden with Satan's intent to ruin Eden; the narrative of the Fall suggests the fall of genre as well, as georgic gives way to tragedy. In turn, Leah Whittington brings together historicist and literary historical conversations, as she shows how Milton draws upon the classical epic trope of supplication both to contrast the characters of Satan, Adam, Eve, and the Son and to engage seventeenth century debates on idolatry and tyranny. Finally, John Luke Rodrigue explores how Milton himself is rewritten as a classic, as eighteenth century composer William Jackson adapts Milton's *Lycidas* into a musical elegy, identifying himself with Milton as a neglected genius who brings plain-style reform to English verse.

In section 3, "History, Politics, and Poetics," Alison A. Chapman looks at the process and protocols of pardons in *Paradise Lost* in the context of seventeenth century juridical practice, arguing that the divine pardons given to Adam and Eve and withheld from Satan implicitly critique contemporary practices. Andrea Walkden then discusses Milton's early miniature epic, "In quintum Novembris," in the context of the Thirty Years' War and 1620s English fears of invasion, showing how Milton's poetic interest in the phenomenon of the feast day links the Gunpowder Plot poem with the later Nativity ode. Finally, Michael Komorowski redates the sonnet "On the New Forcers of Conscience" to 1645, arguing that the sonnet is a product of the tension between Parliament and the Westminster Assembly and evinces sympathy with the Erastian position of state control of the church as a means of curbing Presbyterian excesses and ensuring liberty of conscience.

W. H. Auden's gnomic utterances and postmodern sense of the poet as interpreter of rather than prophet to a fragmented society obviously differ from Milton. But there are links even in the differences. The third section of "In Memory of W. B. Yeats" shows the kind of action that a poem can undertake. Rhymed verses replace prosaic stanzas in a ceremonial farewell: "Earth, receive an honoured guest; / William Yeats is laid to rest." Poetry and poet are situated in a Europe on the verge of world war: "In the nightmare of the dark / All the dogs of Europe bark / And the living nations wait, / Each sequestered in its hate." The poet is urged to descend into this nightmare, to invoke a new vision after all: "Follow, poet, follow right / To the bottom of the night, / With your unconstraining voice / Still persuade us to rejoice." Some ten years after he had reworked Milton's *Lycidas* in his elegy on Yeats, Auden wrote that Milton was "the first poet in English literature whose attitude toward his art [was]...priestly or prophetic...the most sacred of all human activities. To become a great poet was to become not only superior to other poets but superior to all other men."[4] Auden's vision in his elegy on Yeats is not otherworldly and religious, but it nonetheless offers a transformed understanding and individual renewal. The poet calls up a new kind of Eden ("With the framing of a verse / Make a vineyard of the curse"), a new vision that empowers the individual: "In the deserts of the heart / Let the healing fountain start, / In the prison of his days / Teach the free man how to praise." As such, Auden's words would resonate with Milton. Or, rather, Milton's words resonate in Auden, ultimately demonstrating as well as describing the transformative power of poetry.

As this volume proceeds through production, we have learned the very sad news of the July 2014 passing of Stella Revard, a longtime *Milton Studies* board member and a brilliant, much-loved, and much-respected member of the Milton community. For many of us, Stella was a role model, mentor, and friend. Her cosmopolitanism, classical erudition, love of opera, wit, and generosity will be much missed.

Laura L. Knoppers

Notes

1. "In Memory of W. B. Yeats," in W. H. Auden, *Another Time* (New York, 1940). In revising his originally published elegy, Auden added the now (in)famous line, "For poetry makes nothing happen." For a helpful introduction to recent scholarship on Auden, see the essays in Stan Smith, ed., *Cambridge Companion to W. H. Auden* (Cambridge, 2005) and Tony Sharpe, ed., *W. H. Auden in Context* (Cambridge, 2013).

2. On Auden's disillusionment with Yeats, see Edward Callan, "Disenchantment with Yeats: From Singing-Master to Ogre," in *W. H. Auden*, ed. Harold Bloom (New York, 1986), 161–76.

3. Citations of *Lycidas* are taken from Stella Revard, ed., *John Milton: Complete Shorter Poems* (Oxford, 2012). On Auden's use of earlier elegiac sources, see Rachel Wetzseon, *Influential Ghosts: A Study of Auden's Sources* (New York, 2007), chapter 3. On the reworking of Milton's *Lycidas* in particular, see Edward Mendelson, *Later Auden* (New York, 1999), chapter 1.

4. Quoted in Mendelson, *Later Auden*, 7.

Medicine and Science

The Masque and the Matrix: Alice Egerton, Richard Napier, and Suffocation of the Mother

Boyd Brogan

A widow, 44... in May of 1546 seriously suffered from the suffocation of the mother (*suffocatio uteri*). When she was taken for dead and was lying unconscious, I was urgently called to her. However, it was a case of suffocation because of retained seed (*suffocatio ex semine retento*)... I moved [her own burned hair] constantly before her nostrils for her to smell. Then I gave her feet a painful rubbing.... We also applied bindings to her hips.... In the meantime, because of the urgency of the situation, we asked a midwife to come and apply the following ointment to the patient's genitals, rubbing them inside with her finger.... And thus she was against hope brought back to consciousness. For such titillation with the finger is commended by all physicians... particularly for widows and those who live chastely, and nuns.... However, I am of the opinion that this should only be done in very urgent circumstances after other remedies have failed.

— Pieter van Foreest, *Observationum et curationum medicinalium libri*

A senseless, motionless female patient; a male physician, his techniques exhausted, summons a woman for help.[1] Could a scene of this kind—a typical example of the early modern womb disease known as suffocation of the mother—have inspired the puzzling sequence of events that closes John Milton's *A Maske Presented at Ludlow Castle, 1634*? Such a possibility may seem unlikely. How could Milton possibly have risked even the most stylized of depictions of the Earl of Bridgewater's daughter undergoing this kind of treatment—a treatment that van Foreest, like many of his contemporaries, clearly believes to be a kind of therapeutic masturbation?

Other parallels are numerous, however; while recent criticism has sometimes taken it as axiomatic that an unconscious woman in an early modern drama must be suffering from this ailment, few such dramas fit the description as closely as *A Maske*. Previous studies have noted Milton's claustrophobic womb imagery, and discovered references to menstruation or the early modern notion of "female seed."[2] Suffocation of the mother, thought to be caused when seed or menses were unhealthily retained within the womb, or "matrix," offers a point at which these independent suggestions may converge. This was also a disease that had been known for centuries to be "without any possible doubt...caused by chastity"[3]—the virtue to which Milton's Lady is famously committed—and which became particularly well known in England in the early seventeenth century. Two of its features were especially notorious: its similarity to the effects of witchcraft and the deathlike paralysis that constituted its most famous symptom. These points resonate with critical debates about whether the Lady's immobilization is caused by Comus's "numbing spell," or somehow self-inflicted.[4] A subtext of *suffocatio* can also make sense of why Sabrina is necessary: once the paralysis has taken hold it requires a therapy that only a woman can perform.

As van Foreest's closing words of caution suggest, that therapy could be controversial. But this essay will propose that in 1630s England the controversy may have receded. Cases of "the mother" were thought to be unusually frequent in this period, increasing the potential demand for this remedy of last resort. From 1625, moreover, a very different interpretation to van Foreest's was available. On this account, there was nothing sexual about what I will refer to for convenience, in the absence of any standard early modern term, as the "midwife's cure." Aimed merely at opening the cervix to release toxins from the affected womb, it was a humane and medically vital procedure derived from a standard obstetric technique. Assertions to the contrary were anatomically ignorant and associated with "silly superstitious Papists."[5] By 1634 the midwife's cure may have become an accepted part of the medical repertoire, so that its dramatic representation required little more than the entry of a female healer to take charge of proceedings.

The larger point in the context of *A Maske*, however, is that chastity was something that might need curing. Suffocation of the mother was not the only disease of chastity with which early moderns were familiar: greensickness, "women's melancholy," and others helped to establish sexual abstinence as pathological, especially (though not exclusively) for women. The concept behind such diseases was not new,[6] but in the early seventeenth century they underwent a resurgence of interest.

It is here that the key difference between the interpretation that will be proposed and previous readings of *A Maske* is located. The critical debates on the ethical significance of the Lady's chastity are well known. Psychoanalytically minded scholars have found it damagingly self-denying; others have celebrated the Lady's resistance to a threatened rape.[7] Medical contexts throw a different light on both these contentions. Chastity in *A Maske* is problematic, not for the twentieth century psycho-ethical reason that it is suppressing the Lady's desire, but for the seventeenth century physiological one that it is making her ill. Her character's moral stature, in turn, derives not only from her resistance to Comus, but from her willingness to endure illness for her chastity's sake.

Basing these contentions on textual parallels might seem ambitious, but such parallels are not all that links suffocation of the mother to *A Maske*. In 1632, Alice Egerton, who would go on to play the role of the Lady, was diagnosed with this disease by the

Buckinghamshire physician Richard Napier. Her extensive records in Napier's casebooks show that her symptoms began in March of that year and continued at least until May of 1633. Though in 1970 Barbara Breasted found the key to them, in the shape of a letter to Napier discussing Alice's condition,[8] these records have not previously been described.

They do not, in themselves, prove *A Maske*'s medical theme. One might advance an argument similar to John Creaser's on the Castlehaven scandal: such a delicate illness, suffered so recently, was the last thing Milton was likely to write about. I will close with some suggestions as to how and why such a theme might have been chosen, a choice unlikely to have been Milton's.[9] It is worth noting at this point, however, that the correspondences suggested here are more central and obtrusive than the Castlehaven hints that scholars have detected. There is nothing implicit about the theme of a work for which, as Christopher Kendrick suggests, *The Masque of Chastity* would make a plausible title.[10] Alice Egerton suffered from a disease caused by sexual abstinence a year before she performed its leading role. If Milton wanted to avoid recalling this fact he would have had to pick a different topic altogether.

But there may have been no reason to avoid it; one thing a chastity disease might be seen to do, after all, was to demonstrate its victim's chastity. Scholars of both Milton and the Bridgewaters are fortunate that when Alice fell ill with what would prove to be just such a complaint, her care was entrusted to a physician whose casebooks were carefully preserved by his admirer Elias Ashmole.[11] It is to the Egerton entries in those casebooks that I will now turn.

Alice Egerton's Illness

On October 15, 1632, Robert Napier wrote a letter to his physician uncle on behalf of the Countess of Bridgewater. The letter conveyed the countess's fears that her daughter Alice, a patient of Richard Napier's, might be suffering the effects of witchcraft. This letter, transcribed in Breasted's article, has long been known to Miltonists. What has not been realized is its place in a much larger sequence of events preserved in Richard Napier's casebooks.

Early modern medical relationships were rarely straightforward, one-to-one encounters between physician and patient,[12] but the Napiers and Egertons became particularly intertwined. Napier also treated Alice's older sisters, Magdalen and Penelope, as well as their servant Mrs. Quicke and her daughter. But he initially became their physician through the offices of his nephew Robert, who married Penelope at some point between February 6, 1632, when Napier cast an astrological figure to consider whether the marriage would take place, and October of the same year, when in the letter discovered by Breasted he passed his new wife's best wishes to his uncle.[13] Robert's role as an intermediary between Napier and his new Egerton patients coincides with the period in which this marriage was arranged. He first contacted Napier about a "kell," or membrane, in Magdalen's eye, which had left her "almost blynd," in a note received on January 16, 1632 (212/394). He wrote again on behalf of both Magdalen and Alice that September (416/416–17), but the letter of October 15 that followed was the last to concern itself with this topic. After this date, with his marriage now secured, Robert ceased to write on the Egerton girls' behalf, this role being taken up by Mrs. Quicke.

Napier marked his record of his nephew's letter of January 16 "sine consensu," a standard phrase denoting that the patient herself was unaware that her ailment had been brought to the physician's attention.[14] In March, however, Alice also fell sick, and by September 9 parental "consent" to Napier's treatment of both Egerton daughters had been obtained. On that date Napier received from his nephew what seems to have been a more formal, comprehensive letter, sent "by the entreaty of the Countes," detailing both Alice's and Magdalen's health problems. Napier recorded the main points in this letter over a page and a half, an unusually large amount of space, which suggests the significance of his being officially requested to treat these distinguished patients (416/416–17).

It was standard practice for an astrological figure—a square divided into 12 sections known as "houses"—to be drawn up for each consultation.[15] At the center of the first figure that Napier cast in response to his nephew's description of their symptoms, under the words "Quaerit^r de causa morbo[r]u[m]...Magdalenae

Bridgwater Edgerton [asking the cause of the diseases of Magdalen Egerton]," he wrote "Struma," a term for scrofula, or "king's evil";[16] he repeated this in two subsequent consultations, on November 2, 1632, and March 29 the following year (214/118, 214/407).

Magdalen had been "6 y[ears] troubled" with the disfiguring facial swellings that characterized this illness, which had worsened slightly in the past two months. It had begun "after the smale pox," a disease that often led to chronic ill health.[17] As well as continuing difficulties with her sight ("eys darke," Napier tersely recorded), she was suffering from "melancholick ill" and had never menstruated, resulting in "a full pletherick body." Traditional remedies for king's evil — "An Angle [i.e., Angel; a coin] fro[m] king Jams & also this king"[18] — had been unsuccessful. Other treatments to date had included six "issues" (therapeutic incisions or sores), two each in her neck, arms, and feet, repeated bloodletting from hands, arms, and feet, and "leaches at her lips & thighs & fundament." She had also received the usual rounds of "purges pils dyet drinks," the potential hazards of which are indicated by a later note describing the effects of one of Napier's own "vomyte[s]" on her sister: it "rought excedingly," leaving Alice "very sicke" (214/323).

As this incident shows, Napier's care proved no gentler. At one point he prescribed a stock of "40 Leaches for sundry tymes" (211/512); when her condition worsened he recommended "4 leaches to the emrod [haemorrhoid] vaynes" (1488/213). She was to sleep with "the bloody p[ar]te" of a halved pigeon pressed to the soles of her feet, and the other half resting against her neck (1488/213). Other methods included clysters — medicines injected into the rectum — and "Blystering playsters," designed, like the "issues," to create lesions through which the plethoric humours could find an outlet (211/512, 211/521). At one point, following the countess's unilateral decision to place her on a strict diet, even Napier became concerned about his patient's ability to withstand her treatments (214/225). Most of them were administered at home, probably by Mrs. Quicke, who wrote to Napier on February 8, 1633, to ask "when she may apply the Leaches to Lady Magdalen" (214/302).

Alice's condition was even more distressing: for the previous six months she had experienced frequent convulsions, apparently sometimes as many as 20 a day. She also had pain in her right side, and unlike her sister was "very leane" (416/416). Napier's assessment of her symptoms' severity may be indicated by the figures he cast for this entry. Initially his focus appears to have been on Magdalen: both girls' names, ages, and symptoms were recorded in separate columns on the left-hand page, but there is only one figure, marked 8:25 a.m., which is under Magdalen's name and contains her diagnosis. Alice's column looks like something of an afterthought. On the facing page, however, Napier wrote out Alice's details a second time and cast a new figure beneath them, marked 8:45 a.m. (416/417).[19] The decision to cast this second figure for Alice alone may suggest Napier's growing concern as he reflected on her condition.

As with her sister's, the nature of Alice's illness seemed clear. Her entry begins "Mother. a great rising up her throate wth a great swelling," the classic choking symptom from which the name "suffocation of the mother" was thought to derive.[20] Beneath this, Napier noted "hath had it the mother wth convuls[ive] fits halfe a yere 20 fits in a day." The second astrological figure, which he cast for Alice alone, has "the mother" written through its center. Later, on October 1, he received a urine sample from Alice; this entry displays a figure with "matricis suffocatio [suffocation of the matrix]" written through it (214/49).

In spite of Napier's efforts, Alice's symptoms continued. On September 20, "The Lady Alice had 2 fitts" (214/31); on February 8 the following year, Mrs. Quicke inquired "whether the [Lady] Alice sh[ould] take any thing to prev[ent] her fitts before the spri[ng]" (214/302); and on the 21st of the same month Napier recorded that "ye Lady Alice had some sad fits fortnight since" (214/323). Napier may also have had suffocation of the mother in mind when on May 14, 1633, he prescribed a clyster for Alice's "gryping in her belly," and advised, "let her smell to her pomander" when "occasion" required it (1488/215). "Gnawing in the stomacke" was a symptom often considered to warn of an approaching mother-fit, and scent therapy was traditionally associated with it.[21] During the first of what were to be two spells of treatment in residence at Napier's practice at Great Linford, on October 22, 1632, Alice and Magdalen were visited by a "Lady Tyringha[m]" (214/76). This is likely to have been Anne Tyringham, whom Napier was also treating for chronic mother-fits around this time.[22] Her visit may have offered an opportunity to sympathize with a fellow sufferer.

This first Linford visit lasted from around October 12 to November 6, 1632; the undescribed letter that Napier received from the Countess of Bridgewater on October 8 was probably arranging it (214/60). Arrival on or before October 12 is suggested by the fact that on this date Mrs. Quicke received her first consultation (214/68); Robert Napier's letter of October 15 also twice notes that she is "now wth you." Prescriptions for Alice and Magdalen dated November 1 are headed "when they are to goe home" (214/116), and on the sixth, "The Lady Magdalen & the Lady Alice ther wth Mr Cartwright & M^r williams went to Astridg wth Rich & Mr Rudle" (214/122). "Astridg" seems a misspelling of Ashridge, the Egertons' estate. "Rich" is likely to be Robert Napier's younger brother, also called Richard Napier, and also a physician; he regularly helped out at his uncle's practice, which he inherited in 1634. Ralph Ruddle was Napier's medical assistant from 1628. I have not been able to identify Cartwright, but it is just possible that "M^r williams" could be William Gadesden, another assistant.[23] This was a medically competent escort for patients whose health probably remained fragile; a note headed with Magdalen's name on November 1 inquires "wheath^r I can doe her good" (214/118), and again observes "struma in collo" (scrofula of the neck), although her urine was described as "good wth white dregs & a great sediment." Other entries during this stay record a recipe (October 14) and astrological figure (November 3) for Magdalen (214/72, 214/120) and a second consultation, on October 30, for Mrs. Quicke.

The second visit, which was about twice as long, probably began on March 28, 1633, when Napier noted that "the 2 ladys came to me" (214/405); he used a similar phrase to describe Alice and

Magdalen elsewhere (214/146), and the following day's entry for Magdalen states that she "was p[re]sent" (214/407). It finished on or near May 14, when unusually extended instructions for both girls' continued treatment include a "purging dyet Ale" for Alice to be administered "in the same manner as her ladyship tooke it here with us at Linford." These notes also inform their recipient (probably Mrs. Quicke) that "you have thre ounces of co[m]fortable lozenges to give unto the lady Alice," with instructions for dosage (1488/215–[16]).

Witchcraft or *Suffocatio?*

It was during the first of these two stays at Linford, on October 15, 1632, that the letter describing the suspected witchcraft arrived. In it, Robert Napier explained that "the strangenesse of my Lady Alices fitts"[24] was such that it had caused her mother to wonder whether, rather than stemming from a "natural Cause," they might not be due to "the malediction of some evill disposed bodye." The suspect was uncomfortably close to home: it was "on[e] Quicke the husband of the gentlewoman who waytes upon the Ladyes." Though separated from his wife, Mr. Quicke evidently remained a disruptive presence on the fringes of the Egerton household. The letter described him as a "lewd...wicked fellowe" who was vocally hostile to both his estranged wife and her employer, despite being himself "maintayned by the countesse upon charitye." Witchcraft accusations often stemmed from this kind of uneasily dependent relationship, though it was unusual for them to be directed toward a man.[25] It was feared that Alice might not have been his first victim; Mrs. Quicke herself had previously been "strangely handled wth a sicknesse," which her husband was thought to have magically provoked (1730/f.251r).

Napier's record of his first consultation with Mrs. Quicke, three days before he received this letter and hence not influenced by it, does not mention witchcraft, but it confirms that she was experiencing "mutch greefe...Intolerable greefe[.]greefe for her husb: a naughty husb"; a note below this, which might also refer to another patient, states, "full of melanch[oly] & greefe & was mopish" (214/68).²⁶ She also had more straightforwardly physical symptoms: "head ill shooting [pain] head hart & backe" (214/106), though apparently nothing that suggested magic. The sympathetic tone suggested by these notes may have won Mrs. Quicke's trust: she returned for two more consultations and expressed a wish to bring her daughter to see Napier, which she eventually did on April 23 the following year. On that date, Napier noted that "yong marg. Quick" had "gravell" in her urine and suffered from fits during which she "useth to cast [vomit]" (211/58); her mother had an "obstruct[ion] of the splene fu[m]ing up to her head" (211/55), probably implying that her melancholy continued.²⁷

Napier's response to the concerns expressed in his nephew's letter remains uncertain. In a passing reference to the entry that records its receipt, Michael MacDonald asserts that the astrological figure it contains "testified to the truth of [the countess's] fears."²⁸ MacDonald may have felt able to conclude this purely from the astrological symbols (though, if so, his reasoning is not disclosed); however, outside of this possibility the notes here do not appear to show Napier reaching such a conclusion. The figure in question is headed "Utru[m] suspicio ven.[eficium] sit vera [whether the suspected witchcraft is true]"²⁹—a question that probably embraced Mrs. Quicke's symptoms as well as Alice's—but it records nothing beyond this; the question is asked, but no answer has been written (214/75). It seems likely, however, that MacDonald was recalling subsequent entries that, while less definite than he implies, do suggest that Napier lent at least some level of credence to the countess's suspicions.

Napier's attitude to witchcraft was neither uniformly credulous nor skeptical. He regularly treated it, using charms and prayers to do so; but there were also a number of cases in which, like his predecessor Edward Jorden, he concluded that such suspicions were mistaken and a "natural Cause" was at work. The dividing line was not necessarily clear. Many witchcraft treatments were designed to be effective against natural diseases as well, and normal medicines could still be of use even if the illness was thought to have been brought on by magic.³⁰

The majority of the case notes for Alice, Magdalen, and Mrs. Quicke, both before and after the October 15 letter, suggest that Napier felt he was dealing with problems of natural origin. There are three exceptions. In the entry of November 1, 1632, headed "when they are to goe home," recipes for "vomyts" and a "dyet drink" are followed by the words "a Ring for the Lady Alice & a pomander of [tin][31] for the Lady Magd on Sunday next"; on May 14, 1633, as noted, Alice was instructed to "smell to her pomander" if she experienced the "gryping" stomach pain that could signal an approaching mother-fit; and on May 25, Mrs. Quicke inquired "wheath[er] she shall have a new sig.[il] the old being wasted" (214/116, 1488/215, 211/172).

Sigils were metal emblems inscribed with astrological symbols. They were among Napier's standard treatments for witchcraft, and the ring and pomander are likely to have been similarly intended: pomanders, decorative containers filled with aromatics and worn around the neck, were primarily medicinal, but they could also function as sigils.[32] It seems possible that in the November 11 entry the recipients' names have been accidentally transposed, since on May 14 the pomander is referred to in connection with Alice. Since suffocation of the mother was a disease in which natural and supernatural causes were particularly hard to distinguish, and since scent therapy was a traditional remedy for the first and sigils for the second, a pomander might be a useful way of addressing both possibilities. Given the lack of other supernatural implications in Napier's records of these cases, it seems likely that these items were dispensed as concessions to his patients' concerns, rather than reflecting any positive conviction of his own that their illnesses were caused by witchcraft. The fact that two of these entries are dated seven months after the October 15 letter, however, shows that those concerns persisted.

The suspected witchcraft was at the center of the wider tensions to which Alice's case gave rise. The Egertons were used to coping with Magdalen's ill health. But not only did a second daughter's illness double this burden, it also exacerbated the countess's existing difficulties with Mr. Quicke, whose marriage to her daughters' personal attendant evidently made him a difficult person to get rid of. By October 1632 her concerns about him were already playing on the countess's mind; the matter "hath bin often in my Ladyes thoughts," Robert Napier reported. They seem also to have damaged her trust in his wife, regardless of their estrangement, since the October 15 letter also made a point of conveying her wishes for Napier "to conceale this letter, and particularly from M^rs: Quicke" (1730/f.251r). Given Mrs. Quicke's prominent role in caring for Alice and Magdalen, this must have been a difficult situation. Her husband's hostility was already causing her "Intolerable greefe," compounded by her own daughter's poor health. But she was not the only member of the Egerton household burdened with a mixture of sickness and depression: in September 1632 Magdalen had "melancholick ill" (416/416), and the following March she was still suffering from "heavy sad melanch[oly]" (214/407). Ashridge in these years was not an easy place to be.

"Well Without...Physick"

Despite his apparent willingness to treat all possible causes of the Egerton daughters' illnesses, there were early indications that the effectiveness of Napier's methods might be in doubt. As noted, at the end of the first Linford visit, the question "wheath^r I can doe her good" appears in relation to Magdalen. This was a standard query in astrological medicine, and one that was commonly posed by the patient herself,[33] but coming at this stage it does not suggest that things were going to plan.

The month after the girls had returned home, on December 15, Magdalen had a facial swelling, though it responded to treatment (214/225). As mentioned, Alice's fits returned in February (when she was also made "very sicke" by one of Napier's purging drinks), and again in May. But in February Magdalen also fell sick once more: after "taking her strong purg[ing] pils 2 or 3 days," she menstruated, possibly for the first time, but immediately afterwards "her face swelled & was ill." The arrival of "terms" had not solved her problems (214/323). The following month, during the girls' second stay at Linford, she was suffering from bouts of "flushing heate" (1488/213), about which Napier seemed particularly concerned. On April 28, he asked the stars "utru[m] lady Magdalen unqua[m] recuperabit salute[m] [whether Lady Magdalen will ever recover health]" (211/78).

Doubts such as these appear ultimately to have led the countess to assert her own authority over her daughters' health care. This may have seemed neither inappropriate nor entirely unexpected; female patients and their families routinely expected to have considerable say in determining a course of treatment, and "household physic" was often preferred to professional medicine.[34] The tug-of-war began on December 12, 1632, when Napier learned that "The Countes would debar her [Magdalen] of her supp[er]s," a treatment he thought "would be grievous unto her" (214/225). Six months later, the countess again attempted to impose this kind of regime: on June 28, Napier recorded "M[ist]res Quicke utru[m] expediat [whether beneficial] D[omi]nae Magd to abstayne fro[m] supp[er] & to drink water" (211/271). The phrasing suggests that a doubtful Mrs. Quicke had asked for guidance on the potential dangers of the countess's intentions. Despite, or perhaps because of, the effects his own medicines had had on these fragile patients in the past, Napier's opinion of this "grievous" course seems to have remained unchanged, but he was on difficult ground. The next two days' entries contain prescriptions for drinks for Magdalen that are specified, unusually, as "not purg[in]g but corrob[or]at[in]g," or strengthening, and "corroborative ye Animall & vitall parts." The accompanying recommendation to "Let her suppers be during this tyme of bisket bread & reasons [raisins] ye summe," softened by the advice "once in 2 or 3 dayes to take an Sauce before such a slight supper," suggests Napier was playing along with the countess's regimen in an attempt to mitigate it without openly defying her (211/510, 211/513).

If so, however, the diplomacy was in vain, since on August 8 Napier recorded Mrs. Quicke's report that not only had Magdalen "bene forced to use fast... the Countes hath made the lady Magd to keepe an exact dyet & fasting," but also that she "hath abstaynd fro[m] the use of any p[re]scribed by me"; somewhat tactlessly, the letter added that she "semeth to be mutch better for it" and was now "mutch amended." Alice was similarly "well wthout taking any physick"; this is her last mention in the casebooks (211/364). Confusingly, Napier also writes here "craveth a masse of my pils," which seems odd given that his expertise was apparently being rejected, but it might have been Mrs. Quicke who personally expressed this wish. She wrote to Napier again on September 27 and October 25, 1633. The record of the first of these, much of which is lost in the binding, appears to read, "the Earle of Bridgewater and his lady would send their coach"; the second notes only the receipt of "her Letter in the Behalfe of the Lady Magdalen" (211/476, 412/f. 15^r).

This last entry, in October 1633, is the final time that either of the youngest Egerton sisters is named in Napier's records. Were their recoveries complete? The year 1633 also saw Magdalen's wedding to Gervase Cutler,[35] and this may simply have removed her to the care of a new physician, but Alice remained at home. Though the countess seems to have lost faith in him, Napier's death on April 1, 1634, meant that his medical practice passed to his nephew Richard Napier the younger. This Richard Napier was also an Egerton confidante, and his relationship with the countess may have been stronger than his uncle's. Robert's October 15 letter observes that his brother was the first person with whom she had discussed the suspected witchcraft (1730/f. 251^r); although it is just possible that some other brother is referred to, this seems likely to mean Richard. The association seems to have continued, since on October 13, 1635, Robert wrote to Richard "concerneing the Lady Bridgewater" (177/f. 24^r); the countess, who died five months later, may already have been sick. It seems likely, then, that Frances Egerton might have again sought help from Great Linford if her youngest daughter's illness had recurred, but this does not seem to have happened; though the younger Richard seamlessly continued his uncle's casebooks, Alice does not reappear. After August 1633 she appears to have been cured.[36]

Suffocation of the Mother

What was the nature of the disease from which Alice Egerton suffered, and why is it relevant to Milton's drama? Suffocation of the mother—alternative terms include "fits of the mother" and "strangulation of the womb," or matrix[37]—was by no means an early modern invention; well known to medieval physicians, it had been an established part of the medical repertoire for centuries.[38] The numerousness of seventeenth century vernacular descriptions in print, however, may indicate something beyond this period's general enthusiasm for the Englishing of medical knowledge.[39] At least seventeen such descriptions were published between 1583 and 1671, five of them in or prior to 1634,[40] and the fact that Robert Burton's contribution to this list was added only in the third, 1628 edition of the *Anatomy* suggests a growth in interest in the years leading up to *A Maske*. (Though Burton claims to be discussing a condition that is similar but distinct, the similarities are strong enough to justify its inclusion here, as I will discuss). A further two such accounts appeared shortly after its first performance, in 1636 and 1637.[41] Milton himself, of course, could have drawn directly on the Latin works from which these treatises derived,[42] but they indicate that by 1634 a wider audience, including women, might be expected to share in the textual knowledge of an illness which at the time was thought to be unusually prevalent; in 1633 it had been described as "such a disease in our days."[43] Similar ailments had also featured in two newly printed plays, Brome's *Northern Lasse* (1632) and Fletcher and Shakespeare's *Two Noble Kinsmen* (1634).

Some of this notoriety derived from suffocation of the mother's supposed resemblance to witchcraft. This was first suggested in print by Edward Jorden in 1603, following his defense, on this basis, of the suspected witch in the case of a 13-year-old girl named Mary Glover. Jorden's thesis gained publicity with the circulation of two works refuting his interpretation of Glover's symptoms,[44] and it was restated by Helkiah Crooke in 1615 and Burton in 1628. It fades from later accounts, but in 1632 the Countess of Bridgewater's dilemma—was Alice suffering from the "natural Cause" of *suffocatio*, or the "malediction" of a witch?—was very much of its time.

As virtually every contemporary account observes, suffocation of the mother was caused by retention of either menstrual blood or "seed." The latter refers to semen; not, importantly, as deposited by the male partner during sex, but that produced by the woman herself, a belief that remained standard throughout at least the first half of the century, and is taken for granted even in such later texts as Jane Sharp's *Midwives Book* (1671). Though recent studies often ignore it, it was seed that was thought to give rise to the most severe symptoms;[45] hence, van Foreest's apprehension on realizing that he was dealing with a case of *suffocatio ex semine retento*, as well as the common insistence that "to see them...married to good husbands in due time" offers "the best and surest remedy of all" by facilitating regular sexual intercourse.[46] The causes of suffocation of the mother were thus entirely physiological rather than psychological, making the common conflation with modern "hysteria" misleading.[47]

The retained substance, whether blood or seed, would corrupt, giving off poisonous vapors. These had been an important development in the conceptualization of the disease, and their role was often emphasized: in 1670 one description referred to suffocation of the mother simply as "the Vapours."[48] The symptoms they caused were notably diverse,[49] but the choking sensation and convulsions Alice Egerton experienced were typical; others included refusal of food and drink, raving or angry speech, and changes in facial coloring. The most distinctive and consistently described symptom, however, was a paralysis that resembled death so closely that women were supposedly buried or even autopsied while still alive.[50] The paralysis could also be deadly on its own account: though "Many doe recover," Philip Barrough observed in 1583, "many againe doe perishe sodainely in the very fit, or at the least way within fewe houres after" (150). Nothing in Alice Egerton's case notes suggests she ever experienced such paralysis herself—though an example recorded by the physician John Hall suggests "convulsion" could imply it[51]—but for a dramatist it would have offered a usefully recognizable symbol.

A passage in *The Doctrine and Discipline of Divorce* (1643-44) shows that Milton was familiar with chastity diseases a decade after his Egerton commission, when he posited them as an explanation for the "fanatick dreams" of sectaries. Here Milton implies that such people often set out with a sincere "zeal of Religion" that leads them to practice sexual abstinence, even within the legitimate context of marriage ("restraint of some lawfull liberty"). But this results in madness of the kind that suffocation of the mother typically produces: "As by Physick we learn in menstruous bodies, where nature's current hath been stopt...the suffocation and upward forcing of some lower part [produces]...dotage and idle fancies."[52] The suggestion, which Milton is too delicate to state directly, is that retained seed may have similarly toxic effects in men, a less common but not unheard-of idea. *A Maske*'s medical references are both more pervasive and less direct, but Comus's allusion to the Lady's "melancholy blood" (*A Maske* 809), which comes at a key moment in the drama, may be related to the "suffocation" that occurs in "menstruous bodies."

A link between melancholy and suffocation of the mother was suggested in the 1628 edition of the *Anatomy of Melancholy*, in which Burton inserts a new discussion of an ailment called "Maides, Nunnes, and Widowes melancholy," which is described as "like fits of the mother" and "hard to distinguish" from them.[53] Early moderns were aware of a range of chastity diseases with broadly similar features, but the relationship between suffocation of the mother and Burton's "Maides...melancholy"—for convenience I will refer to it as women's melancholy—seems especially close. They shared causation by blood or seed, generation of poisonous vapors, resemblance to witchcraft, and cure by marriage; only the paralysis was missing. Though women's melancholy is introduced as a disease of older women, halfway through his discussion Burton appears to include younger victims, possibly showing the Glover case's influence. Like Milton in *The Doctrine and Discipline of Divorce*, he also suggests that chastity diseases can affect men.[54]

The affinities Burton posited would have been rendered plausible by similarities in the way both conditions were thought to operate. According to Timothie Bright, melancholy occurred when "the grosser part of the bloud...surchargeth the bodie, and yeeldeth up to the braine certaine vapors."[55] At least one author describes the vapors emitted by retained seed as similarly melancholic: William Vaughan discusses a male patient who was cured when "by...carnall copulation the vaporous fumes of the seede are taken away...which doe infect his braine, and lead him into melancholy."[56] Since *suffocatio* was also caused by "vapours" given off when menstrual blood or seed surcharged the body, the connection was there to be made.

Witchcraft was another point of contact. Reginald Scot's *Discoverie of Witchcraft* offered a precedent for Jorden's medical explanation for bewitchment; rather than referring to suffocation of the mother as such, however, it describes witches as suffering from delusions caused by postmenopausal retention of what he calls "their monethlie *melancholike* flux or issue of bloud."[57] Burton may have been influenced by both Scot and Jorden in this respect, since victims of women's melancholy similarly imagine themselves to be "forespoken or bewitched...they see visions, conferre with spirits and divels." Two later discussions of "Melancholy of Virgins and Widdows" or "Melancholy proceeding from the Matrix," along lines very similar to Burton's, also describe victims who "think they see Ghosts" or have "a conceit that they are talking with Angels."[58] Melancholy and suffocation of the mother converged around this shared propensity to make their victims appear bewitched.

A comparable uncertainty presents itself in the case of the Lady's immobilization. Is this "numbing" caused by a "spell"? The Attendant Spirit thinks so, and Comus has threatened it (*A Maske* 558–61), but the moment at which his threat is carried out is unclear. And Comus himself seems to raise the issue immediately before the paralysis occurs. He "fear[s] /...some superior power" is prompting the Lady's speeches, a possibility that briefly drenches him in "cold shuddering dew" (799–801), but then reassures himself by substituting a medical explanation: "'tis but the lees / And settlings of a melancholy bloud" (808–09). Like Jorden's treatise, these lines reinterpret behavior that could imply supernatural activity in medical terms.

In an important article in the *Review of English Studies* in 1990, B. J. Sokol suggests that these "lees" might be menstrual, though he is unable to cite an example of the word itself being used in this context.[59] The term that best supports his hypothesis, however, might be "melancholy." "Lees" was commonly used to describe melancholy, that "grosser parte of bloud";[60] and "melancholy blood," in turn, could refer to menses. Of the two examples I have found, one refers directly to suffocation of the mother, and the other is concerned with a similar complaint. The latter is Scot's description of "witches" whose delusions are caused by stoppage of "their monethlie melancholike flux or issue of bloud." The former occurs in *The Compleat Midwifes Practice*, whose publication in 1656 admittedly postdates *A Maske*; it describes how menses (rather than seed) can be identified as the causal agent if the patient's "courses" are "mingled with a melancholy blood."[61] "Lees /...of a melancholy blood" could thus describe the toxic menses that formed one of the two possible causes of *suffocatio*, a disease that lent its victims the appearance of having been struck by a "superior power." As they waver between medical and supernatural causes for the Lady's behavior, Comus's lines are framing the paralysis that is about to occur in the terms of the standard question to which a case of *suffocatio* was likely to give rise: disease or witchcraft?

There is a natural temptation to derive moments such as this from the sensational accusations in Robert Napier's letter. But the letter's overriding concern, as Breasted observes, is secrecy. The countess was aware of the explosive nature of its contents: "she would not...harbour any such thought carelessly" and was careful to pass on her instructions for Napier to keep them to himself (1730/f.251ʳ). Henry Lawes could have got wind of her fears and indiscreetly passed them on to Milton, but she would hardly have tolerated a drama based on them. *A Maske* owes its magical setting to the Neoplatonic stylings of its genre rather than the suspicions of *maleficium* in the Egerton household, and more specific inferences, such as Comus's uncertainty in these lines, are likely to originate with the emphasis in medical accounts on womb diseases' similarity to witchcraft. Such accounts also may have played a role in the development of the countess's concerns; once Napier had diagnosed suffocation of the mother, a disease so easily confused with "malediction," it could have opened or strengthened the possibility that it might really be the latter that was at work. Frances Egerton's fears resemble those expressed by Comus because they share a source in the medical literature of the early seventeenth century.

Chastity Diseases in *A Maske*

That literature defined suffocation of the mother as a disease of sexual abstinence, and paralysis as its gravest symptom. After refusing Comus's sexual advances, the Lady becomes paralyzed: like "a statue," she is "fixed, and motionless," caught in a "numbing spell" which only Sabrina can "thaw" (*A Maske* 660, 818, 852). The Elder Brother seems inadvertently to anticipate this when he describes how the virgin Minerva "freezed her foes to congealed stone" with "rigid looks of chaste austerity" (448–49). His confidence is misplaced, since it is the virgin herself who becomes frozen; but the speech does establish a connection between chastity and a force that paralyzes. The language of numbing, congealing, and freezing is significant here. Jorden described how one sufferer had "all her sences benummed," and noted that "in this disease of the mother...the parts are benummed or do not feele at all"; it resembled "a *Stifnesse* or *congelation* of the body, wherein they lie like an image in the same forme they were taken." "Image" here has its predominant early modern meaning of "statue" (*OED* 1.a). Jorden's opponent Stephen Bradwell also repeatedly described Mary Glover, whom Jorden had diagnosed with suffocation of the mother, as "stiffe and congealed...congealed stiffe," and "colde and stiffe as a frozen thing."[62] Though Bradwell disputed Jorden's medical explanation, as in Alice Egerton's case the disagreement centered on the cause of the symptoms rather than the symptoms themselves.

Paralysis was the most serious consequence of chastity diseases, but it was not the only one. As has been seen, victims of Burtonian "women's melancholy," an illness closely related to suffocation of the mother, were thought to experience imaginary visions of, or conversations with, spirits, ghosts, or angels. Something like this occurs when the Lady addresses the virtues—"hovering angel girt with golden wings, /...I see ye visibly" (*A Maske* 213–15)—a moment recalled in the Elder Brother's description of the "thousand liveried angels" that appear to the chaste "in...solemn vision," allowing them "oft converse with heavenly habitants" (454–58).

For Burton, such visions formed part of a more general tendency toward "perverse conceipts" and "preposterous judgement." Victims were also "apt to loath, dislike, disdaine," a symptom Jorden also described: they might "prattle, threaten, chide," or "waxe furious and raging." This was clearly a helpful thesis for explaining possession; one contemporary account describes Mary Glover as "scornfullye disdayninge...terriblie threatning."[63] An unsympathetic reader might view the Lady's later speeches in a similar light—one critic refers to their "increasingly extreme positions" and "increasing anger," which concludes "not in argument, but in threat"[64]—as she taunts Comus, in lines he dismisses as "babble" (*A Maske* 806), with the "perverse conceipt" that she could destroy his palace with her words (792–98). The alliance between *suffocatio* and melancholy may be particularly relevant here: as Carol Thomas Neely notes, "a grandiose sense of power" characterizes many accounts of melancholic behavior.[65]

Jorden associated this manner of speech with the patient's being "deprived...of rest"; elsewhere he notes their "offence in eating, or drinking, as if the Divell ment to choake them therewith," a symptom he considered "ordinarie in uterin affects." "Loathing of meat" was also a symptom of suffocation of the mother in 1634's *Workes of...Ambrose Parey*; the later translation of Rivière's *Practice of Physick* (1655) described "want of appetite, and thirst," and especially "an universal loathing of al kind of Drink."[66] Comus describes the Lady's condition in similar terms: "tired all day without repast," she is in need of "refreshment" and "timely rest" (686–88). I will postpone the question of why Milton would furnish his villain with medical insights, but the analysis here is plausible. Having been asked for a drama on a medical theme, it would have been natural to turn to contemporary stage plays on similar topics. In Fletcher and Shakespeare's *The Two Noble Kinsmen*, first printed in the year of *A Maske*'s performance, an attack of women's melancholy is precipitated by hunger and a series of nights in the open. Here, as in John Ford's *The Lovers Melancholy* (printed in 1629),[67] lack of sleep and sustenance play a causative as well as a symptomatic role in melancholy derangement. "I am moped," Fletcher's heroine explains to the audience: "Food took I none these two days, /...I have not closed mine eyes /...Let not my sense unsettle." For the Doctor, "bring[ing] her to eat, to sleep" is essential to restore her health.[68]

When the Lady angrily rejects his similar offer, Comus replies by characterizing her refusal as an act of "lean and sallow Abstinence" (*A Maske* 708). In 1632 Robert Napier described Alice Egerton as "very leane," but Comus's "sallow" may have a related implication. Two later accounts of *suffocatio* describe victims turning "sandy," "yellow," or "swarthy" in the face;[69] Levinus Lemnius's *Secret Miracles of Nature* (1658) also describes a "swarth weasil colour." Thomas Elyot's popular *Castle of Health*, whose last reprinting was in 1610, describes this as characteristic of melancholy in general: "Abstinence is a forbearing to receive any meate or drinke...it maketh the colour salow, it ingendereth melancholy."[70] A dramatist looking for a visual signal for a chastity disease of the kind Burton described as "Maides...melancholy" might take this kind of description as a cue.

Critics have noted other strands of womb imagery. Katherine Eisaman Maus suggests that "Versions of the Lady's body...pervade the masque," noting the situation of Comus's palace in the "navel" of the wood (*A Maske* 519); for Sokol, Comus's invocation of "the dragon womb / Of Stygian darkness" (131–32) furthers the menstrual theme.[71] But this dragon "spits" not menstrual blood itself, but something closer to the toxic by-products it emitted when retained: "thickest gloom," which "makes one blot of all the air" (132–33). Burton used similar terms to describe the "black smoakie vapours" and "fuliginous [sooty] exhalation" given off either by "menstruous blood" or its sister pathogen, "corrupt seed."[72] These gloomy blots of air recall the "smoke" and "rank vapours" of the Attendant Spirit's opening speech (*A Maske* 5, 17) and anticipate the Elder Brother's "black usurping mists" (336) as well as the capacity of Comus's crew to "vomit smoke" in self-defense (654). A womb that spits smoky vapors rather than blood makes sense if the underlying reference is to suffocation of the mother. Crooke twice refers to this key aspect of the disease's operations as a "venemous breath," which might anticipate the halitosis of both Comus's dragon and his henchmen.[73] These passages suffuse the setting of *A Maske* with imagery drawn from the textual tradition of *suffocatio*.

That imagery reaches a height when Comus sinuously shifts the referent of "lean and sallow Abstinence" from food and sleep to sex. Were such abstinence to be taken as a general principle, he insists, nature itself would become "surcharged with her own weight, / And strangled with her waste fertility" (*A Maske* 727–28). As a seduction argument this seems difficult, since the menacing overpopulation he describes—seas overflowing with "spawn innumerable," skies dark with birds, an "over-multitude" of herds (712, 729–30)—sounds more like the result of excessive sexual activity than niggardly restraint (725). But Comus may have medical concepts in mind. Bright described melancholy as arising when gross blood "surchargeth the bodie, and yeeldeth...vapours." Suffocation of the mother occurred via a similar mechanism, but the substance that "surcharge[d] the bodie" could also be female seed. Since Comus's argument seems to describe sexual intercourse, to which he is urging the Lady, as a way of using up a "fertility" that might otherwise become dangerously surcharged, it seems plausible that the "waste fertility" that might do the surcharging is to be identified with toxic seed. This would suggest that the tactfully submerged referent of this passage is Alice Egerton's illness, for which strangulation, rather than suffocation, was a common alternative title: Barrough's 1583 description, for example, is headed "strangling of the wombe"; in 1615 Crooke referred to "strangulation or suffocation of the matrix"; and Johnson's 1634 translation of Ambroise Paré employs the title "strangulation of the wombe" throughout.[74]

It might be thought contradictory for Comus to refer at different moments to both "melancholy blood" and "waste fertility," since blood and seed were considered to be alternative rather than joint causes of *suffocatio*. But every account of the disease was obliged to mention both, and it is in relation to such accounts, in which "menstruous blood" and "corrupt seed" were each invariably foregrounded, that Milton is situating his drama. Linking the Lady's condition to both of them may be medically inaccurate, but it makes that defining relationship all the clearer.

The "Effluxe of Humor"

The Attendant Spirit and the brothers rush in, Comus flees, and the would-be rescuers, nonplussed, are confronted with a "motionless" Lady whom they cannot free (*A Maske* 818). "Some other means" must be found (820), and the male Spirit, having reached the limit of his powers, asks for female assistance. This is the point in Milton's drama that, I am arguing, parallels van Foreest. Like the Attendant Spirit with his haemony, the Dutch doctor has techniques of his own to try—he makes his patient smell her own burning hair, binds her hips, and gives her feet a "painful rubbing"—but when these fail he acknowledges that "the urgency of the situation" requires a method that only a female practitioner can carry out.

The *Observationum libri* has been described as a work to which virtually every medical writer of the period, particularly those writing on women's diseases, would have referred,[75] and van Foreest's dramatic presentation is helpful to clarify my argument. Milton did not, however, have to have this specific example in mind: descriptions of this therapy, and the use of a midwife or other female assistant to carry it out, are a standard feature of both medieval and early modern accounts of suffocation of the mother. Many of these also mention a further element that van Foreest omits: the emission of the toxic seed or menses from the womb as the patient revives.[76] This was sufficiently well known for Stephen Bradwell to use it to dispute Jorden's diagnosis of Mary Glover: the lack of such an "effluxe of humor" in this case was a key argument against the "mischeevous operation" of "generative seed" that suffocation of the mother would imply. Like other commentators, Bradwell seemed hazy about whether seed or blood was involved here, but the argument itself was emphatic. If it was *suffocatio,* then "what (I pray you) removed the residew of diseasefull causes, to wit, generative seed or menstruall bloud...here followed no evacuation of anie such materiall causes in her curation, as...must then have ben." This was key, since "effluxe of humor in the declination of the fitt, is an argument of the generative seede degenerated into a cause of the evell," and this "being utterly absent" was an important sign "that *Marie Glovers* case was not the suffocation from the mother."[77]

Though this "effluxe" could occur independently, as Bradwell describes, it was also what the midwife's actions aimed to achieve. In 1583, Barrough noted that "a certaine humiditie and moistnes" would in any case emerge from the womb on recovery; but if no such recovery was forthcoming, "let a midwife dippe her fingers in these [scented] oyles, and then put them into the mouth of the matrice, rubbing it, long and easilie, that through that provoking, the grosse and clammy humour may be avoided out."[78] A few years previously, in 1575, Paré had given a similar but fuller description, which Thomas Johnson made available to English readers in the year of *A Maske*'s performance:

> [In t]hose who are freed from the fit of the suffocation of the wombe, either by nature or by art...lastly, some moisture floweth from the secret parts with a certaine tickling pleasure; but...[when] the necke of the wombe is tickled with the mydwives finger, in stead of that moysture comes thick and grosse seed...and by little and little all symptoms vanish away....
>
> Let the mydwife annoint her fingers...and with these let her rub or tickle the top of the necke of the wombe...so at length the venemous matter contained in the wombe, shall bee dissolved and flow out...[and] the woman shall bee restored unto themselves againe.[79]

The reference to "venemous matter" is significant. The Lady's marble seat is said by Sabrina to be "venomed"—presumably by the ambiguous "gums" that have somehow become "smeared" on it (*A Maske* 915–16). This "glutinous" (916) substance has sometimes been read as "gluing" the Lady to her chair,[80] but it is not mentioned before Sabrina's freeing her, and its appearance on the seat—rather than within the Lady—may be associated, instead, with this moment of release. Galen had compared the toxicity of even small amounts of retained seed or menses to that of poisonous bites or stings.[81] In English this is usually rendered as "venom," a word that is often repeatedly employed to emphasize the seriousness of the condition. As well as describing the "venemous matter" that flowed from the womb when the midwife's cure had done its work, for example, Paré (in Johnson's translation) notes elsewhere that suffocation of the mother occurs when "seminall matter...acquireth a venemous quality" equivalent to that of "the stinging or bitings of venemous beasts"; the corrupted blood or seed became "a venemous humour."[82]

Jorden similarly observed that the disease came about when menses or seed "corrupteth and putrifieth to a venemous malignity" that emitted "venemous vapour," becoming a "venemous matter" that resembled the "venom" of a rabid dog. In particular, the seed, corrupted in this way, "passeth all the humors of our bodie, in venom...And therefore it is compared to the venom of a serpent." In 1615, as has been seen, Crooke used the same word to describe the paralysis in which both pulse and breathing could be "taken away by a venemous breath...a venemous breath of corrupted seed." The English version of Rivière's *Practice of Physick* opens its section on "Mother-Fits" with an account of this venom's creation: "When Seed and Menstrual Blood, are retained in Women...[they] attain a...venemous quality; from whence venemous Vapors are elevated and carried."[83] Milton could have known neither this last work nor its Latin original before *A Maske*, but it shows how "venom," which also appears in four later treatises up to 1671, had become part of suffocation of the mother's English vocabulary.[84] Modern critics have often identified the gums as semen, but only James Broaddus notes that early modern physiology allowed for this to originate from the Lady as well as her male opponent.[85] Broaddus does not consider suffocation of the mother, but its explanation of why the emergence of "venomed" seed might coincide with a release from paralysis supports his suggestion.

Describing the seed as poison was also an important tactic in ethical defenses of the midwife's cure. Winfried Schleiner, to whom this section of my argument is indebted, has shown that a key issue in this early seventeenth century debate was whether any of the seed that was evacuated during this procedure might still be fertile, the assumption being that fertility was lost as toxicity developed: the problem, it was argued, was that "there may be also healthy semen present," but "only the peccant part may be expelled directly with any justification."[86] But as well as conveying the likely absence of such "healthy semen," the extreme toxicity implied by the word "venom" also provided grounds for desperate measures in itself: as one earlier authority put it, "This practice [the midwife's cure] is only excused and exempted from being counted a sin against nature on condition that it is necessary to prevent death."[87] Paré introduced his description of the midwife's cure with a similar warning: without such a "speedy remedy," the paralysis "many times causeth present death."[88]

The "venomous" quality of the seed thus provided a double justification for its expulsion by the midwife, pointing at once to both its lack of generative potential and the urgency of its victim's predicament. Accordingly, Roderigo à Castro, considering in 1603 "Whether one should by friction applied to the pudendum have the semen flow forth" in such cases, observed "that the semen excreted at that time is not able to generate any more, but is a poisonous [*venenatum*] and useless excrement of the body." Moxius (1612), outlining this side of the argument in order to confute it, asked, "should it not be licit to expel this poisonous [*veneficum*] seed useless for generation, considering that the woman is partially senseless and hardly breathing?" James Primrose, writing half a century later, agreed that it must be legitimate to expel this "poison of the body [*venenum corporis*], an excrement not only useless but harmful."[89] The Lady's "venomed seat" may carry something of these arguments' apologetic weight.

The Ethics of the Midwife's Cure

Emphasizing its venomous nature was not, however, the only way around what Schleiner describes as "the moral dilemma about removing seed." Though medieval physicians may sometimes have been less comfortable with it than he implies, Schleiner argues that the early modern controversy over this technique began in the 1580s and had blossomed into a "lively debate" by 1600; in 1612 Moxius referred to it as "so difficult [an issue] in contemporary medicine that nothing else, in my judgment, comes close," and it was "a very difficult and arduous problem that has by now tortured the minds of many."[90] Schleiner is less clear on an endpoint, but the latest work he discusses that addresses the controversy directly, Zacuto's *De praxi medica*, was published in 1634. Though Schleiner's focus is exclusively on the Latin tradition, works in English mirror this chronology. Barrough (1583) and Johnson's Paré translation (1634) both describe the midwife's cure, but the discussions by Jorden, Crooke, and Burton published between these dates are silent on it. Jorden frankly admitted that some aspects of "the doctrine of this disease" could not be "conveniently disclosed" in "a vulgar tongue," causing him to "purposely omit" certain "Other matters of government of them either in the fit or out of the fit, togither with the cure in regard of the internall causes," almost certainly a reference to the midwife's role. After Johnson's *Workes of...Ambrose Parey*, however, it is described in a further seven English accounts up to 1657. Four of these were printed in the 1650s, but two others appeared in 1636 and 1637, suggesting that the radical spirit of the Interregnum was not the only factor.[91] From the 1630s onward, in England at least, anxiety around the midwife's cure may have begun to subside.

For that to happen, there needed to be a sense that this was a purely medical technique rather than a sexual one. A key intervention here, as Schleiner observes, came with the 1625 publication of Giovanni Battista Cortesi's *Miscellaneorum medicinalium decades*. The originality of Cortesi's defense of the midwife's cure lay in his denial that any sexual stimulation was, or should be, entailed. His plausible argument relied on the point that in women ejaculation—thought to emanate from the ovaries, or female "testicles"—released seed into the womb rather than, as in men, expelling it out of the body altogether. If the problem occurred because seed had been retained in the womb, then ejaculation would only add to it. What was needed, instead, was simply to open the neck of the womb to allow the retained, corrupted seed to flow out. Orgasm would only make this more difficult, by adding to the quantity of the substance one was trying to remove; but it was in any case very unlikely, because the woman in question was by definition seriously ill, and so hardly capable of pleasure. Cortesi also minimized any remaining element of scandal by carefully leaving the question of whether the evacuated substance was in fact "seed" open to question.[92]

Cortesi's reinterpretation may have been based on existing medical practice. Here the question arises as to whether, by the seventeenth century, descriptions of this therapy were intended merely for the titillation of male readers—as scholars such as Helen King and Laura Gowing have suggested may have been typical of the works in which such descriptions appeared[93]—or whether it was actually being performed at this date. Most accounts direct that a scented ointment should be used to facilitate the midwife's touch. If the midwife's cure existed in practice, it would thus be likely to have been subsumed under the category of "unction" or "anointing," in which ointments were applied to the body.[94] Midwives were particularly familiar with this, since anointing the neck of the womb, with a view to stretching it open, was a standard procedure during childbirth.[95] In this respect the fact that it is usually a midwife who is mentioned, rather than simply a female practitioner, may be relevant. A midwife who was required to anoint the neck of the womb and hold it open in a case of *suffocatio* would simply have been applying one of the most basic techniques of early modern obstetrics in a different context.

Practitioners as well as publishers may have been encouraged by Cortesi's description. Though works by male authors such as Barrough and Paré describe the midwife's cure in sexual terms, descriptions in texts aimed specifically at midwives take a different line. These had been available in print since 1540,[96] but the earliest descriptions of the midwife's cure in such works occur much later, in the anonymous 1637 translation of Rüff's *Expert Midwife*, and a work whose author-translators are identified only by their initials, *The Compleat Midwifes Practice* (1656). The latter is particularly important, since although in many respects derivative of earlier material, it was composed by four practicing midwives, two of whom are likely to have begun their training in the early 1620s and 1630s.[97] The text on which *The Expert Midwife* is based, Rüff's *De conceptu et generatione hominis*, dates from the mid-sixteenth century, but its appearance in English in the 1630s may also be significant. Both these works use the term "anointing." They also share Cortesi's caution as to whether the substance to be evacuated is in fact "seed" at all; Rüff calls it "corrupt humours," and *Midwifes Practice* claims that, "after the fit is past, there flows from the womb a matter *like* to that of the seed."[98]

It will be recalled that it was also thought possible for this "effluxe" to occur without the midwife's help, and both these texts take advantage of this to downplay the causal link between them. Rüff suggests that it is the application of foul scents to the nostrils that enables the expulsion of the "humours," before later observing that "Likewise...an Unguent may be prepared wherewith her secrets may be annoynted inwardly which suffereth this swooning." The equivalent passage in *Midwifes Practice* awkwardly asserts that "It is cured by evacuation of the seed, such as are rue and agnus castus, and anointing with odoriferous salves, especially if the woman be to live without the use of man."[99] Here the "evacuation" seems linked to the herbs rather than the "anointing." Rather than aiming at the male reader's voyeuristic enjoyment, these descriptions seem to be attempting the opposite, describing the midwife's cure in as unsexual a manner as possible. Such an approach seems more likely to be aiming to preserve knowledge of a useful technique while avoiding scandal.

Literacy levels among midwives in this period have been debated, but at least some awareness of accounts like these seems likely.[100] Might they have performed such a therapy? Recent studies, concerned to recapture the moral standing and expertise of the early modern midwife, have perhaps unsurprisingly ignored this question.[101] But as well as approaching it simply as an application of her usual obstetrical "anointing" in a new context, a midwife—and the community in which she practiced—might view such participation as preserving respectability rather than eroding it, by shielding the body of the female patient from the gaze and touch of a male physician. This aspect of women's involvement in medical practice—as "chaperone[s]" and "subordinate...manual assistants"—was well established: Monica Green suggests that, from the fifteenth century onward, it tended increasingly to be all that female practitioners were left with, as male dominance over the new field of gynecology progressed.[102]

Scholars such as Margaret Pelling and David Harley have noted the existence in the seventeenth century of husband-and-wife medical teams, and apparently close professional relationships between midwives and physicians.[103] Some of these partnerships seem likely to have originated partly from the need for women to perform such roles. As Pelling notes, their interventions may not always be apparent. In one example, the record states that the surgeon James Winter "gave her [the patient] the unction," but goes on to describe later treatments in terms that suggest both this and subsequent "anoynting[s]" may actually have been carried out by a woman under Winter's direction. In reports like this, "the difference between doing and causing to be done is often blurred"; such examples, Pelling suggests, may hint at "the existence of an unseen population of female carers who carried out the instructions of male practitioners."[104]

Griffith's *Bethel*, printed in 1633, laments that suffocation of the mother is "such a disease in our days," implying that cases were exceptionally numerous.[105] If this was thought to be the case, then the likelihood of physicians diagnosing an unconscious woman with *suffocatio*, and turning to the midwife's cure for a potentially life-saving remedy, would have been similarly increased. Answers may lie hidden in the casebooks, but one real-life example appears to have made it into print. The physician was Shakespeare's son-in-law John Hall, the date was February 15, 1631, and the patient was a girl "aged about 13" named "Mrs. Mary Comb." Though young she might have been married; there is some evidence that in practice not every physician shared the textbooks' confidence in marriage as a cure.[106] The use of "Mrs." does not necessarily imply marital status at this date, however, and it is also possible that here as elsewhere Hall's translator misinterpreted his author's *domina* ("Lady").[107]

Hall's *Select Observations* relates how Mary Comb was "cruelly vexed with the Mother, continuing in the Fit for nine houres, with some light intervals of ease." After trying, like van Foreest, a number of other techniques—a "fume," potion, and plaster—Hall "appoynted...[an] oyntment to anoynt the inner part of the Matrix...By this it returned to its place."[108] By "appoynted" we should clearly understand the entry of one of Pelling's "unseen population of female carers,"[109] and so perceive the parallel between this moment in Hall's contribution to the *Observationes* genre and the scene from one of the most influential examples of that genre,[110] van Foreest's *Observationum libri*, with which this essay began. The date and the patient's age provide a surprising degree of proximity to Alice Egerton's case. So far as I can find, this technique is not recorded for any of the several other cases of suffocation of the mother that Hall's *Select Observations* records;[111] however, nothing in the manner of its telling marks it out as sensitive or unusual. Neither does anything suggest a sexual dimension. Instead, the anointing works as described in *The Expert Midwife* and *The Compleat Midwifes Practice*; rather than provoking an ejaculation, it simply works to restore the womb to its "place."

Hall was known for his Puritan sympathies, and these may have been a factor in his willingness to prescribe this type of treatment.[112] Schleiner's research on the European controversies surrounding it finds no consistent difference between Protestant and Catholic commentators—his chief witness is the influential Wittenberg professor Daniel Sennert—but this may not have been the case in an England in which the demystification of medical knowledge became an important element of the Puritan agenda for social and scientific reform.[113]

Something like that agenda appears to have motivated a comment inserted into a later treatise, Rivière's *Practice of Physick*, by one of its English translators. The relevant passage, which occurs in Rivière's chapter on "Mother-Fits, or Womb-sickness," is worth quoting in full:

> Instead of carnal Conjunction, where that cannot be had, many advise that the Patient be rubbed and tickled by a Midwife in the Neck of her womb, into which the Midwife must put her fingers anointed with Oyls of Spices, that so the offensive Sperm may be voided. But seeing that cannot be done without wickedness (understand by a silly superstitious Papist, that counts it a meritorious good work to burn Mother and Child in her womb alive, as at Jersey, and a wickedness to free a sick body of a little offensive humor) a Christian Physitian must never prescribe the same.[114]

The bracketed interpolation has been assumed to be the work of the most high-profile of this text's three-man translation team, Nicholas Culpeper, but this may be unlikely; Culpeper's own account of suffocation of the mother does not include the midwife's cure, making one of his co-translators, either Abdiah Cole or William Rowland, the more plausible candidate.[115] Regardless of his identity, however, like Cortesi this commentator replaces prurient scruples about rubbing and tickling with the medical objective of evacuating the toxic substance, again described in neutral terms as "a little offensive humour." For him, the treatment of suffocation of the mother is caught up in a polemic between humane, medically minded Protestants, and benighted witch-burning Catholics.

Though Culpeper, and probably his co-translators, held radical views, the "Papist[s]" whose "superstitious" sexual ethics leaves *suffocatio*'s victims to suffer recall the words of a less radical author, Robert Burton. Burton does not mention the midwife's cure, but he shares the sense of the Rivière translator that the discourse of chastity diseases is naturally aligned with Protestantism. The title "Nunnes...melancholy" highlights the traditional association of such diseases with nuns, one of the reasons they were considered "inherently unhealthy."[116] Burton ends by developing this theory into an attack, though one aimed, distinctively, at the institutions rather than their victims:

> How odious and abominable are those superstitious and rash vowes of Popish Monasteries, [which]...binde and enforce men and women...to lead a single life against the lawes of nature [and]...debarre them of that, to which by their innate temperature they are so furiously inclined...better marry then burne, saith the Apostle, but they are otherwise perswaded....what fearefull maladies, ferall diseases, grosse inconveniences come to both sexes by this enforced temperance, it troubles me to thinke of, [but] much more to relate those...notorious fornications...rapes, incests, adulteries...See *Bales* visitation of Abbies, *Mercurialis, Rodericus à Castro, Peter Forestus*, and divers Physitians.[117]

Burton's hostility to celibacy is far from unique, but his use of chastity diseases to support it may be an innovation. Other than the passing mention in Griffith's *Bethel*, there are no comparable medical references where one would expect to find them, in the Protestant marriage literature that flourished in this period.[118] But Burton's inclusion of more traditional accusations—"fornications...rapes, incests, adulteries"—locates his medical discussion firmly within the wider critique of Catholic sexual abstinence conducted through works such as Gouge's *Domesticall Duties* (1622).[119] Milton seems likely to have known this section of the *Anatomy*, since his reference to suffocation of the mother in the *Doctrine and Discipline of Divorce* adapts Burton's argument against "Abbies" to the new target of Antinomianism. And Burton's polemical conclusion, like the translator's criticism of Rivière, shows the essential compatibility of the notion of chastity diseases with the antimonasticism central to Protestant thought. Passages such as these, combined with the numerous vernacular accounts that describe the emission of seed and the midwife's role from the 1630s on, may suggest the particular receptiveness of England's Protestant culture to these controversial aspects of contemporary medicine in the middle decades of the seventeenth century.

Part of that receptiveness involves the sympathy for the victim that both the Rivière interpolator and Burton display. Burton is particularly emphatic here. Wary of being seen to endorse sexual activity per se, he distinguishes two kinds of sufferer. Both are likely to be "noble virgins...in great houses," who are especially "prone to this disease." But where one type can be dismissed as "wanton, idle flurt[s]," the other is just the opposite: "of a strong temperament...very modest of themselves, sober, religious, vertuous, and well given (as many so distressed maides are), yet...this malady will take place...and may not otherwise be helped." It is this class of victims alone that Burton feels able to "pitty," and for whom he speaks "in favour...[and] commiseration...I cannot chuse but condole their mishap."[120]

Strong-minded, religious, and dedicated to the "sober laws / And holy dictate of spare temperance" (*A Maske* 765–66), the distressed noble virgin at the center of *A Maske* fits this second profile, in which chastity diseases testify to virtue, evoking compassion rather than shame. The distinction is sharpened by the "holy dictate of spare temperance," which sounds like Burton's "enforced temperance," but in fact performs the important work of dissociating the Lady from it. Spare temperance is not a doctrine of absolute abstinence, but one that allows "a moderate and beseeming share" (768). That this is not the kind of chastity associated with "Popish Monasteries" is underlined by its assertion against an aggressor who heads a "foundation" of "vowed priests" governed by "canon laws" (136, 807): a classic figure of monastic sexual hypocrisy that readers of Gouge or Burton would recognize. The Lady's endurance of her "mishap" commands respect, rather than mere pity, because she is able to maintain this fine line between sexual virtue and "superstitious...vowes," even under Comus's pressure. The "doctrine of virginity" to which she later alludes (786) has recently been interpreted as a Laudian endorsement of clerical celibacy, but her words here tilt the balance toward arguments like that of Daniel Rogers's *Matrimoniall Honour* (1642): "marriage shall not prejudice nor stain...virginity."[121] Clearly no "wanton...flurt," the Lady also avoids the opposite hazard that attends Burton's virtuous victims, whose special vulnerability is to celibacy rather than seduction.

Nothing in her case notes suggests that Alice Egerton ever experienced the midwife's cure, or the paralysis that would require it. There is likely to have been nothing strange about this; paralysis was only the most severe and lurid of the diverse symptoms associated with her disease. But it was the one that someone commissioned to write a drama themed around suffocation of the mother was likely to notice. Milton, who may never have met any of the Egertons, would not have had access to the specifics of Alice's case. Instead, he would have drawn his depiction of her ailment from a combination of popular knowledge—in 1634 there was probably plenty of this about—and the range of accounts available in print: this is when he is likely to have learned "by Physick" about diseases of menstruous bodies. From both these kinds of source the paralysis and the midwife's cure could have emerged as the most iconic elements of the disease; portraying both offered the simplest, most visually striking means of conveying what the drama was about. Paralysis was easy to show, but perhaps too ordinary a symbol to get the message across on its own: similar devices had featured in previous masques.[122] If Hall's example is representative, however, in the early 1630s the procedure of "anoynt[ing] the inner part of the matrix" may have been sufficiently routine to risk including it, too, in Milton's tactfully stylized depiction. The work of representing this pivotal moment in the disease's sequence could even be achieved in large part simply via the entrance of a female character to whom the responsibility of rescuing the Lady would be transferred.

The work of female practitioners, as has been seen, was often silently passed over; but by doing just the opposite with Sabrina's glorious arrival, Milton might be emphasizing the importance of female intercession at this point in preserving the Lady's modesty. Another kind of reassurance may also be at work: as well as performing a symbolic midwife's cure to rescue the Lady, Sabrina, who lends her aid to "virgin[s] such as was herself" (*A Maske* 855), may present an example of its effectiveness in the story of her own survival. She too was miraculously "revived" from a near death experience by a kind of inward anointing, when "ambrosial oils" were "through the porch and inlet of each sense / Dropped in" (1838–39). Though critics have disagreed about whether she does in fact touch her patient,[123] a fact that might be seen as testifying to the success of Milton's discreet presentation, the release is effected by her "powerful hand" (902). Importantly, however, that hand has "chaste palms moist and cold," in contrast to the "gums of glutinous heat" beneath it (916–17). As Cortesi had argued, the substance that is voided may have sexual connotations, but the hand that effects its expulsion does not.

Occasions

There has been much speculation as to the nature of the "extraordinary occasions" that prevented John Egerton from visiting Ludlow in the years between his appointment as president of the Council in Wales in 1631 and his eventual arrival in 1634. Cedric Brown has conjectured that the earl's own ill health played a part, but that of his youngest daughter is a more likely candidate.[124] Beginning in early 1632 and continuing until the summer of 1633, it fits the time frame. Mrs. Quicke's inquiry, in February of that year, if Alice "sh[ould] take any thing to prev[ent] her fitts before the spri[ng]" suggests they were thought to be seasonal, as some commentators suggested was usual.[125] In that case it would have been spring of 1634 before the family could have begun to feel confident that her long illness, and the household tensions it brought with it, might finally have passed. If it was her recovery that cleared the way for the investiture finally to take place, then it would make sense to include a celebration of that recovery during the associated festivities. And since her illness was associated with chastity, a masque of chastity would be an appropriate form for such a celebration to adopt.

The commission for it is likely to have reached Milton via Henry Lawes, who as Alice's music teacher for the previous seven years would have been familiar with her medical problems,[126] but Lawes may have been transmitting his employers' wishes. The Countess of Bridgewater's library lists for the years 1627–32 contain several volumes of recent plays—an interest likely to derive from her father, the patron of Strange's Men—[127]and her children had participated in masques at court. Both she and Lawes would thus have been likely to be aware of the popularity of medical topics in both these kinds of contemporary dramatic writing. Martin Butler's recent study notes the recurrence of medical tropes in the Caroline masques of the 1630s, and Alan Walworth has traced comparable developments on the commercial stage.[128]

One such play was Ford's *Lovers Melancholy* (1629), which makes its debts to *The Anatomy of Melancholy* explicit in a marginal note. Another was Fletcher's *Faithfull Shepheardesse*, which has sometimes been considered *A Maske*'s single greatest influence.[129] After initial failure it was reissued in 1633 on foot of its successful revival at court, a success to which its medical themes may have contributed. This play's river deity is an obvious antecedent to Sabrina, and one of the things she inherits is his medical approach. Similarly engaged in the rescue of a "virgin pure" who is "almost dead"—in this case from a stab wound—Fletcher's physician-god checks for a pulse, tests her blood quality (result: "unpoluted"), and, noting the wound is unbandaged, staunches it with a healing flower.[130]

Two plays that became available in print on either side of this date, however—Richard Brome's *Northern Lasse* (1632) and Shakespeare and Fletcher's *Two Noble Kinsmen* (1634)—are more directly relevant. Both feature female protagonists suffering from women's melancholy; both their ages are highlighted as 15.[131] This was evidently considered to be a time when such illness was especially likely to strike, but it was also Alice Egerton's age in 1634. These plays offered precedents for stage depictions of 15-year-olds suffering from diseases of sexual abstinence. The abstinence in question results from unattainable desire rather than rigorous virtue, but the force Burton described as "innate temperature" made no such distinctions. *Two Noble Kinsmen* is particularly significant; the acknowledged influence of Fletcher's *Faithfull Shepheardesse* strengthens the possibility that Milton also knew this second work in which its author had a hand, which appeared in print around the same time. Shakespeare's participation has won it modern attention, but the medical focus gives *Kinsmen* a distinctively Fletcherian character.

Though the tone surrounding each is predominantly comic, Brome's Constance and Fletcher's Jailer's Daughter are sympathetic and resourceful characters. Both find themselves the objects of attempts at sexual exploitation based on their illnesses. Constance successfully fights back, but the Jailer's Daughter succumbs in a scene that retains its power to disturb. Both plays are concerned with the possibility that unscrupulous men may take advantage of the sexual cure that the notion of a chastity disease implies. *A Maske* transposes this theme into an elevated key, as Brome's and Fletcher's bumbling wooers are replaced by a more credible seducer, and the consequences of refusal are made plain. The difficulty of undoing the "numbing spell" demonstrates that for the victim of such an ailment, the preservation of sexual honor may carry a mortal risk. The plausibility of the medical argument that Comus draws on in the course of his attempted seduction thus elicits all the more admiration for the Lady's determination to resist it, whatever the cost.

If Alice Egerton's personal circumstances prompted the commissioning of *A Maske* in 1634, a shift in those circumstances may also have prompted a new passage published in 1637. *A Maske*'s textual history lies beyond this essay's scope, though since three of its more vexed passages relate to chastity or celibacy, the medical theme seems likely to be relevant.[132] But the case of the revised epilogue, with its allusion to Cupid and Psyche's marriage (*A Maske* 1002–10), may be more straightforward. This was probably composed for *A Maske*'s 1637 printing.[133] In 1637 Alice turned 18, which, judging from her sisters' examples, the Egertons appear to have viewed as the start of marriageable age.[134] Dowry inflation was making marriages for younger daughters increasingly hard to arrange, but in Alice's case this obstacle would have been removed by her grandmother's death in January of that year, which allowed John Egerton finally to inherit his father's remaining estates.[135] This was a substantial increase in wealth from which Alice's dowry alone stood to benefit, her seven older sisters already having married, and it had arrived at just the right time. Since marriage was often considered the "best and surest remedy" for suffocation of the mother,[136] there may also have been a sense of relief in the Egerton household that the release of funds for Alice's dowry could finally put her recovery beyond doubt.

As it happened, things turned out differently. Following Alice's mother's death in 1636, the need to care for her ailing father would have become increasingly apparent; later, the civil war decimated the stock of potential husbands, as well as damaged the family finances. These were all factors that commonly contributed to what Amy Froide has called that "series of decisions and non-decisions" through which an early modern woman might enter into an extended period of singleness; one that in Alice's case lasted until 1652, when the war was over and her father was dead.[137] But in the year of *A Maske*'s publication, those events could not have been foreseen; the prospect of her marriage would have appeared suddenly to have opened. In 1634 Milton's drama had commemorated Alice Egerton's recovery from illness. In 1637 its new ending may have lightly anticipated what seemed the next occasion she would have to celebrate.

University of Cambridge

Notes

1. Pieter van Foreest, *Observationum et curationum medicinalium libri*, vol. 28 (*De mulierum morbis*), observation 26 (Leiden, 1599), 151–53; cited and translated by Winfried Schleiner, *Medical Ethics in the Renaissance* (Washington, D.C., 1995), 113. I have slightly amended Schleiner's translation. Warmest thanks are due to Colin Burrow, Helen Cooper, Helen Moore, Diane Purkiss, Lauren Kassell, Robert Ralley, and (especially) Thomas Roebuck for their assistance with this article; the faults that remain are my own.

2. Katherine Eisaman Maus, *Inwardness and Theatre in the English Renaissance* (Chicago, 1995), 198–209; B. J. Sokol, "'Tilted Lees,' Dragons, Haemony, Menarche, Spirit, and Matter in *Comus*," *Review of English Studies*, n.s. 41 (1990): 309–24; James Broaddus, "'Gums of Glutinous Heat' in Milton's *Mask* and Spenser's *Faerie Queene*," *Milton Quarterly* 37 (2003): 205–14.

3. Danielle Jacquart and Claude Thomasset, *Sexuality and Medicine in the Middle Ages*, trans. Matthew Adamson (Oxford, 1988), 174; see also Monica Green, introduction to *The Trotula: An English Translation of the Medieval Compendium of Women's Medicine*, trans. Monica Green (Philadelphia, 2001), 27, 40.

4. "Numbing spell": John Milton, *A Maske Presented at Ludlow Castle, 1634*, line 852, in *Milton: The Complete Shorter Poems*, ed. John Carey, 2nd rev. ed. (Harlow, 2007). Further references will be to this edition and will be cited in the text by line number. On the paralysis as self-inflicted, see, e.g., William Oram, "The Invocation of Sabrina," *Studies in English Literature, 1500–1900* 24 (1984): 131; Hugh M. Richmond, *The Christian Revolutionary: John Milton* (Berkeley and Los Angeles, 1974), 72.

5. Lazare Rivière, *The Practice of Physick*, trans. Nicholas Culpeper et al. (London, 1655), 428.

6. Helen King, "Once upon a Text: Hysteria from Hippocrates," in *Hysteria beyond Freud*, ed. Sander L. Gilman et al., 3–90 (London, 1993); King, *The Disease of Virgins: Green Sickness, Chlorosis and the Problems of Puberty* (London, 2004).

7. For psychoanalytic perspectives, see Oram, "Invocation of Sabrina"; Richmond, *Christian Revolutionary*; and esp. William Kerrigan, *The Sacred Complex: On the Psychogenesis of "Paradise Lost"* (London, 1983), 23–72. Opposing views include Leah Marcus, "Justice for Margery Evans: A 'Local' Reading of Comus," in *Milton and the Idea of Woman*, ed. Julia M. Walker, 66–95 (Urbana, Ill., 1988); John Leonard, "Saying 'No' to Freud: Milton's *A Mask* and Sexual Assault," *Milton Quarterly* 25 (1991): 129–40.

8. Barbara Breasted, "Another Bewitching of Lady Alice Egerton, the Lady of *Comus*," *Notes and Queries* 17 (1970): 411–12.

9. John Creaser, "Milton's *Comus*: The Irrelevance of the Castlehaven Scandal," *Milton Quarterly* 21 (1987): 24–34; On the choice of topic, see William B. Hunter, *Milton's "Comus," Family Piece* (New York, 1983), 4–5.

10. Christopher Kendrick, "Milton and Sexuality: A Symptomatic Reading of *Comus*," in *Re-membering Milton: Essays on the Texts and the Traditions*, ed. Mary Nyquist and Margaret W. Ferguson, 43–73 (London, 1987), 46–47.

11. Michael MacDonald, *Mystical Bedlam: Madness, Anxiety, and Healing in Seventeenth-Century England* (Cambridge, 1981), 13–15.

12. See, for example, Wendy Churchill, *Female Patients in Early Modern Britain: Gender, Diagnosis, and Treatment* (Farnham, 2012); Monica Green, *Making Women's Medicine Masculine: The Rise of Male Authority in Pre-Modern Gynaecology* (Oxford, 2008); Margaret Pelling, "Compromised by Gender: The Role of the Male Medical Practitioner in

Early Modern England," in *The Task of Healing: Medicine, Religion and Gender in England and the Netherlands, 1450–1800*, ed. Hilary Marland and Margaret Pelling, 101–34 (Rotterdam, 1996).

13. Bodleian MSS Ashmole 212, p. 430, and Ashmole 1730, f. 251^r. Further references to Ashmole MSS will be given in the text, in the format [MS number]/[page/folio]; hence, the above references would read 212/430, and 1730/f. 251^r. Napier recorded letters received in his patients' case notes; other than the letter from Robert Napier discussed here, where correspondence is referred to it is these summaries that are the source, rather than the original letters themselves, which have not been located. All dates are given in New Style. Some entries discussed may be in the hands of Napier's assistants; I have not attempted to distinguish these. My full transcription of the Egertons' case notes will appear shortly on the *Casebooks Project* website, www.magicandmedicine.hps.cam.ac.uk.

14. Lauren Kassell, *Medicine and Magic in Elizabethan London: Simon Forman, Astrologer, Alchemist, and Physician* (Oxford, 2005), 132; Ronald C. Sawyer, *Patients, Healers, and Disease in the Southeast Midlands, 1597–1634* (Ph.D. diss., University of Wisconsin-Madison, 1986), 244.

15. Kassell, *Medicine and Magic*, 132–33.

16. E.g., Philip Barrough, *The Methode of Phisicke* (London, 1583), 260 ("them which be diseased with Struma or Scrofula").

17. Sawyer, *Patients, Healers*, 381–83.

18. Elizabeth Lane Furdell, *Publishing and Medicine in Early Modern England* (New York, 2002), 85–87.

19. Napier gives Alice's age here as 12, but elsewhere he records her birthdate as June 13, 1619, making her 13 (214/433; this also gives birthdates for Magdalen, August 7, 1615, and Penelope, August 17, 1610). He may have been thinking of her age when her symptoms had begun, six months earlier.

20. E.g., Edward Jorden, *A Briefe Discourse of a Disease Called the Suffocation of the Mother* (London, 1603), f. 5^r: "This disease is called...Suffocation of the Mother...because most commonly it takes them with choaking in the throat." See also King, "Once upon a Text," 28–32.

21. "Gnawing in the stomacke": Jorden, *A Briefe Discourse*, f. 18^r. See also Ambroise Paré, *The Workes of that Famous Chirurgion Ambrose Parey*, trans. Thomas Johnson (London, 1634), 941 ("[pain] ariseth...unto the orifice of the stomacke"); Rivière, *Practice of Physick*, 424 ("noyse in their lower Belly...with belching or inclination to Vomit"). On scent therapy, see King, "Once upon a Text," 25–28, 61. Applying sweet rather than foul smells at the nose was an error that may have been common: cf. Schleiner, *Medical Ethics*, 115.

22. Patients often came to stay with Napier for treatment (Sawyer, *Patients, Healers*, 158). On Anne Tyringham, see, e.g., 214/205, 214/230, 214/259, 214/321.

23. Jonathan Andrews, "Napier, Richard (1559–1634)," *Oxford Dictionary of National Biography* (Oxford, 2004), hereafter cited as *DNB*; Sawyer, *Patients, Healers,* 53–54, 141, 156–67, 266, 435.

24. "Strange" often implied witchcraft: see Ronald C. Sawyer, "'Strangely Handled in All Her Lyms': Witchcraft and Healing in Jacobean England," *Journal of Social History* 22 (1989): 469–70.

25. Sawyer, *Patients, Healers,* 325–27.

26. On "mopishness," a variant of melancholy, see MacDonald, *Mystical Bedlam,* 161–63.

27. E.g., Levinus Lemnius, *The Touchstone of Complexions,* trans. Thomas Newton (London, 1576), f. 138^v ("if the Splene or Mylte should suffer obstruction ... the Mela[n]cholike juyce disperseth it selfe into every part of the body").

28. MacDonald, *Mystical Bedlam,* 210.

29. Napier typically used *veneficium* to mean witchcraft (Sawyer, *Patients, Healers,* 320).

30. Sawyer, *Patients, Healers,* 149, 200, 308–11, 341–42, 523–24; MacDonald, *Mystical Bedlam,* 32, 200–16.

31. Napier here gives the astrological symbol for tin (Kassell, *Medicine and Magic,* xiv).

32. As seen at 212/140–41 (Jennings), where the "pomander" in the first entry is clearly to be identified with the sigil (*S* followed by tin symbol, Napier's standard abbreviation) in the second. For discussion, see Sawyer, *Patients, Healers,* 309–10.

33. Kassell, *Medicine and Magic,* 140 (citing MS Ashmole 1495, f. 31^v).

34. Churchill, *Female Patients,* 140; Green, *Making Women's Medicine Masculine,* 309.

35. British Library MS Add. 24488 (Hunter, *Chorus Vatum*), 350–51.

36. Mary Ann O'Donnell, "Egerton, Frances, countess of Bridgewater (1583–1636)," *DNB*.

37. E.g., Barrough, *Methode of Phisicke,* 150 ("suffocation or strangling of the wombe"); Helkiah Crooke, *Mikrokosmographia* (London, 1615), 218 ("strangulation or suffocation of the matrix, which we call fits of the mother").

38. Jacquart, *Sexuality and Medicine,* 173–77; Green, *Trotula,* 22–30; King, "Once upon a Text," 55–56; Helen Rodnite Lemay, "William of Saliceto on Human Sexuality," *Viator* 12 (1981): 177–78; Lemay, "Anthonius Guainerius and Medieval Gynecology," in *Women of the Medieval World: Essays in Honour of John H. Mundy,* ed. Julius Kirshner and Suzanne F. Wemple, 317–36 (Oxford, 1985), 322–23.

39. Irma Taavitsainen and Paivi Pahta, "Vernacularisation of Medical Writing in English: A Corpus-Based Study of Scholasticism," *Early Science and Medicine* 3 (1998): 157–85; Paul Slack, "Mirrors of Health and Treasures of Poor Men: The Uses of the Vernacular Medical Literature of Tudor England," in *Health, Medicine and Mortality in the Sixteenth*

Century, ed. Charles Webster, 237–73 (Cambridge, 1979), 237–42; Charles Webster, *The Great Instauration: Science, Medicine and Reform, 1626–1660* (London, 1975), 258–59, 262–72, 289.

40. Barrough, *Methode of Phisicke*, 150–51; Jorden, *A Briefe Discourse*; Crooke, *Mikrokosmographia*, 44, 225, 231, 252–53; Robert Burton, *The Anatomy of Melancholy*, 3rd ed. (Oxford, 1628), 193–96; Paré, *Workes*, 939–45, 948, 950; John Sadler, *The Sicke Womans Private Looking-Glasse* (London, 1636), 61–68; Jakob Rüff, *The Expert Midwife* (London, 1637), 61–68 [253–60]; Nicolaas Fonteyn, *The Womans Doctour* (London, 1652), 51–60; William Harvey, *Anatomical Exercitations* (London, 1653), 28, 349, 402, 501–02, 507; Rivière, *Practice of Physick*, 420–31; T. C. et al., *The Compleat Midwifes Practice* (London, 1656), 62–66 [210–14]; Alessandro Massaria, *The Womans Counsellour*, trans. R[obert] T[urner] (London, 1657), 72–79; Nicholas Culpeper, *Culpeper's Directory for Midwives; or, A Guide for Women. The Second Part* (London, 1662), 106–15; Nicholas Sudell, *The Womans Friend* ([London], 1666), 21–25; *An Account of the Causes of Some Particular Rebellious Distempers* ([London], 1670]), 33–41; James Wolveridge, *Irish Midwives Handmaid* (London, 1670), 155–61; Jane Sharp, *The Midwives Book* (London, 1671), 317–28. Where pagination is inconsistent, I have counted pages and marked the "correct" numbers in square brackets. My account is based on these works. See also Kaara L. Peterson, *Popular Medicine, Hysterical Disease, and Social Controversy in Shakespeare's England* (Farnham, 2010); Fissell, *Vernacular Bodies*, 55–63; Lesel Dawson, *Lovesickness and Gender in Early Modern English Literature* (Oxford, 2008), 60–68.

41. Sadler, *Sicke Womans Looking-Glasse*, and Rüff, *Expert Midwife*.

42. On these, see Schleiner, *Medical Ethics*, 107–29.

43. Matthew Griffith, *Bethel; or, A Forme for Families* (London, 1633), 375.

44. John Swan, *A True and Breife Report, of Mary Glovers Vexation* ([London], 1603); Stephen Bradwell, *Mary Glovers Late Woeful Case*, a manuscript treatise dated 1603 (British Library MS Sloane 831), hereafter cited as *Woeful Case*, from the transcription in Michael MacDonald, *Witchcraft and Hysteria in Elizabethan London: Edward Jorden and the Mary Glover Case* (London, 1991).

45. See, e.g., Jorden, *A Briefe Discourse*, f. 20^r; Paré, *Workes*, 939, 942; Rivière, *Practice of Physick*, 421; Jacquart, *Sexuality and Medicine*, 175.

46. Burton, *Anatomy of Melancholy* (1628 ed.), 194. See also Paré, *Workes:* "if she be married, let her...bee strongly encountered by her husband, for there is no remedy more present than this" (945).

47. King, "Once upon a Text."

48. *Account of the Causes*, 33 ("the Vapours, otherwise called...Fits of the Mother"). See also King, "Once upon a Text," 50–51, and Green, *Trotula*, 25.

49. Jorden, *A Briefe Discourse*, f. 2^r.

50. Barrough, *Methode of Physick*, 150. On the wide seventeenth century circulation of stories of *suffocatio* victims mistaken for dead, see King, "Once upon a Text," 63.

51. John Hall, *Select Observations on English Bodies*, trans. James Cook (London, 1657), 222 (cited in Peterson, *Hysterical Disease*, 157–58): "suddenly taken with convulsion of face and eyes, losse of speech, her matrix carryed from its proper place, and so cast, as if she had been the very image of death." "Convulsion" might mean she was paralyzed in a contorted position.

52. *The Doctrine and Discipline of Divorce*, in *The Complete Prose Works of John Milton*, 8 vols., ed. Don M. Wolfe et al. (New Haven: Yale University Press, 1953–82), 2:278–79.

53. Burton, *Anatomy of Melancholy* (1628 ed.), 193 ("ut difficulter possit ab uteri strangulatione decerni").

54. Ibid., 194, 196.

55. Timothie Bright, *A Treatise of Melancholy* (London, 1586), 1–2.

56. William Vaughan, *Approved Directions for Health* (London, 1612), 96–97.

57. Reginald Scot, *The Discoverie of Witchcraft* ([London], 1584), 54; emphasis mine.

58. Burton, *Anatomy of Melancholy* (1628 ed.), 194; Culpeper, *Directory for Midwives...Second Part*, 119 (ghosts); Fonteyn, *Womans Doctour*, 72 (angels).

59. Sokol, "Tilted Lees," 311. Although my hypothesis supports this part of Sokol's argument, it points to different conclusions.

60. Lemnius, *Touchstone of Complexions*, ff. 136^{r-v} ("Melancholike juyce...lyke unto dregges and Lees, yt settleth in the bottom of the vessel...ye setling and refuse of Bloud"); Vaughan, *Approved Directions for Health*, 122 ("The Melancholick humour...resembling the lees of blood").

61. T. C., *Compleat Midwifes Practice*, 67 [215].

62. Jorden, *A Briefe Discourse*, ff. 4^r, 14^r, 13^r; Bradwell, *Woeful Case*, 10, 12, 6.

63. Burton, *Anatomy of Melancholy* (1628 ed.), 194; Jorden, *A Briefe Discourse*, f. 13v; Swan, *True and Briefe Report*, 40–41.

64. Oram, "Invocation of Sabrina," 132–33.

65. Carol Thomas Neely, *Distracted Subjects: Madness and Gender in Shakespeare and Early Modern Culture* (Ithaca, N.Y., 2004), 77. This exchange may, of course, have been added at a later date; see S. E. Sprott, *A Maske: The Earlier Versions* (Toronto, 1973), 5, 30.

66. Jorden, *A Briefe Discourse*, f. 13^v, $A4^r$; Paré, *Workes*, 939; Rivière, *Practice of Physick*, 423.

67. See, for example, mad Meleander's challenge to Corax to prove himself similarly deranged: "If thou canst wake with me, [and] forget to eate...Thou shalt be a companion fit for me" (John Ford, *The Lovers Melancholy* [London, 1629], 61).

68. John Fletcher and William Shakespeare, *The Two Noble Kinsmen*, ed. Robert Kean Turner and Patricia Tatspaugh (Cambridge, 2012), 3.2.25–29, 4.3.78–80; further references will be to this edition.

69. Massaria, *Womans Counsellour*, 74; Sharp, *Midwives Book*, 321.

70. Levinus Lemnius, *The Secret Miracles of Nature* (London, 1658), 18 (in 1634 Milton could have known the Latin original of this work, *Occulta naturae miracula* [Antwerp, 1559]); Thomas Elyot, *The Castle of Health* (London, 1610), 83.

71. Maus, *Inwardness and Theatre*, 200–01; Sokol, "'Tilted Lees,'" 316.

72. Burton, *Anatomy of Melancholy* (1628 ed.), 193.

73. Crooke, *Mikrokosmographia*, 253, 236.

74. Barrough, *Methode of Phisicke*, 150; Crooke, *Mikrokosmographia*, 218; Paré, *Workes*, 939–43.

75. Schleiner, *Medical Ethics*, 114–15. These included Jorden, who regularly notes van Foreest as a source (e.g., ff. 5^r, 9^v, 22^r).

76. For medieval accounts, see Beryl Rowland, ed., *Medieval Woman's Guide to Health: The First English Gynecological Handbook* (London, 1981), 95; Mary Wack, *Lovesickness in the Middle Ages: The Viaticum and Its Commentaries* (Philadelphia, 1990), 131; Jacquart, *Sexuality and Medicine*, 176; Lemay, "Anthonius Guainerius," 323; Green, *Making Women's Medicine Masculine*, 253. Early modern descriptions include Barrough, *Methode of Phisicke*, 150–51; Paré, *Workes*, 942, 945; Sadler, *Sicke Womans Looking-Glasse*, 73–74; Rüff, *Expert Midwife*, 66–67 [258–59]; Fonteyn, *Womans Doctour*, 6; Rivière, *Practice of Physick*, 424–28; T. C., *Compleat Midwifes Practice*, 66 [214]; Massaria, *Womans Counsellour*, 75; Sudell, *Womans Friend*, 20. Barrough, Paré, Rüff, Rivière, and *Compleat Midwifes Practice* also describe the emission, as do Culpeper, *Directory for Midwives... Second Part*, 109–10; and Wolveridge, *Irish Midwives Handmaid*, 157.

77. Bradwell, *Woeful Case*, 99, 138, 104.

78. Barrough, *Methode of Phisicke*, 150–51.

79. Paré, *Workes* (trans. Johnson), 942, 945.

80. Debra Shuger, "'Gums of Glutinous Heat' and the Stream of Consciousness: The Theology of Milton's *Maske*," *Representations* 60 (1997): 2; Leonard, "Saying 'No' to Freud," 130.

81. Galen, *De locis affectis*, 6.5. For discussion, see King, "Once upon a Text," 43; Green, *Trotula*, 24.

82. Paré, *Workes*, 950, 939–40.

83. Jorden, *A Briefe Discourse*, ff. 5^v, 20^{r-v}; Crooke, *Mikrokosmographia*, 253, 326; Rivière, *Practice of Physick*, 420.

84. The original, Latin, version of *Practice of Physick* is *Praxis medica* (Paris, 1640). The four later treatises are T. C., *Compleat Midwifes Practice*, 64 [212]; Culpeper, *Directory for Midwives... Second Part*, 108–09, 114; Sudell, *Womans Friend*, 21; Sharp, *Midwives Book*, 240, 318, 322–23.

85. Broaddus, "'Gums of Glutinous Heat,'" 207–11. For an overview of this literature, see Michael Gillum, "Yet Once More, 'Gumms of Glutenous Heat,'" *Milton Quarterly* 44 (2010): 47, 50n2.

86. Juan Rafael Moix (Moxius), *De methodo medendi per venae sectionem morbos muliebres acutos* (Geneva, 1612), 508; cited and translated by Schleiner, *Medical Ethics*, 121, 156n34.

87. Jaques Despars, *Expositio supra librum canonis*, bk. 3, fen. 21, tr. 4, ch. 17; cited and translated in Jacquart, *Sexuality and Medicine*, 176.

88. Paré, *Workes*, 942.

89. Roderigo à Castro, *De universa mulierum medicina* (Hamburg, 1603), 108; Moxius, *Methodo medendi*, 508; James Primrose, *De morbis mulierum* (Rotterdam, 1655), 218; all cited, translated, and discussed by Schleiner, *Medical Ethics*, 118, 123, 155n24, 157n45. There is no connection here with Napier's use of *veneficium* as a term for witchcraft.

90. Schleiner, *Medical Ethics*, 107, 119–20; on physicians' discomfort, see Lemay, "William of Saliceto," 178; Moxius quotations from *Methodo medendi*, 502, 508, cited and translated by Schleiner, *Medical Ethics*, 121, 156n34, 156n32.

91. Quotations from Jorden, *A Briefe Discourse*, ff. 18^v, 25^v. The relevant works are Sadler, *Sicke Womans Looking-Glasse* (1636); Rüff, *Expert Midwife* (1637); Fonteyn, *Womans Doctour*, Rivière, *Practice of Physick*, T. C., *Compleat Midwifes Practice*, and Massaria, *Womans Counsellour* (all 1650s); Sudell, *Womans Friend* (1666).

92. Giovanni Battista Cortesi, *Miscellaneorum medicinalium decades*, 816–18; cited and discussed in Schleiner, *Medical Ethics*, 127–28. See also Helen King, "Galen and the Widow: Towards a History of Therapeutic Masturbation in Ancient Gynaecology," *EuGeSta* 1 (2011): 205–35.

93. Helen King, "The Politick Midwife: Models of Midwifery in the Work of Elizabeth Cellier," in *The Art of Midwifery: Early Modern Midwives in Europe*, ed. Hilary Marland, 115–30 (London, 1993), 121; Laura Gowing, *Common Bodies: Women, Touch and Power in Seventeenth-Century England* (London, 2003), 84.

94. Margaret Pelling, *Medical Conflicts in Early Modern London: Patronage, Physicians, and Irregular Practitioners, 1550–1640* (Oxford, 2003), 219–20.

95. Doreen Evenden, *The Midwives of Seventeenth-Century London* (Cambridge, 2000), 82. For examples, see T. C., *Compleat Midwifes Practice*, 84–85; Thomas Raynalde, *The Birth of Man-Kinde* (London, 1634; orig. pub. 1545), 98–102, 106, 111; Rüff, *Expert Midwife*, 80–81.

96. Evenden, *Midwives*, 6.

97. Evenden suggests they were licensed in 1632 and 1638, respectively; up to seven years' training was required beforehand (ibid., 8, 55).

98. Rüff, *Expert Midwife*, 66 [258]; T. C., *Compleat Midwifes Practice*, 66 [214]; emphasis mine.

99. Rüff, *Expert Midwife*, 66–67 [258–59]; T. C., *Compleat Midwifes Practice*, 66 [214].

100. Evenden, *Midwives*, 6–7; David Harley, "Provincial Midwives in England: Lancashire and Cheshire, 1660–1760," in Marland, *Art of Midwifery*, 27–48 (31, 34).

101. An exception is Caroline Bicks, *Midwiving Subjects in Shakespeare's England* (Aldershot, 2003), 78–79.

102. Green, *Making Women's Medicine Masculine*, 258, 265, 291.

103. Pelling, *Medical Conflicts*, 214–16; Harley, "Provincial Midwives," 29.

104. Pelling, *Medical Conflicts*, 220–21, 349–50; the example is from *Annals of the Royal College of Physicians of London*, 5 vols., trans. J. Emberry and S. Heathcote (London, 1953–), 3:295 (Dec. 10, 1630). This is not to say that physical contact between physicians and female patients never occurred: see Churchill's nuanced discussion (*Female Patients*, 64–71, 76–79, 86–89).

105. Griffith, *Bethel*, 375.

106. Katherine E. Williams, "Hysteria in Seventeenth-Century Case Records and Unpublished Manuscripts," *History of Psychiatry* 1 (1990): 388–92, 400; Churchill, *Female Patients*, 183–84, 215–16, 223, 228.

107. "Mrs.," OED 1.b ("A title prefixed to the name of an unmarried lady or girl," first citation 1550); Joan Lane, *John Hall and His Patients: The Medical Practice of Shakespeare's Son-in-Law* (Stratford-upon-Avon, 1996), xxx.

108. Hall, *Select Observations*, 198–200.

109. Cf. the undated entry in Napier's casebooks recording Magdalen's "clyster taken by my appoy[n]t[ment] at London" (211/521). There are no comparable entries for Alice.

110. Gianna Pomata, "Sharing Cases: The *Observationes* in Early Modern Medicine," *Early Science and Medicine* 15 (2010): 204, 217–18; see also Churchill, *Female Patients*, 7, 17.

111. Hall, *Select Observations*, observations 39, 42, 61, 96 (first century); and 28, 31, 57, 61, 63, 71, 80 (second century). See also "counsels" observations 7 and 66.

112. Lane, *John Hall*, xvi–xvii, xxv.

113. Schleiner, *Medical Ethics*, 125–26, 133–34; Webster, *Great Instauration*, 246–50, 256–64.

114. Rivière, *Practice of Physick*, 427–28.

115. Audrey Eccles, *Obstetrics and Gynaecology in Tudor and Stuart England* (London, 1982), 79; Culpeper's account of *suffocatio* is in *Directory for Midwives...Second Part*, 106–15.

116. Green, *Making Women's Medicine Masculine*, 312.

117. Burton, *Anatomy of Melancholy* (1628 ed.), 195–96.

118. Griffith, *Bethel*, 375. Anthony Fletcher's otherwise excellent discussion seems mistaken in this respect: "The Protestant Idea of Marriage in

Early Modern England," in *Religion, Culture and Society in Early Modern Britain: Essays in Honour of Patrick Collinson,* ed. Anthony Fletcher and Peter Roberts, 161–81 (Cambridge, 1994), 176.

119. William Gouge, *Of Domesticall Duties* (London, 1622), 184: "Fearefull have been the effects [of monastic celibacy]...fornication, adulterie, incest."

120. Burton, *Anatomy of Melancholy* (1628 ed.), 194–95.

121. Gordon Campbell and Thomas N. Corns, *John Milton: Life, Work, and Thought* (Oxford, 2008), 82; Daniel Rogers, *Matrimoniall Honour* (London, 1642), 386; see also John Leonard, "'Good Things': A Reply to William Kerrigan," *Milton Quarterly* 30 (1996): 124. A likelier candidate for this Laudian subtext, and one that also seems likely to share *A Maske*'s medical theme, is *Il Penseroso*'s figuration of "divinest Melancholy" as a nun who turns to marble (*Il Penseroso* 12, 31, 42).

122. Martin Butler, *The Stuart Court Masque and Political Culture* (Cambridge, 2008), 355–56.

123. Cf. Erin Murphy, "Sabrina and the Making of English History in *Poly-Olbion* and *A Maske Presented at Ludlow Castle,*" *Studies in English Literature, 1500–1900* 51 (2011): 102–03; Mary Loeffelholz, "Two Masques of Ceres and Proserpine: *Comus* and *The Tempest,*" in Nyquist and Ferguson, *Re-membering Milton,* 34; Matthew Steggle, "'Gums of Glutinous Heat' and Euripides' *Medea,*" *Notes and Queries* 46 (1999): 330.

124. Cedric Brown, *John Milton's Aristocratic Entertainments* (Cambridge, 1985), 28–29.

125. Barrough, *Methode of Phisicke,* 150; Jorden, *A Briefe Discourse,* ff. 21r–v.

126. Gordon Campbell and Thomas N. Corns, *John Milton: Life, Work, and Thought* (Oxford, 2008), 73, 79.

127. Heidi Brayman Hackel, "The Countess of Bridgewater's London Library," in *Books and Readers in Early Modern England: Material Studies,* ed. Jennifer Anderson and Elizabeth Sauer, 138–59 (Philadelphia, 2002), 140, 147–54.

128. Butler, *Stuart Court Masque,* 292, 315, 336, 344; Walworth, "'To Laugh with Open Throate': Mad Lovers, Theatrical Cures and Gendered Bodies in Jacobean Drama," in *Enacting Gender on the English Renaissance Stage,* ed. Viviana Comensoli and Anne Russell (Chicago, 1999), 53–72.

129. In Ford's play, the words "Vid. Democrit. Junior"—Burton's pseudonym in the *Anatomy*—appear alongside the physician Corax's description of melancholy (*Lovers Melancholy,* 40). For Fletcher's influence on *A Maske,* see, e.g., *The Complete Poems of John Milton,* ed. John Carey and Alastair Fowler (Harlow, 1968), 170–71.

130. John Fletcher, *The Faithfull Shepheardesse* (London, [1610]), F3ᵛ.

131. Fletcher, *Two Noble Kinsmen,* 5.2.38, 2.4.7; Richard Brome, *The Northern Lasse,* ed. Harvey Fried (New York, 1980), 3.2.13, 2.1.89. On the former, see esp. Neely, *Distracted Subjects,* 69–98.

132. The Lady's address to chastity (*A Maske* 195–224), her speech on the "doctrine of virginity" (779–804), and her comparison of evening to a "votarist" (187–89), which may imply a monk or nun. I will address the issues here in a future essay.

133. Sprott, *A Maske: The Earlier Versions*, 8.

134. None of the Egerton daughters was married younger than 18, with the possible exception of Mary Egerton (m. 1627), for whom I have not found an exact birthdate. See Alix Egerton, *Milton's "Comus": Being the Bridgewater Manuscript, with Notes and a Short Family Memoir* (London, 1910), 15, 20–21; O'Donnell, "Egerton, Frances"; Brown, *Aristocratic Entertainments*, 186n66.

135. Louis A. Knafla, "Egerton, John, First Earl of Bridgewater (1579–1649)," *DNB*. On dowries, see Olwen H. Hufton, *The Prospect Before Her: A History of Women in Western Europe, 1500–1800* (London, 1997), 64–66, 106–08.

136. Burton, *Anatomy of Melancholy* (1628 ed.), 194.

137. Knafla, "Egerton, John"; Judith Spicksley, "The Early Modern Demographic Dynamic: Celibates and Celibacy in Seventeenth-Century England" (Ph.D. thesis, University of Hull, 2001), 127–28, 228; Amy Froide, *Never Married: Singlewomen in Early Modern England* (Oxford, 2005), 49–52, 183, 186 (quotation at 183).

"His Footstep Trace": The Natural Theology of *Paradise Lost*

Katherine Calloway

> No man ever taught, that *Adam*'s fall (which was a breach of his *religious duty towards God*) was a deficiency from the study of *Experimental Philosophie:*...as if *Natural* and *Experimental Philosophie,* not *Natural Theology,* had been the *Religion* of *Paradise.*
> —Henry Stubbe, *A Censure upon the history of the Royal Society,* 1670

Much recent work on John Milton has emphasized the harmony between *Paradise Lost* and the methods and aims of modern science. These studies have more than corrected the misimpression—imputed to a 1956 book by Kester Svendsen—that Milton was "part of a popular cultural lag, an old order not yet superseded in either common imagination or the literature of science."[1] Instead, scholars have shown that Milton was aware of contemporary work in natural history, cosmology, and physics; and, what is more, he employed in his own poetic effort the same collaboration-dependent method that was the hallmark of the new science.[2] One or two voices have warned against taking these claims too far,[3] but on the whole the new critical consensus is that Milton, like many early modern Protestants, moved things forward rather than backward, scientifically speaking. Yet while these critics carefully avoid homogenizing the "New Science," there is still a strand of scientific reform that needs to be extricated and brought into our understanding of Milton's relationship to science: a Baconian suspicion and marginalization of natural theology. Although Milton was not the reactionary Svendsen argued he was, his epic demonstrates an awareness that science could be directed to nontheological ends, a redirection that he epideictically decries. Taking instead the view of those scientific reformers who practiced natural theology, Milton works out in his poem a rubric for applying human science to theological understanding while resisting the anthropocentrism and modern notion of reason underlying many contemporary prose works of natural theology.

Milton among the Natural Theologians

When Milton wrote in *On Christian Doctrine* that God "has left so many signs of himself in the human mind, so many traces of his presence through the whole of nature, that no sane person can fail to realize that he exists," he was rehearsing a commonplace.[4] Natural theology, the application of human reason (as distinct from revelation) toward knowledge of the divine, was inferred from the writings of Saint Paul and justified the practice of philosophy during medieval Christendom. In the seventeenth century, the enterprise changed in response to new understandings of how human reason best operated: the old ontological and cosmological demonstrations of God's existence were transformed into the Cambridge Platonists' midcentury attacks on Hobbesian materialism and the increasingly popular works of physico-theology that proliferated in the latter half of the century. Making use of the growing body of discoveries in cosmology, natural history, and physics, authors of physico-theology argued that the world was too intricately designed to be the result of necessity or chance. The movement of the stars, the structure of the human eye, and the generation of a fetus had long been known to be wondrous, but nobody knew how wondrous until natural philosophers had unfolded the process in unprecedented detail.[5]

Natural philosophy thus continued to be motivated by the imperative to gain theological insight even as its methods came to rely more and more on phenomenological observation of the natural world.[6] But some scientific reformers were concerned about the legitimacy of inferring theological precepts from their discoveries. A distaste for natural theology is discernible in Francis Bacon, who had argued for excluding investigation of final causes from the practice of natural philosophy for pragmatic reasons (a battle that his side eventually won, at least as far as the Royal Society's provenance was concerned). Bacon insisted that divine things were more important than worldly things, and even conceded that natural theology was useful toward correcting pagan superstition and as "an effectuall inducement to the exaltation of the glory of God," but he lamented a misallocation of intellectual resources. What natural theology could show — that there is a God and that pagan superstition is wrong — it had already shown, and much labor was being wasted on those arguments, labor that would more profitably be applied to natural philosophy proper.[7] Some later reformers' objections were more thoroughgoing: human learning could never reach to divine things, they argued, rendering natural theology impossible and its practitioners prideful.[8]

Advancement of science and exclusion of the divine from its scope might thus go together, with the charge of pride being leveled against those who wished to apply the nascent sciences to divine things. As Bacon explained, "That men and Gods were not able to draw Jupiter down to the Earth, but contrariwise, Jupiter was able to draw them up to Heaven, so as wee ought not to attempt to drawe downe or submit the Mysteries of God to our Reason; but contrarywise, to raise and advance our reason to the Divine Truth."[9] In other words, the scientist's inquisitive gaze should be directed downward rather than upward, working to understand the region that God has given humans. In pursuing a godlike understanding of the world, "Divine Truth," humans show that they are created in God's image. To turn that inquisitiveness toward God himself, by contrast, constitutes a presumptuous attempt to "draw Jupiter down to the Earth."

This interpretation of human creation *imago dei*—humans are intended to take a God's-eye view of creation, not presuming to apply their science to divine things—was not the only one available to early modern scientists; a competing interpretation was held by scientific reformers who continued to give a legitimate place to natural theology. In their view, human creation in God's image did entail a God-like ability to perceive and understand the nature of things, an ability evident (among other ways) in Adam's mastery of the garden and naming of the animals. But the end to which knowledge was directed was theological. Far from relegating divine things to the sphere of revelation, practitioners of natural theology believed that the primary reason to practice science in the first place was for greater knowledge of final causes. A high-profile advocate of this view is Robert Boyle, who turned his pen to natural theology from time to time and who endowed a famous lecture series to continue the enterprise after his death. In his 1663 *Usefulness of Philosophy*, Boyle argued that only through scientific training can one properly read the book of nature for its deeper meaning, rendering science a worthy occupation.[10] Making the converse point was Richard Baxter, who argued in his 1667 *Reasons of the Christian Religion* that to conduct science without reference to its metaphysical implications is "to gaze on the glass and not see the image in it; or to gaze on the image, and never consider whose it is: or to read the book of the creation, and mark nothing but the words and letters, and never mind the sense and meaning."[11] For Baxter, not only was it appropriate to draw theological conclusions from scientific observations; there was no use practicing science to any other end.

If two competing interpretations of human creation *imago dei* among scientific reformers might thus be described as "godlike knowing" and "god-knowing," the young Milton was on the "god-knowing" side of the spectrum. As already mentioned, in *On Christian Doctrine* Milton wrote that no sane person would fail to draw theological conclusions from reason and observation.

Further, the vision for human learning Milton lays out in *Of Education* aligns with that of Baxter.[12] Long ago, Balachandra Rajan compared Milton's famous claim, "The end then of learning is to repair the ruins of our first parents by regaining to know God aright, and out of that knowledge to love him, to imitate him, to be like him, as we may the nearest by possessing our souls of true virtue, which being united to the heavenly grace of faith makes up the highest perfection" (YP 2:378–79),[13] with the following passage from Baxter's 1673 *A Christian Directory*: "The great means of promoting love of God is duly to behold Him in his appearances to man in the ways of Nature, Grace and Glory. First therefore learn to understand and improve His appearances in Nature, and to see the Creator in all His works, and by the knowledge and love of them, to be raised to the knowledge and love of Him."[14] Both men trace the course toward knowledge of God from observation of the natural world. Baxter foresees the use of the natural sciences in divinity—"What an excellent book is the visible world for the daily study of a holy soul!"—in terms that anticipate the naturalist John Ray's heady inferences of God's wisdom from every bird and flower.[15] Elsewhere, Baxter sets observation over cogitation explicitly: "The Soul in Flesh is so much desirous of a sensitive way of apprehension that we have great need of the clearest evidence, and the most suitable, and the most frequent, that possibly can be given us," he writes in his 1667 *Reasons of the Christian Religion*, adding that "it is foolish to reason against sense and experience or to deny that which is, because we think that it should be otherwise."[16] Likewise, Milton famously argues in *Of Education* that "our understanding cannot in this body found it selfe but on sensible things, nor arrive so cleerly to the knowledge of God and things invisible, as by orderly conning over the visible and inferior creature" (YP 2:368–69). In sum, Milton's theory of learning harmonized in many ways with that of the reformers. Already in the 1640s, however, he had distinguished himself from those who marginalized final causes, aligning himself instead with practitioners of natural theology who agreed that knowledge of God was the end of human learning.

As we turn to the Milton of the 1660s, it bears remembering that seventeenth century natural theologians often agreed about little else.[17] As a result, to say that Milton located himself among those who saw value in applying reason to theological ends is still to leave much in question. What types of natural theology might he have sanctioned? Seventeenth century specimens include the efforts of Henry More and Ralph Cudworth logically to prove God's existence against Epicurean materialism by appealing to an idea innate in the human mind, as well as arguments leveled by Newtonians later in the century asserting the staggering improbability that such a perfectly designed cosmos could exist without a perfect designer. They include the celebratory tour through the marvels of natural history found in John Ray's *Wisdom of God* as well as the self-scrutinizing arguments of Richard Baxter against the antinomians. Here I examine *Paradise Lost* alongside contemporary prose works of natural theology, discovering where Milton aligns with and diverges from these works.

Natural Theology and *Paradise Lost*

One piece of evidence that *Paradise Lost* was in conversation with contemporary works of natural theology is that some early readers saw it that way. For instance, several lines from the epic would appear on the frontispiece of John Wesley's 1763 *A Survey of the Wisdom of God in Creation:* "These are thy glorious works, Parent of good / Almighty! Thine this universal frame, / Thus wondrous fair! Thyself how wondrous then!"[18] But already in 1692 *Paradise Lost* was being brought into the service of physico-theology by a young Richard Bentley. Bentley, whose 1732 "edition" of *Paradise Lost* is known for its managerial footnotes and rampant emendations, cited the epic alongside contemporary scientific work in his inaugural Boyle Lectures, later published together as *The Folly of Atheism*. Addressing the objection that a perfect God would have created a perfectly spherical earth rather than one "distinguished with Mountains and Valleys," he calls readers' attention to Milton's Eden and heaven. If the poet cannot "imagine Paradise to be a place of Pleasure, nor Heaven it self to be Heaven" without "Valleys and swelling Accents," he argues, then surely the world is better formed with such accents than without them.[19] For Bentley, one way in which *Paradise Lost* might justify God's ways is by presenting a world that declares God's wisdom and providence.

But Bentley came to believe the epic needed emendation in order to present such a world. Among other changes in his 1732 edition of *Paradise Lost*, he took issue with the ambiguity of the cosmos as presented in book 8 and worked to bring Adam's conversation with Raphael in line with Newtonian physics.[20] Such exertions on Bentley's part suggest that *Paradise Lost* sits uneasily with at least his own type of physico-theology. This "astro-theology," which subsequent Boyle lecturers such as William Whiston and William Derham saw themselves as perfecting, argued from the mathematically predictable behavior of superlunary bodies that there must be a God. Deploying a line of reasoning later used by intelligent design theorists, they spoke of tiny particles in an immense void and the impossibility that these could coagulate into the present world on their own; they spoke of the inexplicability of the force of gravity except that it be "the immediate *Fiat* and Finger of God."[21] Bentley, in pursuit of the most accurate and authoritative information possible, famously corresponded with Isaac Newton while composing his lectures, receiving informal tutoring in mathematics as well as Newton's blessing on his theological project.[22] If Bentley viewed *Paradise Lost* as a serious effort to justify God's ways, his impulse to mend Milton's cosmos is not surprising. The question is where he went wrong: in straining to harmonize the poem with contemporary science, or in his underlying conviction that Milton's cosmos should declare a creator.

If the latter is the case—if Milton's cosmos intentionally thwarts human rational effort to arrive at theological conclusions—then the poem aligns at least to some extent with those scientific reformers who were suspicious of a "god-knowing" application of the human rational faculty. The beginning of book 8 does seem tightly to constrain, if not to undermine, this faculty and begs for comment from those who want to understand Milton's relationship to scientific advancement. Interestingly, one way to read the passage is to cast Raphael as an advocate of a Baconian "god-like knowing" that brackets final conclusions as inappropriately prideful. Focusing on the harmony between Baconian method and Raphael's prescription of epistemic humility, John Gillies characterizes Raphael's speech as "a masterpiece of scientific awareness," explaining, "Raphael begins by applauding the spirit of free inquiry: 'To ask or search I blame thee not...whether heaven move or earth, / Imports not, if thou reckon right' (8.66, 70–71). What looks like an evasion (it doesn't matter which cosmological hypothesis is right) is in fact a Baconian regard for methodological rigor ('if thou reckon right'): the answer is less important than the integrity of the question and the methods used to pursue it." Analysis of this passage by Gillies and others has shown that Raphael sets himself against philosophically conclusive "model-spinning" and advocates instead the more receptive methods of Baconian science:[23] Raphael is untroubled by Bentley's evident need for the universe to turn out to be one way and not another. But careful bounds are set on his scientific open-mindedness in the lines that Gillies elides:

> To ask or search I blame thee not, for Heav'n
> Is as the Book of God before thee set,
> Wherein to read his wondrous Works, and learne
> His Seasons, Hours, or Dayes, or Months, or Yeares.
> *This to attain,* whether Heav'n move or Earth,
> Imports not, if thou reck'n right.[24] (*PL* 8.66–71; emphasis added)

To "reck'n right," then, is not only to use a particular methodology, but also to seek knowledge of God by reading his wondrous works. What does not tend toward this end, "the rest," has been concealed from "them who ought / Rather admire" (8.74–75).[25] Raphael therefore asserts that the universe, no matter what its precise composition and movement, *will* always turn out to be one way (evincing God) and not another (evincing chance or necessity). What distinguishes Milton's reading of the book of nature from Richard Bentley's—as we shall see more fully in a moment—is Bentley's concern that a particular cosmology might put God's existence and providence into question.

Instead, Milton begs the question and presumes that all truth comes from God, and that any advancement in knowledge will return humans to God. Raphael explicitly says that God's glory is the end of human knowledge when he promises to tell Adam—in language reminiscent of the earliest aims of the Royal Society—"what thou canst attain, which best may serve / To glorify thy Maker, and infer / Thee also happier" (*PL* 7.115–17).[26] The doctrine that all truth originates in God, implicit in Milton's theology of creation *ex deo*, is evident in this and other episodes of learning in the poem, to which we now turn. In tracing how and to what end human reason functions in those episodes, I come to three conclusions. First, both before and after the Fall humans are obliged and encouraged to apply their reason toward theological ends—that is, to practice natural theology. Second, in both cases reason is not epistemically conclusive and must be supplemented by instruction that originates in God. (The only lesson in the poem not so supplemented is the experiential lesson of God's ability to suppress rebellion, and it is the self-originating nature of that lesson that leaves the rebels condemned.) This suggests that Milton's conception of "reason" may differ fundamentally from the conception operating in works purporting to prove God's existence, whether from an innate idea or from the structure and operations of the natural world. Finally, the poem suggests that fallen humans must rely more exclusively than before on sense and revelation over intuition and deduction.

Unfallen Natural Theology in *Paradise Lost*

Unfallen humans show a proclivity for rightly interpreting the data before them. Prelapsarian Adam and Eve are "natural theologians" in the sense that theology comes naturally to them: they use their intellects with great efficiency in drawing accurate conclusions about God. This proclivity is not unlike the "actual knowledge" on which the Cambridge Platonist Henry More rests his influential work of natural theology, *An Antidote against Atheism* (1653):

> Suppose a skilful *Musician* fallen asleep in the field upon the grasse,...but his friend sitting by him that cannot sing at all himself, jogs him and awakes him, and desires him to sing this or the other song, telling him two or three words of the beginning of the song, he presently takes it out of his mouth, and sings the whole song upon so slight and slender intimation: So the *Mind* of *man* being jogg'd and awakened by the impulses of outward objects is stirred up into a more full and cleare conception of what was but imperfectly hinted to her from externall occasions; and this faculty I venture to call *actuall Knowledge* in such a sense as the sleeping Musicians skill might be called *actuall skill* when he thought nothing of it.[27]

Adam experiences such a "jogging" after he has waked into existence. From the first he knows that he exists "Not of my self; by some great Maker then," a deduction that Roy Flannagan notes demonstrates his innate rational faculty (*PL* 8.278). Further, he knows that nothing he sees is that Maker: like Satan on Mount Niphates, he first addresses the sun, but rather than both praising and envying the sun as Satan does, Adam charges the sun to testify along with all created things "how may I know him, how adore, / From whom I have that thus I move and live" (8.280–81). Fresh from the ground, Adam has already outstripped the pagan world in theological understanding.

Adam's dialogue with God further shows him to have the kind of reason More attributes to the considerate natural theologian. More sets out to describe the physical world—stars, earth, plants, animals, humans—in terms that illustrate that "there can be no fitter excogitated." "Whereas the rude motions of matter a thousand to one might have best cast it otherwise," More declares, "yet the productions of things as such as our own Reason cannot but approve to bee best, or as wee our selves would have design'd them."[28] Later, discussing human anatomy, he pronounces, "supposing the same matter that our bodyes are made of, if it had been in our own power to have made our selves, we should have fram'd our selves no otherwise then we are," adding regarding the eye specifically: "what could [one] have excogitated more accurate?"[29] For More, human reason is capable of testing and approving the design it finds in the world and would be capable of noticing a deficiency in this design, if there were any. This is precisely what happens once Adam has surveyed all the animals: "In these," he says, "I found not what me thought I wanted still," and the reader comes to find that in leaving Eve uncreated, God intended to test Adam's "excogitative" abilities through Socratic interrogation (*PL* 8.354–55, 437).

Milton's God does not merely incline unfallen humans to practice natural theology, however; he obliges them to do so in a context in which other ways of thinking about creation are possible. In Eve's dialogue with Adam about the stars, and in Adam's dialogue with Raphael on the same topic, the possibility of gaining knowledge without reference to God is raised and decried. Closing a sonnet that ties several features of the natural world to her relationship with Adam,[30] Eve asks, "wherefore all night long shine these, for whom / This glorious sight, when sleep hath shut all eyes?" (*PL* 4.657–58). She does not ask the question of natural philosophy, "how," but the questions of natural theology: "wherefore" and "for whom." But her implicit assumption that creation ultimately exists for the sake of humankind needs correction. Adam answers Eve that stars may fittingly and usefully shine, so long as creatures besides the two humans have the ability to glorify God. Adam assumes that a "glorious sight" could be considered superfluous only if, absent spectators, the sight produced no praise of God (4.676). The problem is not that a creature might be useless to humans, but that a creature might be useless to God.

Similarly, when Adam asks Raphael how "wise and frugal" Nature could allot such vast space to less worthy bodies, the angel emphasizes the subordinate nature of humankind. Raphael answers that heavenly motions "speak / The Makers high magnificence," reminding Adam that "he dwells not in his own" and concluding "Heav'n is for thee too high" (8.26, 100–01, 104, 172). Kester Svendsen has been taken to task by scholars for claiming that Raphael here "dismisses the controversy [over heliocentrism] as insignificant and impertinent to man's duty to God and to himself."[31] Yet while Svendsen may indeed be unnecessarily dismissive of science in the poem, Raphael's admonitory tone nonetheless calls for a more tempered view of Milton's scientific enthusiasm. One might rewrite Svendsen and summarize Raphael's view as: scientific inquiry is significant insofar as it is pertinent to the humans' duty first to God, and derivatively to themselves. While Svendsen's terse proclamation misses the possibility that natural philosophy may aid humans in praising God, rendering "asking and searching" a highly significant human duty, his modern-day critics may obscure the centrality of God's glory in the cosmos of *Paradise Lost*.

This conception of natural theology—theocentric rather than anthropocentric—differs fundamentally from Henry More's but aligns with that of Richard Baxter in his 1667 *Reasons of the Christian Religion*. The glory and praise of God are conspicuously absent from More's *Antidote against Atheism*, which focuses instead on the glory of humankind.[32] Confronted (like Milton's Adam and Eve) with phenomena of no apparent use to humans, More takes a tack far different from Adam's. He argues that this lack of usefulness is only apparent: seemingly superfluous or harmful things simply require more human art, skill, and reason to tease out a use, and the very challenge presented by such things is itself useful in exercising human intellect.[33] More makes exceptional provision for the lower animals' right to enjoy themselves,[34] a move spurned by Baxter, who structures his argument around humans' proprietary right over beasts as metonymic for God's proprietary right over humans. Baxter argues that man may do with his beasts as he sees fit, adding: "Man is also (subordinately) their Benefactor, and their End: and they are more for Him than for themselves." Later he completes the metonym, drawing the necessary implication for natural theology: "Therefore Gods Works must be more valued and studied, as they are the Glass representing the Image of his perfections, and shewing us his chief essential amiableness, than as they are beneficial and useful to us, and so shew us only his benignity to us."[35] The sentiment here echoes Adam's answer to Eve's question about the stars' shining "unbeheld in deep of night" (*PL* 4.674). "Though men were none," Adam says, "heav'n would

[not] want spectators, God want praise" (4.675–76). It also echoes Raphael's declaration to Adam that all but a "small partition" of the world is "Ordain'd for uses to his Lord best known" (8.106). In short, whatever answer science might supply for Adam's question about geocentrism, figuratively, the universe does not revolve around him.

Having placed Adam and Eve in a world in which the attempt to practice science—even experimental science—without reference to a higher end is redirected, Milton also addresses whether science alone can achieve that higher end. Although possessing a propensity to reason from "outward objects" and "external occasions" to the knowledge of a creator using something like Henry More's actual knowledge, Adam's first few hours of life also argue for the limitations of his reason. Newly created, he ends his monologue with a question rather than an answer, a pattern that will be repeated in Eve's and his reasoning regarding the stars. Having inferred from the wondrousness of creation that there must be a creator, he stops short of knowledge of that creator's name and character, asking if anyone can tell him these things. He then enters a trance and sees a "Presence Divine," who declares, "Whom thou soughtst I am" (8.314, 316). The presence subsequently explains to Adam his identity and place in the newly created world. The implications of this scene of empirical inquiry and divine revelation for seventeenth century justification for advancement of knowledge are profound. Even if, as some thought, *scientia* might restore to humans their unfallen powers of intellect, Milton suggests that they would still require revelation through a divine word.

In limiting the powers of human reason in this way, Milton falls within the range of positions taken by seventeenth century scientific reformers. Just as his theological justification for natural philosophy resonates with the work of Robert Boyle and Richard Baxter, against those who wished to marginalize natural theology, his emphasis on the limits of reason involves him in a polemic stretching the length of the century, from Francis Bacon to the natural historian John Ray. Both of these scientists contemplate Ecclesiastes 3:11: "Yet cannot man find out the worke which God worketh from the beginning to the end."[36] Quoting the verse in his 1691 *Wisdom of God Manifested in the Works of Creation*, Ray emphasizes human limitations: "To Trace the Footsteps of his Wisdom in the Composition, Order, Harmony, and Uses of every one of [God's works]," he declares, "would be a Task far transcending my Skill and Abilities; nay, the joynt Skill and Endeavours of all men now living, or that shall live after a Thousand Ages, should the World last so long."[37] Bacon, by contrast, had explained in *The Advancement of Learning* that Solomon did not mean here to "derogate from the capacitie of the mind" but to acknowledge the many "Inconveniences" that oblige people to work collaboratively from generation to generation.[38] Human knowledge generally, if not the knowledge of any particular human, "may comprehend all the universall nature of thinges," Bacon goes on to argue, provided that humans remember their mortality, apply their knowledge for human benefit, and "doe not presume by the contemplation of Nature, to attaine to the misteries of God." While Raphael would applaud Bacon's call for humility, prelapsarian Adam famously suggests that the goal of "contemplation of created things" is precisely to "ascend to God" (*PL* 5.511–12), and Raphael does not correct him. In Eden, humility arises naturally from humans' inability to perform that exercise uninstructed rather than from a self-imposed bracketing of theological concerns.

Moreover, although the question of whether humans could ever comprehend "all the universal nature of things" remains open in *Paradise Lost*, the view in the poem seems closer to Ray's than to Bacon's. In the first place, as already noted, Raphael's caution in book 8 sets such an achievement far enough off to be a dim possibility at best. Second, "comprehend," with its etymological resonance of exhaustive thoroughness, is emphatically bounded or reserved for God the three times the word appears in the poem (see *PL* 3.705, 5.505, and 7.114). And finally, there is a fundamental difference between the two scientists' understandings of the relationship between God and nature: Bacon paraphrases the Teacher's "work which God worketh" strongly as a "supreme or summarie law of Nature," begging a central theological question;[39] Ray paraphrases the same line, equally tellingly, as "the Footsteps of his Wisdom." Here, too, Milton's language is closer to Ray's: divine footsteps, not natural law.

The distance between Milton's language and the law-infused physical metaphors of modern science suggests that Milton may not merely have been setting limits on the human capacity to measure and master an objective nature (and thence to draw necessary conclusions about the divine); he may have understood by "reason" something entirely different from the capacity to measure and master. In an exposition of Milton's "scriptural reasoning," Phillip Donnelly highlights passages in Milton's prose and poetry that point to a conception of reason as fundamentally relational, a "poetic gift of peaceful difference" subsisting in the ability to "participate in the ontic goodness of creation."[40] Modern science, by contrast, rests on the notion that matter subsists in a state of chaos, and that an ordered world must have been brought to order by violent coercion. The logic of prose works of natural theology such as Henry More's and Richard Bentley's rests on this necessary inference of an ordering principle from the fact that matter has come to be ordered at all; in this view, reason can operate independently of revelation to pronounce on the existence of such a principle. If, however, chaos and violent coercion do not exhaust the possible realities, if reason has an aesthetic dimension and is fundamentally relational, then reason is not simply curtailed in that it cannot function apart from conversation; reason consists in conversation. In either case, whether Milton (like John Ray) simply curtails reason as the ability to draw logically compulsive conclusions, or "reason" for him consists in relational participation in a reality that is neither necessary nor random, even unfallen humans cannot rely on reason alone.

Fallen Reason and Natural Theology

If right reason in *Paradise Lost* is theocentric and eminently concerned with final causes, fallen reason jettisons "the God hypothesis" as a viable way to understand the nature and purpose of the cosmos, replacing it with self-centered teleology, pagan superstition, and a desire to "discerne / Things in thir Causes" (*PL* 9.681–82). The serpent claims to have this ability as he works on Eve's reason, for example, concluding:

> The Gods are first, and that advantage use
> On our belief, that all from them proceeds;
> I question it, for this fair Earth I see,
> Warm'd by the Sun, producing every kind,
> Them nothing. (9.718–22)

The impious old argument for spontaneous generation, which Richard Bentley would address in *The Folly of Atheism*,[41] stands in stark contrast to Adam's immediate recognition that he and the sun have a greater author. Satan's alternative reading of nature here gives Eve an opportunity to exercise her reason and her "actual knowledge" in defense of God's wisdom. Eve should recognize a God-free origin hypothesis as diabolical, having heard about Satan's claim to be "self-begot, self-rais'd / By our own quick'ning power" (5.860–61). Such passages as these have formed a locus of critical discussion about a putative link between Satan's "Missourism," as Stanley Fish calls it—"Show me, seeing is believing"[42]—and sin. Karen Edwards argues, contra Fish, that Eve required more, not less, empirical acuity in order to see the serpent's deception.[43] On the one hand, Fish's point that Eve should not have *needed* to scrutinize the serpent's vocal chords in order to determine that she should not violate a direct command from God still stands; on the other hand, Edwards's observation that such scrutiny would have shown the serpent to be a charlatan demonstrates a readiness on Milton's part to paint a cosmos that will not unduly try the human capacity to obey.

In the end, what undoes Eve is the kind of teleological anthropocentrism underlying much seventeenth century physico-theology as well as empirical natural philosophy.[44] While Raphael cautions against the assumption that everything exists for the benefit of humankind, Satan makes the same assumption as he approaches the newly created world and its inhabitants:

> Oh Earth, how like to Heav'n, if not preferr'd
> More justly, Seat worthier of Gods, as built
> With second thoughts, reforming what was old!
> For what God, after better, worse would build?
> Terrestrial Heav'n, danc't round by other Heav'ns
> That shine, yet bear thir bright officious Lamps,
> Light above light, for thee alone, as seems
> In thee concentring all their precious beams
> Of sacred influence: As God in Heav'n
> Is center, yet extends to all, so thou
> Centring receav'st from all those Orbs; in thee,
> Not in themselves, all thir known virtue appeers
> Productive in Herb, Plant, and nobler birth
> Of Creatures animate with gradual life
> Of Growth, Sense, Reason, all summ'd up in Man. (*PL* 9.99–113)

These lines, engaging humanity's "centring" for the third time in the poem, invite close consideration. Much of what Satan says accords with Raphael's explanation of the relative excellence of heavenly bodies at the beginning of book 8: the sun does, according to Raphael, exist more for the sake of humans than for itself, enabling the generative processes whereby vegetable, animal, and rational life is sustained on earth. Man's superiority over the other two types of life, too, is clear and unquestioned both in Raphael's account here and in the Creator's words to the newly created Adam. The crucial difference between that view and the one expressed by Satan lies in the relationship between earth and heaven: Satan speaks as though these are realms under separate jurisdictions. In 1.261–63 Satan had hoped that, while God is sovereign in heaven, he himself might "reign secure" in hell; here in 9.99–113 he suggests that human beings may likewise reign secure in their "terrestrial heav'n." The reader has seen, however, that much in this pendant world points to an end besides life on earth: the stars shine all night with no "known virtue" to humans and in order to argue "the Maker's high magnificence," not "for thee alone," as Satan says to the earth. Richard Baxter had asserted a metonymic relationship between human dominance over the earth and divine dominance over humankind; instead of a metonym, Satan sees an analogy ("As God in heav'n...so thou"). He hopes that there is more than one center.

And if for Satan earth is a "terrestrial heav'n," Eve is a "Goddess humane" (9.732), the center of the world he wants to comprehend without reference to any other heavens or other gods. Her acquiescence to this view after the Fall is evident when she tells Adam that the serpent "Hath eat'n of the fruit, and is become,...Endu'd with human voice, and human sense, / Reasoning to admiration" (9.869, 9.871–72). On the surface, Eve's remark seems to mean that the serpent's apparent ability to reason evoked her own admiration of (or wonder at) the serpent's new prowess; the absence of clarifying pronouns, however, opens up another interpretation—especially since Eve was so moved by his words of rapturous admiration for herself. For the whole of their existence, the two humans have understood that reasoning naturally leads to admiration in the reasoner: their own reasoning had always led to greater admiration of God. Perhaps Eve appeals to the serpent's performance of such "reasoning to admiration" as evidence of his credibility. The serpent's reason, however, did not lead to his admiring God; it led to his admiring Eve, and this redirection should have marked his knowledge as suspect. Adam, likewise admiring Eve rather than God, soon submits to the same perversion.[45] In short, fallen reason in *Paradise Lost* often co-opts the teleological language used to justify science in Milton's England, setting up humankind as the end of a self-sustaining order.

The humans having redirected toward themselves the reasoning admiration that properly belongs to God, the question arises: how, if at all, might reason be applied to redress this problem? If human reason is now misdirected in its end, are its power and method also perverted? Or might the rational faculty still be in working order, capable of recovering theological truth, if by grace humans were once again willing to seek it? These questions face not only Adam and Eve in the last three books of the poem but also Milton as well as his contemporaries in the Royal Society.

Unsurprisingly, in *Paradise Lost* the kind of natural theology attempted by Henry More, already dangerously anthropocentric in its end, becomes less viable in its method after the Fall. The incompatibility is evident on both sides: in *An Antidote against Atheism*, More omits to mention the Fall, an omission that suggests the "actual knowledge" he attributes to humans could easily be subject to its adverse effects. While it may seem prudent, perhaps necessary, to leave human fallenness out of natural theology, many early works of physico-theology tackle the subject unflinchingly. John Wilkins, a founding member of the Royal Society and Bishop of Chester from 1668, refers to the Fall in his 1675 *Principles and Duties of Natural Religion* and asserts the necessity of revelation to complement his arguments.[46] What is more, Richard Bentley's Boyle Lectures begin with an entire sermon on Psalm 14:1 ("The fool hath said in his heart, 'There is no god'"), referring later to our participation in "the miseries of *Adam*'s Fall" and flatly asserting, "We do not contend to have the Earth pass for a Paradise."[47]

Nor was this humility confined to physico-theology. Nathaniel Culverwell, often classified as a Cambridge Platonist, makes this apology in his 1652 *An Elegant and Learned Discourse on the Light of Nature:*

> Far be it from me to extenuate that great and fatal overthrow, which the sons of men had in their first and original apostasie from their God;...but this we are sure, it did not annihilate the soul, it did not destroy the essence, the powers and faculties, nor the operations of the soul; though it did defile them, and disorder them, and every way indispose them....The whole head is wounded, and akes, and is there no other way but to cut it off? The Candle of the Lord does not shine so clearly as it was wont, must it therfore be extinguisht presently? is it not better to enjoy the faint and languishing light of this Candle of the Lord, rather then to be in palpable and disconsolate darknesse?[48]

Human reason, often figured as "the candle of the Lord" in contrast with the greater light of revelation,[49] has grown yet dimmer since the events of Genesis, book 3. The exploration of human reason in the final books of *Paradise Lost* resonates with Culverwell's rhetorical questions: "disconsolate" is exactly what Adam and Eve will be without enlightenment from Michael (*PL* 11.113–15).

The nature and medium of Michael's instruction, and Adam's participation in the lesson, thus helps to illuminate the role Milton allowed the "Candle of the Lord," human knowledge, in fallen human conversation. The process of fallen learning, of repairing the ruins by regaining to know God aright, begins in book 11.

The trope of lost light appearing in contemporary works of natural theology appears in Adam's lament when he learns that he and Eve are to be expelled from paradise: the garden was their "onely consolation left / Familiar to our eyes, all places else /...desolate" (*PL* 11.304–06). Adam's first experience of the sun had led him to the knowledge of "some great Maker" and now he foresees a desolate experience of separation from God—"As from his face I shall be hid" (11.316). Looking toward the land outside of Eden, Adam puts to Michael the central question of natural theology: "In yonder nether world where shall I seek / His bright appearances, or footstep trace?" (9.328–29). This seems to have been a pertinent question, for Michael offers a consoling answer:

> *Adam*, thou know'st Heav'n his, and all the Earth,
> Not this Rock onely; his Omnipresence fills
> Land, Sea, and Aire, and every kinde that lives,
> Fomented by his virtual power and warmd.   (11.335–38)

Michael's speech accomplishes several things. It highlights the smallness and backward-looking nature of Adam's desire to tie God's presence to particular sites in Eden. It repudiates Satan's suggestion that the earth belongs to humanity. And it complements Raphael's earlier remarks to Adam about the literal sun, whose "virtue on it self workes no effect, / But in the fruitful Earth; there first receavd, / His beams, unactive else, their vigor find" (8.95–97). Raphael needed only to point out that the sun serves the world rather than the other way around; the fallen Adam must further be told that, at a deeper level, it is the Creator's presence and not the literal sun that sustains creation.

Having recalled to Adam God's presence and activity in the natural world, the angel begins to instruct him in the appropriate way to read the world for that presence and activity. In mentioning

God's power, Michael aligns briefly with Francis Bacon, who argued that natural theology should demonstrate God's power and wisdom rather than tracing his image in any particular feature of the world.⁵⁰ But although the natural theology Michael will model for Adam foregoes the old doctrine of correspondences, it is also far from the broad-ranging, downward-gazing comprehension of "things in their causes" that Bacon advocates in the *Advancement of Learning*. Calling Earth "no despicable gift," Michael conveys that it was never God's intention for Adam to look down, understanding the earth in the comprehensive and detached (one might say "objective") way available to one standing on Pisgah.⁵¹ Adam then learns from experience how little can be understood from such a vantage point during the two books he spends on "a Hill / of Paradise the highest" (*PL* 11.377–78): he repeatedly misinterprets the data before him and must be corrected by Michael. Adam's repeated failures in understanding show the insufficiency of human effort generally, figured in the sweeping away of "Earths Kingdomes and thir Glory" in favor of "nobler sights" in lines 411–12 (see also 11.384). But crucially, while Adam's vision proves incapable on its own of leading him to truth, he is nonetheless required to look. The first half of Adam's lesson is conducted by a series of images, which he must attempt to interpret himself before he learns what they signify. By this means Michael combines the book of Scripture and the book of Nature into one hermeneutic project for Adam. He sees through a glass darkly, but he sees.⁵²

Eventually, however, Adam's sight fails. At the end of book 11 Michael comments that "objects divine / Must needs impaire and wearie human sense" and says he will continue to reveal sacred history orally (*PL* 12.9–10). This point in the narrative parallels the scene in book 8 when prelapsarian Adam has exhausted his rational resources and needs a "Presence Divine" to explain the authorship of creation. Here, revelation must supplement visual observation if Adam is to apprehend "objects divine," the presumed end of his lesson. In a striking moment of metacommentary, Michael correlates Adam with Abraham, the biblical type of faith's triumph over sight, when he narrates how Abraham was asked to leave his "native Soile," setting out from Ur "not knowing to what Land, yet firm believes" (12.129). Michael adds parenthetically, "I see him, but thou canst not," intimating Adam's need to receive Michael's narrative with the same faith with which Abraham received his call (12.127–28). (The injunction also applies to Milton's audience, as he tells of things invisible to mortal sight.)[53] This elevation of the aurally received words over images jars with the Royal Society's motto *nullius in verba*, "not in words alone."[54] As was the case before the Fall, it is reason that cannot stand alone and must be supplemented by a divine word. Still, sight is not denied Adam in the final two books of *Paradise Lost:* he is to work by candlelight, to use Culverwell's image, considering how his light is spent.

In sum, even after the Fall, humans are obliged to engage in a distinctly sense-based natural theology, reading the world before them—usually from up close—for evidence of the divine presence, but always with the caveat that direct revelation is required to supplement that reading. Already these limitations of fallen learning distance the natural theology of *Paradise Lost* from some "rational theology" of the Cambridge Platonists and later works of astrotheology; but *Paradise Lost* operates differently even from less ambitious prose works. Those works still follow the general logic: there is a world; therefore, there must be a powerful creator. The world is well designed; therefore, that creator must be wise. Bacon had pointed out that, once these things have been demonstrated, not much remains for natural theology to do—except to add heft to the "well designed" part of the argument. It was on these grounds that physico-theology proliferated (against Bacon's wishes) later in the century, or else on the grounds that some audiences had not yet been reached by existing iterations. Though by volume these works spend more time outlining or establishing empirical data than had their predecessors, at their core they are still old deductive arguments. In *Paradise Lost*, by contrast, the very word "argument" means "narrative," and the "must be" drops out. There is a world, the narrator says; there is a powerful and wise creator; this is how that Creator did it.

This removal of the "therefore," the transmutation of deductive argument into narrative assertion, explains how Milton's poetic natural theology can be more empirical and scientifically open-minded than its prose counterparts, even as Raphael insists that rational observation will always end in admiration of the Creator.[55] Already the physico-theologians took a relatively receptive and humble posture next to the logically compulsive reasoning of philosophers such as Descartes and Cudworth; Milton's poem embodies this humility and receptivity yet more fully.[56] His theological conclusion does not rest on the particular structure and operations of the natural world, but in the story of human participation in a reality originating in God.

The distance between Milton's more rigorously empirical natural theology and his contemporaries' more rationalistic arguments is vividly illustrated by the case of Bentley's *Paradise Lost*. In a syllogism in which God's providence is a conclusion, much depends on establishing the premise: the world must be shown to be well designed. Though Bentley admits that earth "need not pass for a Paradise," it is nonetheless important for him that the world be shown at its best, that Milton's argument not suffer more than it must because of misinformation. Thus does Bentley fret over lines such as 10.710–12: "Beast now with Beast gan war, and Fowle with Fowle, / And Fish with Fish; to graze the Herb all leaving, / Devourd each other." "Did *All* leave grazing the Herb?" Bentley asks in a footnote, "The major part of them, as they do still, kept to their former Food. And then, *Devour'd each other?* That's impossible, and nonsense." He amends the lines to read: "To graze the Herb some leaving, / Devour'd the others."[57] For the most part, he implies, the world still functions admirably, evincing God's wisdom and power. Bentley saw what was at stake in the poem, but he located Milton's great argument in the objective, calculable structure and operations of the natural world rather than in the dynamic interaction between God and humans that forms the substance of Michael's "argument."

And if the argument's substance is not syllogistic logic but narrative, its end is not finally to establish God's power and wisdom but his unfolding "ways"—and the defining characteristic of his ways is love.⁵⁸ Raphael had counseled Adam to be "lowly wise"; in his summary speech, Michael likewise emphasizes the presence of God's footsteps in the lowlands:

> Yet doubt not but in Vallie, and in plaine,
> God is as here, and will be found alike
> Present; and of his presence many a signe
> Still following thee, still compassing thee round
> With goodness and paternal Love, his Face
> Express, and of his steps the track Divine.   (*PL* 11.349–54)

Although natural theology in the period typically focused on divine power or wisdom, Richard Baxter emphasized love in his natural theology as in his natural philosophy.⁵⁹ Baxter's theory of natural theology, as we have seen, comes the closest to Milton's own, and Baxter pays particular attention to the relationship between knowledge and love in the second part of his 1689 *Knowledge and Love Compared*, whose first three chapters unfold: "(1) Knowledge is a means to a higher End, according to which it is to be estimated; (2) the end of Knowledge is to make us Lovers of God, and so to be known of him, and (3) therefore Knowledge is to be sought, valued and used as it tendeth to our Love of God."⁶⁰ Milton's poem artistically represents Baxter's theoretical explanation, depicting appropriate and inappropriate love of knowledge and even drawing an analogy to appropriate and inappropriate carnal knowledge. Human sexual intercourse and human reason are both relational, and both naturally produce "offspring," the offspring of reason being admiration and love of the Creator. Both, when redirected toward exclusively self-serving ends, are sinful. But in both cases, it is wrong to defame "as impure what God declares / Pure" (*PL* 4.746–47).

Much might be said for understanding Milton's view of *scientia* in these terms. From the dialogues between Adam, Eve, and Raphael concerning the stars, the lesson emerges that knowing too much is sinful because—and only because—it is loving too little. Far from decrying knowledge, Adam and Raphael understand knowledge's instrumentality toward greater love of God and therefore urge a subordinate love of knowledge. Likewise, rightly conducted, Eve's "reasoning to admiration" would have led her to greater love of God because of her greater knowledge of him. The Fall marked the first instance of knowledge that did not lead to love of God, and from that moment the rule of love must be applied more rigorously to test whether knowledge has exceeded its bounds. *Paradise Lost*, perhaps the best-known treatment of amative desire for knowledge in the West since Dante, narrates a spectacular disordering of those two loves, but it also provides examples of proper ordering in prelapsarian Adam, Raphael, and Michael.

But though Milton's poem anticipates Baxter's treatise on the instrumental value of knowledge toward the intrinsic good of love, the two men differ fundamentally on the nature of the relationship between knowledge and love. Baxter presumes it to be linear. Imagining the comprehensive knowledge toward which science tends, he exclaims:

> If we had a sight of all the Orbs, both fixed Starrs and Planets, and of their matter, and form, and order, and relation to each other, and their communications and influences on each other, and the cause of all their wonderous motions: If we saw not only the nature of the Elements, especially the active Element, Fire; but also the constitution, magnitude, and use, of all those thousand Suns, and lesser Worlds, which constitute the universal World: And, if they be inhabited, if we knew the Inhabitants of each: Did we know all the Intelligences, blessed Angels, and holy Spirits, which possess the nobler parts of Nature; and the unhappy degenerate Spirits, that have departed from light and joy, into darkness and horrour, by departing from God; yea, if we could see all these comprehensively, at one view; what thoughts should we have of the wisdom of the Creator?[61]

Baxter is not suggesting that humans will ever achieve this comprehensive view, but he rhetorically wishes that we would, assuming that our admiration of God would be greater in proportion to our knowledge. In book 8 of *Paradise Lost*, Raphael raises the same hypothetical situation to assert exactly the opposite: if the unfallen Adam could fathom all mysteries and all knowledge, he might yet have no better thoughts of the wisdom of the Creator than he does now (*PL* 8.66–178). Raphael speaks as well to the seventeenth century physico-theologian: knowledge of physics and natural history may increase, Milton suggests, but this does not necessarily mean knowledge and love of God will increase proportionately. Bacon too noted this disjunction but did not see it as implying a need to curtail the pursuit of knowledge.

Michael, by contrast, asserts that other activities should interrupt learning as the humans journey toward knowledge of God with wandering steps and slow. At the end of the poem, Adam learns that his task is "to love with feare the onely God...and on him sole depend" (12.562–64). He hence acknowledges that God is the author of light and life, that humans will always uncover divine activity in nature if they reason rightly. In response, Michael repeats Raphael's assertion of the nonlinear relationship between knowledge and love, adding a final exhortation:

> This having learnt, thou hast attaind the summe
> Of wisdome; hope no higher, though all the Starrs
> Thou knewst by name, and all th' ethereal Powers,
> All secrets of the deep, all Natures works,
> Or works of God in Heav'n, Air, Earth, or Sea,
> And all the riches of this World enjoydst,
> And all the rule, one Empire; onely add
> Deeds to thy knowledge answerable, add Faith,
> Add vertue, Patience, Temperance, add Love,
> By name to come call'd Charitie, the soul
> Of all the rest. (12.575–85)

Even as they exit the garden, Adam and Eve carry the capacity for *caritas*, which breathes life into the rest of the virtues and will ultimately enable their souls to enter a state of rest again. *Caritas* is also, Michael asserts, the "track divine" of God's footsteps. As we have seen, an impulse behind much seventeenth century science was the drive to restore God's image in humanity, an image that was defaced by the Fall. Adding "Deeds to [his] knowledge answerable," Adam will recover that divine image by imitating divine love.

Westmont College

Notes

I am grateful to Dennis Danielson, Phillip Donnelly, and the anonymous readers at *Milton Studies* for their helpful comments on this article.

1. Kester Svendsen, *Milton and Science* (Cambridge, Mass., 1956), 226.

2. Harinder Singh Majara, *"Contemplation of Created Things": Science in "Paradise Lost"* (Toronto, 1992); John Rogers, *The Matter of Revolution: Science, Poetry, and Politics in the Age of Milton* (Ithaca, N.Y., 1996); Stephen Fallon, *Milton among the Philosophers: Poetry and Materialism in Seventeenth-Century England* (Ithaca, N.Y., 1996); Karen Edwards, *Milton and the Natural World* (Cambridge, 1999); Catherine Gimelli Martin, "'What If the Sun Be Centre to the World?': Milton's Epistemology, Cosmology, and Paradise of Fools Reconsidered," *Modern Philology* 99 (2001): 231–65; John Gillies, "Space and Place in *Paradise Lost*," *ELH* 74 (2007): 27–57; Angelica Duran, *The Age of Milton and the Scientific Revolution* (Pittsburgh, 2007); and Joanna Picciotto, "Milton and the Paradizable Reader," *Labors of Innocence in Early Modern England* (Cambridge, Mass., 2010), 400–507.

3. Ann Baynes Coiro, "'To repair the ruins of our first parents': *Of Education* and Fallen Adam," *SEL* (1988): 133–47; Stanley Fish, "Why We Can't All Just Get Along," in *The Trouble with Principle* (Cambridge, Mass., 1999), 243–62; and William Poole, "Milton and Science: A Caveat," *Milton Quarterly* 38 (2004): 18–34. Picciotto qualifies Poole's argument, but affirms that Milton was not himself an "aspiring virtuoso" (*Labors of Innocence*, 725n21).

4. John Milton, *On Christian Doctrine*, in *Complete Prose Works of John Milton*, 8 vols., ed. Don M. Wolfe et al. (New Haven, Conn., 1953–82), 6:130. All citations from Milton's prose are to this edition, hereafter cited in the text as YP, followed by volume and page number.

5. See, respectively, Richard Bentley, *The Folly and unreasonableness of atheism demonstrated from the advantage and pleasure of a religious life, the faculties of humane souls, the structure of animate bodies, & the origin and frame of the world: in eight sermons preached at the lecture founded by the late honourable Robert Boyle, Esquire* (London, 1699), 208–10; Henry More, *An Antidote against atheisme; or, An appeal to the natural faculties of the minde of Man, whether there be not a God* (London, 1653), 94–95; and John Ray, *The Wisdom of God Manifested in the Works of Creation, Being the Substance of some common Places delivered in the Chappel of Trinity-College, in Cambridge* (London, 1691), 56–61.

6. Peter Harrison, *The Bible, Protestantism, and the Rise of Modern Science* (Cambridge, 1998), 168–69. Scott Mandelbrote, "Early Modern Natural Theology," in *The Oxford Handbook of Natural Theology*, ed. Russell Re Manning (Oxford, 2013), summarizes a spate of recent

arguments that natural theology "granted legitimacy to an emerging scientific culture of 'modernity'" (76).

7. Francis Bacon, *Advancement of Learning* (London, 1605), 31, 23.

8. Godfrey Goodman, John Webster, and John Owen all argued in this direction. See William Poole, *Milton and the Idea of the Fall* (Cambridge, 2005), 1; Scott Mandelbrote, "The Uses of Natural Theology in Seventeenth-Century England," *Science in Context* 20, no. 3 (2007): 452–54; and J. I. Packer, *The Redemption and Restoration of Man in the Thought of Richard Baxter* (Exeter, 2003), 90–92.

9. Bacon, *Advancement of Learning,* 23.

10. Robert Boyle, *Some Considerations Touching the Usefulnesse of Experimental Natural Philosophy* (London, 1663), 4; see also Mandelbrote, "Uses of Natural Theology," 463.

11. Richard Baxter, *Reasons of the Christian Religion* (London, 1667), 108.

12. This is not to deny the ecclesiastical and political differences between Milton and Baxter, some of which are surveyed in John Peter Rumrich's "Uninventing Milton," *Modern Philology* 87 (1990): 258. However, the sense Rumrich gives of Baxter's view of human reason seems more in harmony with the Baxter of *The Arrogancy of Reason* (London, 1655) than with the Baxter of *The Unreasonableness of Infidelity* (London, 1655), *The Reasons of the Christian Religion* (London, 1667), and *More Reasons of the Christian Religion and No Reason against it* (London, 1672). As Rumrich points out, Baxter is a difficult man to categorize.

13. For an explanation of the precedence of this aim over that of fitting "a man to perform justly, skilfully and magnanimously all the offices both private and publike of peace and war," see Stephen Schuler, "Sanctification in Milton's Academy: Reassessing the Purposes in *Of Education* and the Pedagogy of *Paradise Lost,*" *Milton Quarterly* 43 (2009): 39–56.

14. Richard Baxter, *A Christian Directory* (London, 1673), 149. Quoted in Balachandra Rajan, "Simple, Sensuous and Passionate," *Review of English Studies* 21, no. 84 (1945): 290.

15. John Ray's 1691 *The Wisdom of God Manifested in the Works of Creation,* arguably the most influential work of English physico-theology, was less concerned with providing airtight logical proof than with evoking wonder in a believing audience. See Katherine Calloway, "John Ray: God's Naturalist," in *Natural Theology in the Scientific Revolution* (London, 2014).

16. Baxter, *Reasons,* 7, 92. With the scientific reformers, Baxter held that scholastic philosophizing often obscured the truth rather than illuminating it and insisted that education, the chief Christian occupation, should stay close to sense perception. See also Packer, *Redemption and Restoration,* 69–71; N. H. Keeble, *Richard Baxter, Puritan Man of Letters* (Oxford, 1982), 43, and Mandelbrote, "Uses of Natural Theology," 455–56.

17. Mandelbrote writes summarily that early modern natural theology "was a contested arena, in which a number of different standpoints might be justified on the basis of the history of classical or Christian thought.... Those different positions reflected in part disagreements about how one should read the evidence of nature, and what weight one should give to the Bible and to reason as lights to guide one in doing so" ("Early Modern," 86).

18. John Wesley, *A Survey of the Wisdom of God in Creation* (London, 1763), frontispiece.

19. Bentley, *Folly of Atheism*, 276.

20. Joseph D. Boocker, "Milton and the Newtonians," presented at the Ninth International Milton Symposium, July 7–11, 2008, London.

21. Bentley, *Folly of Atheism*, 101.

22. In his first letter to Bentley (Dec. 10, 1692), Newton writes, "When I wrote my treatise about our systeme, I had an eye upon such principles as might work with considering men for the beleife of a Deity"; see *Correspondence of Richard Bentley*, ed. J. H. Monk (London, 1842), 47; see also Henry Guerlac and M. C. Jacob, "Bentley, Newton, and Providence: The Boyle Lectures Once More," *Journal of the History of Ideas* 30, no. 3 (1969): 311.

23. Gillies, "Space and Place," 35. Duran, *Age of Milton*, writes, "Raphael's refusal to affirm a final answer cannot then responsibly be interpreted as curtailing the 'contemplation of created things'" (195). Edwards, *Milton and the Natural World*, states, "Raphael commends the *process* of poring over God's book; he declines to halt the process by providing a solution for Adam" (66).

24. John Milton, *Paradise Lost, The Riverside Milton*, ed. Roy Flannagan (Boston, 1998). All subsequent references to Milton's poetry are from this edition and are cited parenthetically in the text.

25. See also Maura Brady, "Space and the Persistence of Place in *Paradise Lost*," *Milton Quarterly* 41 (2007): 177–78.

26. Angelica Duran notes early Royal Society members' interest in "the glory of God and the benefit of Mankind" in "Reformed Catechism and Scientific Method in Milton's *Of Education* and *Paradise Lost*," in *Science, Literature and Rhetoric in Early Modern England*, ed. Juliet Cummins and David Burchell, 75–96 (London, 2007), 76n3.

27. More, *An Antidote against Atheism*, 13–14. Readers may notice a resonance between More's theory of potential knowledge here and that found in Aristotle's *De anima*.

28. Ibid., 49, preface.

29. Ibid., 94–95. The eye has long been a locus of natural-theological debate, with both John Ray and Milton's Samson wondering why such an important organ was left so vulnerable (while, years later still, Darwin expressed wonder that the eye could be produced casually). See Ray,

Wisdom of God, 183–84. Prelapsarian Adam is not yet vexed by this problem.

30. Angelica Duran, "The Sexual Mathematics of *Paradise Lost*," *Milton Quarterly* 37 (2003): 56–60. Sustained discussion of the peculiarities of unfallen feminine natural theology is outside the scope of this study; I wonder, however, whether Eve's recognition of Adam's derivative authorship (*PL* 4.635–38) is meant to be metonymic for human recognition of God's absolute authorship.

31. Svendsen, *Milton and Science*, 44.

32. More, *An Antidote against Atheism*, 101. More never mentions divine glory and criticizes those who "no more rellish the glory and praise of Men, then if we had done nothing or were not at all in being."

33. See, for example, ibid., 54–58, 72–73, esp. 65: "If human Industry had nothing to conflict and struggle with, the fire of mans Spirit would be half extinguished."

34. Ibid., 81–82.

35. Baxter, *Reasons*, 5, 107–08. Baxter's foundational analogy between the propriety rights of humans over animals and that of God over humans lends perspective to Adam's much-celebrated naming of the animals. Adam's knowledge of the nature of "numberless" creatures is indeed formidable, especially by the standards of seventeenth century natural history. Milton's emphasis of Adam's command not only highlights prelapsarian knowledge, but also points by analogy to the breadth and depth of divine knowledge.

36. This is Bacon's phrasing, which closely follows the Geneva Bible. Ray would quote the Authorized Version: "No man can find out the work that God maketh from beginning to end."

37. Ray, *Wisdom of God*, 8. For a discussion of Ray's conversation with Seneca in this quotation, see T. P. Harrison, "Seneca and John Ray," *Arion* 8, no. 3 (1969): 450–51. The lines from Ecclesiastes were engraved over old the Cavendish library in central Cambridge.

38. Bacon, *Advancement of Learning*, preface: "And although hee [Solomon] doth insinuate that the supreme or summarie law of Nature, which he calleth, *The worke which God worketh from the beginning to the end*, is not possible to be found out by Man; yet that doth not derogate from the capacitie of the minde; but may bee referred to the impediments as of shortnesse of life, ill coniunction of labours, ill tradition of knowledge ouer from hand to hand, and many other Inconueniences, whereunto the condition of Man is subiect."

39. This is the question of determinism versus theological voluntarism: of whether, as Stanley Fish, *Surprised by Sin* (Cambridge, Mass., 1998), once put it, "God cannot work effects contrary to those creatures are able to discern in nature" (251).

40. Phillip J. Donnelly, *Milton's Scriptural Reasoning: Narrative and Protestant Toleration* (Cambridge, 2009), 15.

41. Bentley, *Folly of Atheism*, 24, 92. Bentley points out the indignity of believing "that men first proceeded, as Vermin are thought to do, by the sole influence of the Sun out of Dirt and Putrefaction" and asks, "Who were there then in the world, to observe the Births of those First Men, and calculate their Nativities, as they sprawl'd out of Ditches?" Bentley's "sole" pun is either unintentional or marks a departure from his usual crusade to obliterate double-intending language.

42. Fish, *Trouble with Principle*, 244.

43. Edwards, *Milton and the Natural World*, 33. In a way, Fish and Edwards are rehearsing the old argument between Henry Stubbe and Thomas Sprat regarding whether the Fall constituted "a breach of Religious Duty *towards God*" or, as Stubbes bluntly puts it, "a deficiency from the study of Experimental Philosophy." See Mandelbrote, "Early Modern," 75–76; on the debate regarding the provenance of the Royal Society, see also Robert Crocker, *Henry More, 1614–1687: A Biography of the Cambridge Platonist* (Boston, 2003), 152–56.

44. For the relationship between anthropocentric teleology and early empirical science, see P. Harrison, *The Bible*, 161–204. Book 2 of More's *Antidote against Atheism* is an example of anthropocentric physicotheology; for a discussion of currents counter to this trend, see John Hedley Brooke, "'Wise Men Nowadays Think Otherwise': John Ray, Natural Theology and the Meanings of Anthropocentrism," *Notes and Records of the Royal Society* 54, no. 2 (2000): 199–213.

45. "If death / Consort with thee, death is to me as life" (9.953–54); as discussed above, Adam's fall also marks an experimental "trial" unassisted by instruction from God (9.961).

46. John Wilkins, *On the Principles and Duties of Natural Religion* (London, 1675), 257–260, 394–95.

47. See Bentley, *Folly of Atheism*, 242, 271. Bentley had precedent for framing his argument with Psalm 14:1 in Anselm's *Proslogion*.

48. Nathaniel Culverwell, *An Elegant and Learned Discourse on the Light of Nature* (London, 1652), 3–4. It was Culverwell's tempered enthusiasm for reason that first led C. A. Patrides to question whether he fit into the group: see Patrides, *The Cambridge Platonists* (Cambridge, 1969), 11–12. Since then, A. Rupert Hall, *Henry More: Magic, Religion and Experiment* (Oxford, 1990), has helpfully divided the Cambridge Platonists into a philosophical "Christ's" and a theological "Emmanuel" school; Culverwell belongs in the latter (58).

49. See Robert A. Greene, "Whichcote, the Candle of the Lord, and Synderesis," *Journal of the History of Ideas* 52, no. 4 (1991): 617–44, on how this trope functioned in seventeenth century philosophy.

50. See Bacon, *Advancement of Learning,* 22.

51. Satan encountered a similar problem in attempting to understand the earth from on high: approaching the newly created world, he takes in the cosmos in one view (*PL* 3.541, 552, 561), and the narrator points out that he sees the earth "in breadth" only (3.561), for only God's sight is able to discern "abstrusest thoughts" (5.712).

52. Considering Michael's postlapsarian pedagogy, Coiro, "'To Repair the Ruins,'" points out Michael's relatively subdued tone regarding human achievement. By contrast, Duran, *Age of Milton,* 109, sees the dialogic and hopeful nature of books 11 and 12.

53. We may note in passing that when T. S. Eliot famously accused Milton of having an "auditory imagination abnormally sharpened at the expense of the visual," he perhaps missed a theological point about human knowledge—as well as, as Picciotto shows in *Labors of Innocence,* 405, 436–38, an invitation to readers to labor with Milton in constructing paradise rather than passively receiving a complete picture. See T. S. Eliot, *On Poetry and Poets* (New York, 2009), 162.

54. This motto also sits uncomfortably with Jesus' response to Satan in *Paradise Regain'd,* another work that highlights Satan's predilection for surveying things from lofty heights: "Man lives not by Bread only," Jesus retorts, "but each Word / Proceeding from the mouth of God" (*PR* 1.349–50).

55. Donnelly, *Milton's Scriptural Reasoning,* 81–82, comments on the importance of "assert" in "assert Eternal Providence," arguing that this assertion must be accepted before one can engage Milton's theodicy.

56. Well into the seventeenth century empirically grounded natural theology was a strange idea: philosophers from the Cambridge Platonists to Herbert of Cherbury all began their reasoning about the divine internally, although they appealed variously to innate intuition, rational geometric proof, or something in between. But apologists for empiricism were pointing out that their methods were humbler than those purely cerebral activities, offering a needed external check to the human mind, and such humility had to appear particularly appropriate in natural theology, which pursues knowledge of high things and should take all the more care not to overstep its bounds. See Brooke, "'Wise Men Nowadays,'" 209, and Mandelbrote, "Uses of Natural Theology," 453–54.

57. Richard Bentley, ed., *Milton's Paradise Lost: A New Edition by Richard Bentley D.D.* (London, 1732), 333.

58. On the centrality of love in Michael's narrative, see Donnelly, *Milton's Scriptural Reasoning,* 173–77.

59. Baxter, *Reasons,* 80–81, acknowledges that God's love sits above his omniscience and omnipotence. Like Milton in *Paradise Lost* 3.103–15, Baxter observes an analogous placement of will above intellect and

entity in humans. On the importance of Tommaso Campanella's "three primalities of being"—Power, Wisdom, and Love—in Baxter's physics, see Simon Burton, *The Hallowing of Logic: The Trinitarian Method of Richard Baxter's "Methodus Theologiae"* (Boston, 2012), 96–115.

60. Richard Baxter, *Knowledge and Love Compared* (London, 1689), table of contents.

61. Baxter, *Reasons*, 23.

CLASSICS FOR THE CONTEMPORARY AGE

Milton's Tended Garden and the Georgic Fall

Seth Lobis

"Understanding Milton's words," Annabel Patterson writes, "is, and should remain, a work in progress."[1] In this essay my aim is to contribute to that work in progress as well as to another –understanding Milton's representation of work. The word on which I wish to focus is "tend" and its various cognate and pseudocognate forms. In book 9 of *Paradise Lost* Milton weaves these forms into an elaborate and intricate verbal narrative. Bringing this narrative pattern to light yields broader insights into Milton's engagement with and development of the georgic mode as well as his representation of the Fall. He uses "tend" and its variants to establish a contrast between Adam and Eve's prelapsarian labor, which involves tending the garden of Eden, and Satan's fallen labor, which involves intending to do Adam and Eve harm and bending or directing himself to that end. The overarching contrast is between a georgic ethic of care and stewardship and what might be called a georgic *anti*-ethic of temptation and ruination.[2]

Previous accounts of Milton's exploration of georgic in *Paradise Lost* have not, it seems to me, done full justice to book 9, and the primary subject of the separation colloquy at the beginning of the book—labor—has often been acknowledged and then passed over in critical discussions, as if it were little more than a prompt for more abstract and philosophical subjects like duty, freedom, self-sufficiency, and the quality of virtue.³ But if Milton's matter required him to account for the separation of Adam and Eve before the Fall, he did not use their work in the garden merely as a pretext; labor figures as a central part of Milton's representation of prelapsarian life and as a central marker of the changes wrought by the Fall. In a number of ways book 9 provides especially strong support for Barbara Lewalski's influential case that *Paradise Lost* constitutes an encyclopedia of literary modes and that "each mode is introduced by explicit signals."⁴ The signal at the beginning of book 9, "I now must change / Those Notes to Tragic" (9.5–6), seems explicit indeed.⁵ "The verse epistle," Lewalski writes, "indicates not only that the mode of Books Nine and Ten is tragic, but also that those books are designed with reference to the paradigms and conventions of tragedy as a genre."⁶ In tuning into signals outside of the verse epistle, I want to refine and enhance this account of the generic "design" of book 9. Milton sets the tragedy of the Fall within a georgic framework. In Alastair Fowler's terms, he writes the Fall as tragedy with "georgic modulation."⁷ In so doing, Milton adapts a Hesiodic paradigm, according to which georgic is organized around a Fall narrative, correlating labor with crime and punishment, as in Genesis. Milton's strategic use of "tend" and its variants throughout book 9 not only highlights the georgic modality of his narrative of the Fall but also invests georgic with a new ethical and psychological depth. While maintaining a focus on the physical and material dimensions of labor in the epic, Milton emphasizes that georgic is also—to evoke Bacon's stirring formulation—of the mind.⁸ For Milton, the work of tending is bound up in the complexities of inclination, intention, and temptation.

Milton's use of "tend" and its variants represents an innovation in the language of georgic relative to Virgil, his primary precursor, as well as a deviation from his biblical sources, where the key verbs are "dress," "keep," and "till" in English, *operari* and *custodire* in Latin. In the *Georgics* Virgil generally uses two verbs to convey the idea of tending plants or animals—*colere,* the etymon of "culture," and *curare,* with the double sense of caring for and caring about; *cura,* a keyword in the poem that epitomizes its much-discussed tonal complexity, can mean "worry" or "anxiety" as well as "serious attention" or "the devotion of care."[9] In *Paradise Lost* Milton makes "tend" a new georgic keyword. It has two main semantic branches. "Tend" in the sense of having an inclination or disposition toward derives ultimately from the Latin *tendere,* which has a root sense of stretching—hence, the tension of a string or bow. In his late sixteenth century *Thesaurus linguae Romanae & Brittanicae,* Thomas Cooper defines *tendo* as "to extende: to stretch out" as well as "to go: to go forward: to go on."[10] The latter sense is evident in Satan's appeal to the fallen angels in book 1—"Thither let us tend / From off the tossing of these fiery waves" (*PL* 1.183–84)—and is linked to verbal phrases such as *tendere gressum* or *cursum* or *passus,* to direct one's steps. The second branch denotes "applying oneself to the care and service of," "ministering to," and, in an agricultural context, "fostering" or "cultivating." In these senses, "tend" is an aphetic form of the verb "attend," deriving most immediately from the French *attendre.*[11] Milton sets the two semantic branches in apposition as well as in opposition; he generally limits Satan's idiolect to the first branch and orients him against the second. For Satan, the care and responsibility implied by the second sort of tending are inimical in large part because it implies a hierarchical relation downward in the scale of being—the higher tending the lower. The second sort of tending suggests a downward mobility at odds with his ambition and more broadly presumes an ontological connectedness and contingency that he denies. By contrast, Adam and Eve's ministerial tending goes to the heart of Milton's prelapsarian ecological ideal—much illuminated by scholars since the late 1990s[12]—according to which God and all of his creatures, including nature itself, are dynamically interconnected and united by a common love.

For Milton, prelapsarian labor signifies not only delight and devotion but also concern and responsibility; just as God takes care of Adam and Eve, so they take care of the garden. After they disobey God, we see the corruption of this righteous caretaking, as the polarities of georgic didacticism reverse, and Milton shows us, in effect, how *not* to tend the garden.[13] The development of the narrative of "tending" in the latter half of book 9 ultimately suggests that the effects of the Fall extend to genre itself. After the Fall, the ontological and ethical divide between Edenic and satanic georgic collapses. Milton signals not only the birth of tragedy but also the fall of georgic.

When Adam and Eve are introduced early in book 9 of *Paradise Lost*, the mode is overtly georgic. The separation colloquy begins as a discussion of labor practices, in which Eve presents to Adam an agricultural strategy that effectively inaugurates the didactic strain of georgic; having applied her mind to the challenge of laboring in the garden, she sets out to inform and instruct Adam.[14] Eve's opening words turn on two instances, and two senses, of the verb "tend":

> *Adam*, well may we labour still to dress
> This Garden, still to *tend* Plant, Herb and Flour,
> Our pleasant task enjoyn'd, but till more hands
> Aid us, the work under our labour grows,
> Luxurious by restraint; what we by day
> Lop overgrown, or prune, or prop, or bind,
> One night or two with wanton growth derides,
> *Tending* to wilde. Thou therefore now advise
> Or hear what to my minde first thoughts present,
> Let us divide our labours.   (*PL* 9.205–14; my emphasis)

This passage has unsettled readers in part because it makes Eve seem like a proto-management consultant, concerned with productivity and efficiency in a way that hardly seems consistent with a fallen view of pre-fallen labor. Kevis Goodman, citing Marcuse, has referred to this moment in the poem as "the intrusion of a 'performance principle.'"[15] But a negative reading of the passage is discouraged in at least two ways: first, the narratorial prelude to it confirms Eve's assessment of "Thir growing work," which "much...outgrew / The hands dispatch of two Gardning so wide" (9.202–03); and, second, Eve's language directly evokes that of

Genesis 2:15: "And the Lord God took the man, and put him into the garden of Eden to dress it and to keep it." As several readers have observed, when Milton conveys this verse in the voice of God in book 8, the language is subtly different: "This Paradise I give thee, count it thine / To Till and keep, and of the Fruit to eate" (8.319–20). The Geneva and Authorized versions read "dress" instead of "till," with the latter first appearing after the Fall in Genesis 3. If Milton's point in book 8 is, as Richard DuRocher puts it, to "[assert] that agricultural labor is part of the unfallen way of life,"[16] it may be that his having Eve use the Authorized term here in book 9 serves to reinforce her particular piety and scriptural sufficiency. At the same time, the repeated "still" and the homonymic "till" keep Milton's variation in view, further conveying the goodness and pleasantness of prelapsarian labor.

By putting emphasis on the word "tend," Milton makes the biblical account of labor more fully and clearly his own. The verb also appears in Adam's version of the divine commandment in book 4: "let us ever praise him, and extoll / His bountie," he says, "following our delightful task / To prune these growing Plants, and tend these Flours" (436–38). Expressing her goodness, Eve's language dutifully echoes Adam's and God's. She uses "prune" as well as "tend," and her phrase "pleasant task" answers Adam's "delightful task." But we also hear Eve's own voice distinctly in this passage. This vocal and verbal personalization in part reflects Milton's broader aim to show the complementary, and soon-to-be conflicting, dimensions of relationality and individuality that define human nature. The duality is conveyed more explicitly at the end of the passage, when Eve first solicits Adam's "advice" and then offers the suggestion of her own "minde." Eve is obedient to the word, both God's and Adam's, but she is also self-expressive, deploying a language that richly reflects her unique role, to adapt Adam's phrase, as student and manager of household good. When she says the words "Lop overgrown, or prune, or prop, or bind," the line resolving into a series of crisp iambs and orderly monosyllables, what might be regarded simply as an instance of poetic amplification is also an expression of the variety, harmony, and expertness of Eve's work. Eve's work encompasses a delightful diversity of activities, and here we might recall Diane McColley's claim: "Eve is distinguished from all other Eves by the fact that she takes her work seriously."[17]

Seriousness certainly does not imply a loss of innocence, but Eve's subsequent language—"with wanton growth derides / Tending to wilde"—seems incongruously negative. Patrick Hume glosses the phrase as "Scorns our scant Correction, and mocks our Manuring, over-running our Walks with wild ungovern'd growth."[18] With its "luxurious" alliteration, overgoing that in the lines from book 4 to which Hume alludes, it is as if the "wild ungovern'd growth" of the garden has overrun his paraphrase. Given that governing growth is precisely what Adam and Eve have been working to accomplish, Hume's use of "ungovern'd" here strikes me as misplaced. "Tending to wilde," the initial trochee putting particular emphasis on the verb, points back directly to "tend Plant, Herb and Flour." But the repetition comes with a significant difference. There is a shift from transitive to intransitive and from one sense or semantic branch to another, the rhetorical figure antanaclasis; "tending" here denotes not taking care of or cultivating something, but having a disposition to do something—in this case to grow wild. Milton is not engaging in mere rhetorical ornamentation here, nor is he opposing the two senses; rather, he is establishing a logical, and ecological, connection between them. The tendency of the garden to grow profusely and luxuriantly occasions Adam and Eve's tendance of it. Their tendance both restrains and releases the garden's tendency. In this sense the earth and its first inhabitants are shown to be more deeply and intimately interconnected. In her opening words Eve comes up with a way to attain a more perfect economy, a more precise concordance between cultivation and growth, their labor and the garden's nature. Her concern that there is a disparity or disequilibrium between the two can be roughly likened to Adam's concern, before the birth of Eve, that there is a "unitie defective" (8.425) in his order of being. No defect or improvidence exists; rather, the unfolding of creation in time promotes learning and reasoning and maximizes delight or, as Adam puts it in his response to Eve in book 9, "delight to Reason joyn'd" (243). Urging calm and patience, he emphasizes God's providence in looking ahead to the time when their children will be able to extend the reach of their labor, and the harmony between human tendance and nature's tendency will find greater fulfillment. In the end, the "tendency to wild" does not divide humanity from the natural world; it unites them—as the garden grows, so will the human race, according to a common and divine procreative principle, and both require the work of tending.[19]

Eve's call to separate has rightly been read as the beginning of a significant philosophical conversation, but the passage should be understood not only in terms of what follows it but also in terms of what immediately precedes it. The language of Satan's monologue leading up to his forced "entry" into the mouth of the serpent resonates in Eve's opening dialogue. Yet the work implied by his talk of tending is crucially different from hers—Milton sets up a pointed contrast between the two:

> Man he made, and for him built
> Magnificent this World, and Earth his seat,
> Him Lord pronounc'd, and, O indignitie!
> Subjected to his service Angel wings,
> And flaming Ministers to watch and *tend*
> Thir earthly Charge: Of these the vigilance
> I dread, and to elude, thus wrapt in mist
> Of midnight vapor glide obscure, and prie
> In every Bush and Brake, where hap may finde
> The Serpent sleeping, in whose mazie foulds
> To hide me, and the dark *intent* I bring.
> O foul descent! that I who erst *contended*
> With Gods to sit the highest, am now *constraind*
> Into a Beast, and mixt with bestial slime,
> This essence to incarnate and imbrute,
> That to the hight of Deitie aspir'd;
> But what will not Ambition and Revenge
> Descend to?   (9.152–69; my emphasis)

Here, in familiar pseudoaristocratic terms, Satan rejects the divine ethic of tending and serving. For him, to tend or to serve is to deign and to lose dignity. Providence amounts to "subjection," care to debasement. When, according to Satan, God charged his "flaming Ministers to watch and tend" humankind, he committed an act of tyrannical subjugation. But, here as elsewhere, Satan has it wrong. His defiant complaint replays in miniature that after the exaltation of the Son, when he decries God's imposition of "prostration vile" (*PL* 5.782). Correcting the satanic image of God, Abdiel forcefully objects that

> by experience taught we know how good,
> And of our good, and of our dignitie
> How provident he is, how farr from thought
> To make us less, bent rather to exalt
> Our happie state.   (5.826–30)

Whereas Abdiel offers assurance that God is "provident" not only of his creatures' "good" but of their "dignitie" as well, Satan is not so sure and not so faithful. "O indignitie," he cries out (9.154). We can hear Satan's "indignitie" as an antonymic echo of Abdiel's "dignitie," but the more important counterpoint, I think, comes in Adam's lines from book 4: "Man hath his daily work of body or mind / Appointed, which declares his Dignitie, / And the regard of Heav'n on all his waies" (4.618–20). Tending a lower order of creation does not debase humankind; rather, it manifests its dignity. Moreover, Adam and Eve's tendance makes plain the tendance and attention of "Heav'n." As Raphael explains, there is an upward tendency in the scale of nature, but its moral coherence depends on tendance and attention in the other direction. Nowhere is this virtuous condescension more apparent than in the case of the Son. Whereas after the Fall the Son "disdain'd not to begin / Thenceforth the form of servant to assume" (10.213–14), Satan is so full of disdain for service that he would rather "incarnate and imbrute" himself in the form of serpent—"prostration vile" indeed—than "watch and tend" lowly, puny humankind. Satan cannot or simply refuses to learn the fundamental and transvaluative Christian lesson that to lower oneself physically is to raise oneself morally and spiritually, that to tend to others is to extend and exalt the self.

The benevolent kind of tending that Satan rejects is replaced by a malevolent alternative, what he refers to as his "dark intent."

Setting the unfallen couple's tending against Satan's intending, Milton establishes two opposed georgic modes. The root sense of *tendo* comes into play if we think of an intent as a stretching or bending of the mind toward some end—hence a purpose or design. Whereas Adam and Eve "tend Plant, Herb and Flour," Satan "prie[s] / In every Bush and Brake" in order to conceal his evil "intent" (9.206, 159–60). We can see this opposition in Adam's response to Eve's appeal to divide their labors, where he initially refers to "the work which here / God hath assign'd us" and to the "good workes" that Eve endeavors "to promote" in him, but then proceeds to the "malicious Foe" who, as he puts it, "seeks to work us woe and shame / By sly assault" (9.230–31, 234, 253, 255–56). In book 9, we see Satan inwardly laboring in his intent and outwardly laboring to carry it out; Milton calls attention to the gap and the tension between the two, the "work of mind" and the "work of body"—a point to which I will return. No such problematic gap exists between Adam and Eve's intention to tend the garden and their tendance of it.

The contrast that Milton draws between Adam and Eve's labor and Satan's is a contrast between creation and destruction, care and harm, growth and death, and the contrast is developed and heightened by the poet's strategic use of the word "tend" and its variants. From "Serpent" to "intent" to "descent" to "contended" to "constraind," Milton constructs a strikingly echoic sequence that conveys a kind of negative georgic worldview. The building of Pandaemonium, with the fallen angels "Rifl[ing] the bowels of thir mother Earth" (*PL* 1.687), and the invention of gunpowder, with the rebel angels "in a moment up...turn[ing] / Wide the Celestial soile" (6.509–10), are notable counterpoints to Adam and Eve's pious, constructive tending of the garden, but Milton's representation of an antithetical georgic mode needs, I think, to be seen as a wider and more sustained project that reaches a climax in book 9.[20] The satanic georgic begins when Satan "contended / With Gods to sit the highest" (9.163–64). "Contend" is a deeply satanic word, established from the outset of the poem in Satan's opening speech, where he refers to his "fixt mind / And high disdain," which "with the mightiest rais'd me to contend, / And to the fierce contention brought along / Innumerable force of Spirits arm'd" (1.97-98, 99-101). The poet's use of polyptoton, "contend, / ...contention," is emphatic.

Having failed in his contention, Satan intends revenge, which leads him to this point in the poem, where he constrains himself by descending into the serpent. "Constraind" represents an etymological translation of "contended"; Milton brings to the fore the root sense of straining to suggest the costs and consequences of satanic labor—an effect that is reinforced by the internal rhyme of "intent" and "descent." The aural theme sinuously extends through "contended," "essence," "Revenge," and "Descend"; internal rhyme, assonance, and consonance work together in the passage to enact Satan's "constraint." Satan's work is not a "pleasant task," but what Adam calls "irksom toile" (9.242). It is not freeing and open-ended, but binding and confining, to evoke Milton's stricture on rhyme in the note on "The Verse." And Satan's work is wickedly and narrowly teleological. His emphasis on "revenge"—the word is repeated in the passage—provides concrete support for Lewalski's claim that in books 9 and 10 Milton "underscores the Satanic perversion" of two tragic "paradigms," the Aristotelian and the Christian, by presenting Satan, in her words, "as hero of his own revenge tragedy."[21] But Milton, I want to emphasize, gives Satan's revenge both tragic and georgic dimensions. He represents Satan's revenge as a malicious kind of work, and its negative georgic character is highlighted by the close but contrastive verbal relationship between the two passages that we have been examining.

The ground of satanic georgic is less the garden than it is the mind. Through Satan in particular Milton undertakes an intensive psychologization of the georgic mode, amplifying a Protestant emphasis on interiority. Driven by his designs on the unfallen couple, Satan singlemindedly invades what Milton calls "Thir tendance or Plantation for delight" (9.419), but when he finds Eve, he discovers that his work becomes unexpectedly more difficult:

> Her graceful Innocence, her every Aire
> Of gesture or lest action overawd
> His Malice, and with rapine sweet bereav'd
> His fierceness of the fierce intent it brought. (9.459-62)

Satan's struggle with intention is a sign and consequence of his fallenness. On the one hand, Milton seems to be suggesting Satan's potential or capacity for good; on the other, he is highlighting the complex and problematic relationship between intention and action that defines the work of the fallen mind.[22] It was Shakespeare, above all, who provided Milton with a range of potent representational models of this problem, and I would suggest that *Richard III* was particularly important in this case. In the soliloquy that ends the first scene of that play, Richard refers in the space of ten lines to his "deep intent" and his "secret close intent" (1.1.153, 162), setting in motion his furious, murderous campaign. Satan brings to his a rather more Hamletic subjectivity, but he recovers his resolve quickly and without lingering doubt:

> Shee fair, divinely fair, fit Love for Gods,
> Not terrible, though terrour be in Love
> And beautie, not approacht by stronger hate,
> Hate stronger, under shew of Love well feign'd,
> The way which to her ruin now I tend.   (*PL* 9.489–93)

This use of "tend," which gets line-ending emphasis, and which chimes with the quasi-anagrammatic "indented" three lines later, is deeply antithetical to Eve's in her description of her work in the garden. Whereas Eve's tending is dutiful and constructive, Satan's is overtly sinful and destructive. Whereas her aim is care and order, his, as he makes clear, is "ruin." The clear, concise iambs of Eve's speech come into contrast with the "indented" syntax and chiastic involution of Satan's. Satan Englishes the Latin verbal phrase *tendo cursum* here, negating the moral force of Eve's meaning. The neutral sense of movement and direction is darkly colored and corrupted by his evil intent. Satan's laborious journey from hell to earth, from intention to action, from premeditated guile to temptation, has reached its final destination.

The climax of Satan's work in the epic is the temptation of Eve, and "tempt" is a crucial part of the verbal pattern that I have been following in book 9. In seventeenth century linguistic consciousness "tempt" and "tend" were etymologically linked.[23] "Tempt" descended from the verb *tento*, a morphological twin of *tentum*, the past participle of *tendo*. In the *Dictionarium etymologicum*

Latinum, which went through multiple revisions and reprintings in the first half of the seventeenth century, Francis Holyoake defined *tento* as "To assay, prove or try, to handle, or feele often, to tempt one to doe evill" and gave its derivation as follows: "ex teneo vel tendo, tentum."[24] Milton furthers this etymological connection through syntactic proximity. During the separation colloquy Adam urges Eve to stay by his side so as "to avoid / Th' attempt it self, intended by our Foe" (9.294-95). Adam thus shows that he properly understands the tempter's intent. Framing Satan's temptation, Milton uses an analogous etymological figure:

> he glad
> Of her attention gaind, with Serpent Tongue
> Organic, or impulse of vocal Air,
> His fraudulent temptation thus began. (9.528-31)

This figure is soon followed by a slight variant, with "tempter" rather than "temptation": "Say, for such wonder claims attention due. / To whom the guileful Tempter thus reply'd" (9.566-67). The rhetorical labor of Satan's temptation begins with, and depends on, gaining Eve's attention, literally the stretching or bending of her mind to his words. Then, having gained her attention, Satan uses the language of tendance to tempt her to his side. He relates that, allured by the tree, he approached it,

> When from the boughes a savorie odour blow'n,
> Grateful to appetite, more pleas'd my sense
> Then smell of sweetest Fenel, or the Teats
> Of Ewe or Goat dropping with Milk at Eevn,
> Unsuckt of Lamb or Kid, that tend thir play. (9.579-83)

The verb "tend" seems to come here as a tangential afterthought in a dependent, relative clause that follows the third "or" in the passage. But if it reads as tangential, it is far from inconsequential. Satan's use of "tend" is an ethical move, in the rhetorical sense, designed to establish his good character and dispose Eve favorably to him and his speech. He relates to her as one similarly versed in the ways of rural care. In effect Satan is conveying to Eve that he, too, participates in the moral world of georgic. This idea, or illusion, allows him to appeal to sensory pleasure, the major emphasis of the passage, with less risk that she will be put off and withdraw her attention. Satan's subtle georgic gesture helps to clear the way for the main thrust of his temptation.

After Eve eats the fruit, Milton shows that the success of Satan's georgic project entails the corruption of hers—Edenic georgic falls along with Eve. Milton develops the verbal narrative to highlight the extent of her lapse into sensory self-indulgence: "Back to the Thicket slunk / The guiltie Serpent, and well might, for *Eve* / Intent now wholly on her taste, naught else / Regarded" (9.784–87). This scene effectively reverses that in book 5 in which Eve receives Raphael and prepares dinner, "on hospitable thoughts intent / What choice to chuse for delicacie best" (5.332–33). The considerate and temperate host has become a mindless, ravening guest.[25] Only now does Eve withdraw her attention from the serpent, and the internal rhyme of "Serpent" and "Intent," emphatically heading its line, highlights Eve's guilty association with Satan. In her first fallen lines, Milton reveals the debasement of Eve's conception of labor, and for the first time she uses "tend" in a fallen sense:

> O Sovran, vertuous, precious of all Trees
> In Paradise, of operation blest
> To Sapience, hitherto obscur'd, infam'd,
> And thy fair Fruit let hang, as to no end
> Created; but henceforth my early care,
> Not without Song, each Morning, and due praise
> Shall tend thee, and the fertil burden ease
> Of thy full branches offer'd free to all.   (9.795–802)

Instead of obeying and reverencing the "sovran Planter"—the georgic epithet that God receives in book 4 (line 691)—through her work in the garden, Eve now worships the "Sovran" plant. She produces an idolatrous parody of the morning hymn that she and Adam sing in book 5; whereas there the second-person address is to God, here it is to the tree.[26] Having recognized in the morning hymn God's supremacy—"these thy lowest works...declare / Thy goodness beyond thought, and Power Divine" (5.158–59)—Eve now turns the proper vertical order of creation upside down, treating "lowest" as highest, exalting not the true "Power Divine," but rather "the power / That dwelt within, whose presence had infus'd / Into the plant sciential sap, deriv'd / From Nectar, drink of Gods" (9.835–38). Eve has become not only an occult etiologist but also a pagan nature worshipper.[27] She may have gained knowledge, but she has not found wisdom, as her misguided and misdirected "care" makes clear. The satanic discourse of "ease" and "freedom" has infiltrated and contaminated the georgic dialect. The ethic of care coded by the word "tend" has lapsed into error; "tend" has lost its proper "end"—the internal rhyme suggesting, as in Satan's speech, a constraint belied by the rhetoric of freedom. Georgic is now, Milton suggests, a fallen mode.

Milton highlights the fall of georgic in his account of Adam and Eve's reunion after she has fallen, during that strange, brief period in which the two are worlds apart, ontologically mismated. Here Milton provides a strong generic signal, in Lewalski's sense, that the poem has been operating in the georgic mode—and that, were it not for Eve's fatal bite, it would still. Adam has woven Eve a floral garland, Milton writes, "to adorne / Her Tresses, and her rural labours crown / As Reapers oft are wont thir Harvest Queen" (9.840–42). If Roland Mushat Frye is right that "Milton's development of this garland episode is...unique in literary treatments of the Fall," the poet has gone out of his way to emphasize the georgic dimension of his narrative.[28] There is an intense poignancy to Adam's "rural" gesture. He has emerged from the separation colloquy full of love for Eve, not merely accepting her will to work but prepared to honor it. He sets out to glorify her labor and does so by undertaking traditional woman's work—weaving. In this sense Adam makes of separation an opportunity for greater sympathy and closeness with Eve. He comes to embody more fully the epithet that the poet gives him during the separation colloquy: "So spake domestick *Adam* in his care / And Matrimonial Love" (9.318–19). The garland he weaves is meant to enhance Eve's prime virtue—beauty—but it is more than mere ornament; it represents a recognition of, and reward for, her "rural labours." Milton adds to the literal sense of the verb "crown" the stronger figurative sense of "complete" and "confirm,"[29] with a hint of the proverbial idea that "the end crowns the work." And he does so in part for the sake of the tragic irony that the introduction of "Reapers" underscores.

Thomas Newton noted a parallel to this scene in *Iliad* 22, where Andromache, unaware that Hector is dead, weaves flowers for him.[30] When Andromache hears sounds of suffering in the distance, her shuttle falls to the ground. So Adam's heart leaps, "divine of somthing ill"; he discovers the "fatal Trespass"; and "From his slack hand the Garland wreath'd for *Eve* / Down drop'd, and all the faded Roses shed" (*PL* 9.845, 889, 892–93). Milton's use of "crown" and "Harvest Queen" also evokes Claudian's *De raptu Proserpinae*, in which Proserpina "twines a wreath of flowers and crowns [coronat] herself therewith, little seeing in this a foreshadowing of the marriage fate holds in store for her."[31] Commenting on Milton's reference to "*Proserpin* gathering flours" in book 4 (line 269), Empson writes, "Proserpina, like Eve, was captured by the king of Hell, but she then became queen of it, became Sin, then, on Milton's scheme; Eve, we are to remember, becomes an ally of Satan when she tempts Adam to eat with her."[32] Eve sets out not only to tend the tree but also to tempt Adam, and the end of her temptation crowns Satan's evil work.

Yet the georgic character of the passage as a whole suggests the particular relevance and resonance of a third source, the account of Pandora in Hesiod's *Works and Days*, the beauty who, like Eve, brought ruin to humankind.[33] Among the "gifts" received by Pandora was a floral garland: "the beautiful-haired Seasons crowned [*stephon*] her all around with spring flowers."[34] The allusion draws the reader's attention back to book 4, when "With Flowers, Garlands, and sweet-smelling Herbs / Espoused *Eve* deckt first her Nuptial Bed," the unfallen bride "More lovely than *Pandora*, whom the Gods / Endowd with all thir gifts, and O too like / In sad event" (*PL* 4.709–10, 714–16). Paragoned to Pandora in the manner of a dissimile, Eve has now effectively become Pandora. If Eve is the true archetype of beauty, she is also the true source of sin. And Adam effectively becomes an unwitting actor in a pagan pageant, the gift giver ironically participating in his own destruction, not realizing that he is about to lose everything. Milton creates the sad, even awkward, effect that the poem has passed Adam by; he thinks he is still in the familiar georgic mode of book 4, but the notes have changed. When he catches up, when the garland "From his slack hand... / Down drop'd" (9.892–93), Milton signals to the reader that georgic has dropped, too.

Hesiod marks the donation of Pandora as a critical turning point in the history of human labor. Prior to it, work did not oppress: "For previously the tribes of men used to live upon the earth entirely apart from evils, and without grievous toil." These lines are echoed by Hesiod's account of the "golden race," who lived like gods, "with a spirit free from care, entirely apart from toil and distress," and who "had all good things: the grain-giving field bore crops of its own accord, much and unstinting."[35] In book 4 Milton set out to tell the true original of this story. After the reference to Pandora, he immediately returns to the joy of prelapsarian labor, as Adam and Eve pray to God, who made both night and day, "Which we in our appointed work imployd / Have finisht happie in our mutual help / And mutual love, the Crown of all our bliss" (4.726–28). Labor is intimately tied to love. For the unfallen couple, tendance is bliss. In representing Adam and Eve's prelapsarian work in this way, Milton clears up ambiguities in Hesiod's account and in Virgil's complex engagement with it in *Georgics* 1, where the " 'aetiology of *labor*' " digression (lines 118–59) leaves uncertain the question of the presence and nature of work in the Golden Age.[36] Whereas Virgil suggests that Jupiter put an end to the Golden Age so that "his kingdom" would not "slumber in heavy lethargy [nec torpere gravi passus sua regna veterno],"[37] Milton both renews the Hesiodic theme of punishment for transgression and claims priority to it. With the Fall, Adam and Eve's blissful work becomes "grievous toil," and georgic assumes a new ambivalence and complexity, colored by the darkness of both tragedy and elegy.

Milton reinforces the idea of generic corruption in his account of Adam's fall. But he deploys the verbal pattern differently, shifting the emphasis from fallen tendance to fallen intention. After eating the fruit, Adam is impelled not by idolatrous fervor, but by "Carnal desire" (*PL* 9.1013). The narratorial frame marks a momentous change in the workings of his mind: "So said he, and forbore not glance or toy / Of amorous intent, well understood / Of Eve, whose Eye darted contagious Fire" (9.1034–36). Milton conveys that intention has become tainted and troubled by passion; the phrase "amorous intent" has a satanic ring to it, recalling his "dark intent" and "fierce intent." After the Fall, Milton suggests, there are no longer only good intentions. Adam and Eve's first experience of fallen sex is itself a kind of parody of pre-fallen labor; they are "wearied" by it and then "Oppress'd" by "grosser sleep / Bred of unkindly fumes" (9.1045, 1049–50), rather than, as before, enjoying the "gift of sleep" after the "happie" conclusion of their day's "appointed work" (4.735, 727, 726). Milton evokes the darker Virgilian conjunction of *amor* and *labor*.[38] And when the fallen couple wake up, they do not pray to God in the free form Milton imagines, combining "various style" and "holy rapture" (5.146, 147); instead, they fight with each other in "words constraind" (9.1066). Intimating Adam's new fallen kinship with Satan, Milton subtly echoes Satan's complaint earlier in the book about being "constraind / Into a beast" (9.164–65). In both cases the emphasis is on loss and lack of freedom—psychological as well as physical. The root sense of "tend" assumes the fallen sense of "strain."

Milton's generic inscription of the Fall is underscored by a simile that has long drawn the attention of scholars, who have noted its variety not only of possible sources but also of resonances and ramifications.[39] On the first day after the Fall, Milton marks the interruption of the georgic routine that had characterized prelapsarian life. Instead of going off into the garden to tend the trees and plants, Adam now has a new idea about the luxurious foliage of Eden; it can serve to hide him and his sin. He and Eve then approach the Indian fig tree, or banyan, which, "Braunching so broad and long," produces "a Pillard shade / High overarch't, and echoing Walks between" (9.1104, 1106–07); as Milton continues, echoing a passage in John Gerard's *Herball* (1597): "There oft the *Indian* Herdsman shunning heate / Shelters in coole, and tends his pasturing Herds / At Loopholes cut through thickest shade" (*PL* 9.1108–10). Here georgic and pastoral modes merge.[40] Gerard's lines add labor to Pliny's account of the Indian fig tree, which forms an "enclosure [saepem]" where "the shepherds dwell in summer, as it is at once shaded and protected by the fence of the tree":

> [the] great wood or desart of trees...the Indians do vse for couerture against the extreme heate of the sunne, wherewith they are greeuously vexed: some likewise vse them for pleasure, cutting downe by a direct line a long walke, or as it were a vault, through the thickest part, from which also they cut certaine loope holes or windowes in some places, to the end to receiue thereby the fresh coole aire that entereth therat; as also for light, that they may see their cattle that feedeth thereby, to auoid any danger that might happen vnto them, either by the enimie or wilde beasts.[41]

Milton condenses this account, and although he omits its harsher notes, the point of his inclusion is to highlight the fallenness of the world that Adam and Eve will soon inhabit, a world of extreme elements in which the work of "tending" is harder and more perilous—the world, indeed, of Virgilian georgic. There is a grim contrast between this tableau and the image of Adam and Eve resting in their "shadie Bowre...till this meridian heat / Be over, and the Sun more coole decline" (5.367, 369–70), or, their "sweet Gardning labour" concluded, sitting "Under a tuft of shade that on a green / Stood whispering soft" (4.328, 325–26). After the Fall, heat and cold cease to be pleasant variables and become oppressive opposites, the excesses of "Solstitial summer" and "Decrepit Winter" (10.656, 655). As Joshua Scodel has shown, the idea of the "'tempering' of various extremes" runs throughout the *Georgics*, in both "hard" and "soft" figurations, and significantly informs Milton's treatment of the georgic mode from *L'Allegro* and *Il Penseroso* onward.[42] The "*Indian* Herdsman" confronts an intemperate climate from which he frequently ("oft") seeks, and needs, relief.[43] He is forced to "tend" indirectly, semiobscurely, and at a distance. Georgic enters into the epic at this point as a markedly fallen mode.

What Milton emphasizes at the end of book 9 is the end of the happy "rural" way of life that Adam and Eve have known. Insofar as they are fighting with each other, they are laboring in the satanic mode. The book closes with an image of tragic strife:

"Thus they in mutual accusation spent / The fruitless hours, but neither self-condemning, / And of thir vain contest appeer'd no end" (9.1187–89). Whereas before the Fall Adam and Eve their "appointed work...finisht happie in...mutual help / And mutual love" (4.726–28), now they are locked in a seemingly endless bout of "mutual accusation." Their fruitful work has stopped; they are wasting "fruitless hours" in verbal battle. The noun "contest" has appeared twice before in the poem, both times referring to satanic militarism. Satan's evil work has now in some sense become theirs. "Contest" provides an appropriately complex conclusion to the verbal narrative that we have been following in book 9: it is close in sense to "contend" and "contention"; the base "test" is a synonym for "tempt" in the sense "make trial of"; and there is a subtle suggestion of "contempt" as well.

Eventually, Adam and Eve's "contest" does come to an end, as Milton's theodicy requires. In the next book Adam addresses Eve: "But rise, let us no more contend, nor blame / Each other, blam'd enough elsewhere, but strive / In offices of Love" (10.958–60). Love at last succeeds lust and hate. And Adam gains an insight into the providential dimension of the judgment against him, declaring, "My labour will sustain me; and least Cold / Or Heat should injure us, his timely care / Hath unbesaught provided" (10.1056–58). He foresees a redemptive vision of georgic in the fallen world, a vision of the Christian husbandman. If the work of tending will no longer be what it once was, the attendance of the Son persuades Adam that it will bear new fruit.

Claremont McKenna College

Notes

I am grateful to Debora Shuger for her comments on an earlier version of this essay.

1. Annabel Patterson, *Milton's Words* (Oxford, 2009), 9.
2. Anthony Low, *The Georgic Revolution* (Princeton, N.J., 1985), similarly associates Satan with a negative georgic mode, though his emphasis falls on the military-political: "As [Milton] uses Satan and his followers

to warn his readers against the false glitter of epic, so he also uses him to warn against a false pursuit of imperial georgic. For Satan is a laborer as well as a warrior, who understands full well that an empire cannot be built without sweat and toil" (314).

3. On the georgic presence in *Paradise Lost*, with varying emphases—from specific echoes of Virgil to parallel poetic, ethical, and political commitments to the epic's progression of modes—see Barbara Kiefer Lewalski, *"Paradise Lost" and the Rhetoric of Literary Forms* (Princeton, N.J., 1985), 196–98; Low, *Georgic Revolution*, 310–22; Stella P. Revard, "Vergil's *Georgics* and *Paradise Lost*: Nature and Human Nature in a Landscape," in *Vergil at 2000: Commemorative Essays on the Poet and His Influence*, ed. John D. Bernard, 259–80 (New York, 1986); Kevis Goodman, " 'Wasted Labor'?: Milton's Eve, the Poet's Work, and the Challenge of Sympathy," *English Literary History* 64 (1997): 415–46; Joshua Scodel, *Excess and the Mean in Early Modern English Literature* (Princeton, N.J., 2002), 255–63; and Juan Christian Pellicer, "Virgil's *Georgics* II in *Paradise Lost*," *Translation and Literature* 14 (2005): 129–47. In terms of style and structure, a more intimate affinity has been proposed between the *Georgics* and *Paradise Regained*; see Low, *Georgic Revolution*, 322–52; and Louis L. Martz, "*Paradise Regained*: Georgic Form, Georgic Style," in *Milton Studies*, vol. 42, ed. Albert C. Labriola, 7–25 (Pittsburgh, 2002).

4. Lewalski, *Rhetoric of Literary Forms*, 19.

5. All references to *Paradise Lost* are to Barbara K. Lewalski, ed., *John Milton: "Paradise Lost"* (Malden, Mass., 2007); hereafter cited in the text.

6. Lewalski, *Rhetoric of Literary Forms*, 220.

7. Alastair Fowler, "The Beginnings of English Georgic," in *Renaissance Genres: Essays on Theory, History, and Interpretation*, ed. Barbara Kiefer Lewalski, 105–25 (Cambridge, Mass., 1986), 123.

8. On Bacon's idea of "Georgickes of the mind," see Andrew Wallace, "Virgil and Bacon in the Classroom," *English Literary History* 73 (2006): 161–85.

9. *Oxford Latin Dictionary*, corrected ed. (1996), s.v. *cura*. On the importance of this term in the *Georgics*, with special reference to Lucretius, see Monica R. Gale, *Virgil on the Nature of Things: The "Georgics," Lucretius and the Didactic Tradition* (Cambridge, 2000), 144–85. For uses of *curare* and *colere* and their variants in the poem, see, for example, Virgil, *Georgics* 1.3–4, 50–52, 121–24; 2.35–37, 397–439; 3.123–57, 286–87; 4.116–19. In the sense of tending plants and animals, Virgil also uses *nutriri* (2.425) and *agitare* (3.287); on the significance of the singular use of the former, see Richard F. Thomas, ed., *Virgil: Georgics*, vol. 1 (Cambridge, 1988), 237.

10. Thomas Cooper, *Thesaurus linguae Romanae & Brittanicae*, 2nd ed. (London, 1578), Iiiiii 3r.

11. *OED*, s.v. "tend, v.1."

12. On Milton's epic ecological vision, see especially Jeffrey S. Theis, "The Environmental Ethics of *Paradise Lost:* Milton's Exegesis of Genesis I–III," in *Milton Studies*, vol. 34, ed. Albert C. Labriola, 61–81 (Pittsburgh, 1997); Ken Hiltner, *Milton and Ecology* (Cambridge, 2003); Diane Kelsey McColley, *Poetry and Ecology in the Age of Milton and Marvell* (Burlington, Vt., 2007); and Ken Hiltner, ed., *Renaissance Ecology: Imagining Eden in Milton's England* (Pittsburgh, 2008).

13. On the complex didacticism of the *Georgics*, see Katharina Volk, *The Poetics of Latin Didactic: Lucretius, Vergil, Ovid, Manilius* (Oxford, 2002), 119–56.

14. Referring to the "Georgical Committee of the Royal Society" and the agricultural commitments of the Hartlib Circle, Diane Kelsey McColley, "Milton's Environmental Epic: Creature Kinship and the Language of *Paradise Lost*," in *Beyond Nature Writing: Expanding the Boundaries of Ecocriticism*, ed. Karla Armbruster and Kathleen R. Wallace, 57–74 (Charlottesville, Va., 2001), writes, "Eve's program of redressing the Garden of Eden corresponds with that of the georgic revival" (68).

15. Goodman, "'Wasted Labor,'" 427.

16. Richard DuRocher, "Careful Plowing: Culture and Agriculture in *Paradise Lost*," in *Milton Studies*, vol. 31, ed. Albert C. Labriola, 91–107 (Pittsburgh, 1995), 93. On the significance of "till," see also Karen L. Edwards, "Eden Raised: Waste in Milton's Garden," in Hiltner, *Renaissance Ecology*, 263–64.

17. Diane Kelsey McColley, *Milton's Eve* (Urbana, Ill., 1983), 110. See also McColley, *Poetry and Ecology*, 209–10; and William Poole, *Milton and the Idea of the Fall* (Cambridge, 2005), 10–12.

18. Patrick Hume, *Annotations on Milton's "Paradise Lost"* (London, 1695), 250.

19. On Milton's account of labor and Edenic "wildness," see Dennis Burden, *The Logical Epic: A Study of the Argument of "Paradise Lost"* (Cambridge, Mass., 1967), 44–45; and Barbara Kiefer Lewalski, "Innocence and Experience in Milton's Eden," in *New Essays on "Paradise Lost*," ed. Thomas Kranidas, 86–117 (Berkeley and Los Angeles, 1969), 89–95.

20. Theis, "Environmental Ethics," 75–76.

21. Lewalski, *Rhetoric of Literary Forms*, 224.

22. In this sense the poet is aligned, and effectively aligns himself, with Satan. The verse epistle in book 9 records Milton's anxiety about carrying out his intention to write sacred epic: "unless an age too late, or cold / Climat, or Years damp my intended wing / Deprest" (44–46). Revard associates this anxiety with "Vergil's fear that personal limitations may somehow prevent him from fulfilling his epic plans" ("Vergil's *Georgics*," 277). On Virgil's sustained engagement with Homer in the *Georgics*, see Thomas, *Virgil: "Georgics,"* 1:5–6. Virgil's account of Orpheus in *Georgics* 4, a critical figure for Milton, powerfully raises the question of the poet's

work, on which see Christine G. Perkell, *The Poet's Truth: A Study of the Poet in Virgil's "Georgics"* (Berkeley and Los Angeles, 1989), esp. 80–89; and Goodman, "'Wasted Labor.'"

23. The etymological connection between "tend" and "tempt" has since been rejected. See the illuminating note on the etymology of "tempt" in the *OED*.

24. Francis Holyoake, *Dictionarium etymologicum Latinum, antiquissimum & novissimum*, 2nd ed. (London, 1648), Mmmm 4v.

25. On the scene in book 5, see Laura Lunger Knoppers, *Politicizing Domesticity from Henrietta Maria to Milton's Eve* (Cambridge, 2011), 148–53.

26. For the idea that after the Fall Eve conceives the work of tending "with consumer's eyes," see Hiltner, *Milton and Ecology*, 46.

27. On occultism in the account of Eve's temptation and fall, see Karen L. Edwards, *Milton and the Natural World: Science and Poetry in "Paradise Lost"* (Cambridge, 1999), 19–20.

28. Roland Mushat Frye, *Milton's Imagery and the Visual Arts: Iconographic Tradition in the Epic Poems* (Princeton, N.J., 1978), 287.

29. *OED*, s.v. "crown, v.1.," def. 9.

30. Thomas Newton, ed., *Paradise Lost. A Poem, in Twelve Books*, vol. 2, 2nd ed. (London, 1750), 193n.

31. Claudian, *De raptu Proserpinae* 2.140–41; Claudian, *Rape of Proserpine*, trans. Maurice Platnauer (Cambridge, Mass., 1922), 329.

32. William Empson, *Some Versions of Pastoral* (New York, 1960), 165.

33. In his edition of *Paradise Lost*, John Leonard notes all three sources, but gives priority to Claudian. See John Leonard, ed., *John Milton: "Paradise Lost"* (London, 2000), 414n.

34. Hesiod, *Works and Days*, lines 69–126, ed. and trans. Glenn W. Most (Cambridge, Mass., 2006), 93.

35. Ibid., 95, 97.

36. On this ambiguity, see Perkell, *Poet's Truth*, 92–100. Although *Georgics* 2, with its more idealizing perspective and more "optimistic" tone, undoubtedly informed Milton's representation of work in the world before the Fall, I think that Revard underplays Milton's movement away from Virgil and the differences between Golden Age Italy and prelapsarian Eden; see "Vergil's *Georgics*," esp. 262–64. On the relationship between the primitive ideals of Hesiod and Virgil, see Thomas, *Virgil: "Georgics*," 1:6, 16–21, 87–93 (with helpful references to other sources); Stephanie A. Nelson, *God and the Land: The Metaphysics of Farming in Hesiod and Vergil* (New York, 1998), 64–88, 111–24; and Gale, *Virgil on the Nature of Things*, 61–67, 154–62.

37. Virgil, *Georgics* 1.124; Virgil, *Georgics*, trans. H. Rushton Fairclough, rev. G. P. Goold (Cambridge, Mass., 1999), 106–07.

38. See Revard, "Vergil's *Georgics*," 272.

39. For a summary of scholarly responses, see Kester Svendsen, *Milton and Science* (Cambridge, Mass., 1956), 30–32; and Alastair Fowler, ed., *Milton: "Paradise Lost,"* 2nd ed. (Harlow, 1998), 534n.

40. On the blending of georgic and pastoral, both in Virgil and in early modern English literature, see, for example, P. J. Davis, "Vergil's *Georgics* and the Pastoral Ideal," *Ramus* 8 (1979): 22–33; and Alastair Fowler, "Georgic and Pastoral: Laws of Genre in the Seventeenth Century," in *Culture and Cultivation in Early Modern England: Writing and the Land*, ed. Michael Leslie and Timothy Raylor, 81–88 (Leicester, 1992).

41. Pliny, *Natural History*, 12.22–23, trans. H. Rackham (Cambridge, Mass., 1945), 4:16–17. John Gerard, *The Herball or Generall Historie of Plantes* (London, 1597), 1330–31. Edwards casts doubt on the claim for Gerard's influence (*Milton and the Natural World*, 149–51), but Milton's use of the word "loopholes" especially, I think, tells in favor of Gerard.

42. Scodel, *Excess and the Mean*, 80.

43. Edwards, too, notes the force of "oft" in the simile (*Milton and the Natural World*, 152).

Milton's Poetics of Supplication

Leah Whittington

Halfway through Satan's opening speech in book 1 of *Paradise Lost*, the rhetoric of his address takes a thrilling turn: putting aside the bewilderment of defeat and his dismay at his grim new surroundings, Satan shifts into a tone of renewed determination and defiance. This passage, which Empson admired for its "sheer splendor," and which many readers continue to see as a high point of satanic charisma,[1] has received considerable attention from Miltonists interested in situating the politics of *Paradise Lost* in the context of the English civil wars and their aftermath.[2] In framing his opposition to God in terms of resistance to physical gestures of submission, Satan notoriously evokes the antisupplicatory rhetoric of Milton's prose pamphlets:

> What though the field be lost?
> All is not lost; the unconquerable will,
> And study of revenge, immortal hate,
> And courage never to submit or yield:
> And what is else not to be overcome?
> That glory never shall his wrath or might
> Extort from me. To bow and sue for grace
> With suppliant knee, and deify his power
> Who from the terror of this arm so late

> Doubted his empire, that were low indeed,
> That were an ignominy and shame beneath
> This downfall.³   (*PL* 1.105–16)

When Satan refuses "to bow and sue for grace / With suppliant knee," he appeals to the same opposition between the erect posture of free people and the crouching of slaves that Milton deploys throughout his political writings. In *Eikonoklastes*, Milton argues that the English people show their propensity for servitude in their eagerness to "to fall flatt and give adoration to the Image and Memory" of their former king.⁴ In *The Readie and Easie Way*, he famously points to the "perpetual bowings and cringings of an abject people" as one of the many horrors of monarchy (YP 7:426). Critics have eschewed direct parallels between Satan and specific historical figures, insisting instead that Satan's shifty politics make him impossible to pin down to a specific historical analogy.⁵ Critical consensus sees Satan's bursts of republican rhetoric as part of Milton's effort to demonstrate the importance of maintaining a rigorous distinction between the spheres of earthly and heavenly government. Satan's antikneeling diatribe is part of the poet's program to develop a quality of watchfulness in the reader; as David Loewenstein argues, Milton "constantly challenges engaged readers by showing them how to discern the treacherous ambiguities and contradictions of political rhetoric and behavior, including their more revolutionary manifestations."⁶

The difficulty is that Milton makes it as hard as possible to do this work of discernment; the world of *Paradise Lost* is infinitely and self-consciously misreadable. If Milton ultimately wants his readers to separate the norms of heaven and earth, his strategy of accommodation—"likening spiritual to corporal forms" (*PL* 5.573)—precisely encourages the conflation of them.⁷ This essay, therefore, approaches the question of Satan's antisupplicatory rhetoric from a different direction. I argue that in order to understand Satan's opening speech and his persistent opposition to gestures of subordination, we must consider what it means to be a suppliant—to perform and receive acts of supplication—in the larger economy of the poem. This task requires seeing Satan's resistance to the "suppliant knee" not only in connection with seventeenth century religious politics, but also as part of Milton's engagement with the classical epic tradition. Miltonists interested in the classical heritage of *Paradise Lost* have pointed out that the epic scene of supplication, when a warrior defeated on the battlefield begs his conqueror to show mercy, is among the many epic tropes and conventions that the poem appropriates and transforms.[8] But just as historicist critics have largely ignored the epic contexts for Satan's opposition to begging and beseeching, so classicizing critics tend to neglect the seventeenth century reverberations of classical supplicant scenes.[9] The aim of this essay is to bring these two conversations together, as Milton did in *Paradise Lost*, in order to shed further light on the poem's complex negotiation of forms of hierarchy and inequality. Satan's initial rejection of the "suppliant knee" is only one facet of the poem's larger movement through the patterns of ascent and descent, up and down, elevation and reduction. His attitude toward supplicatory gestures comes into view as a shadowy version of Adam and Eve's discovery of supplication as the mechanism of restoration after the Fall, and of the principle of exaltation as humiliation by which God envisions the unfolding process of redemption on the cosmic and universal scale. This investigation generates a vivid picture of the power of inherited forms to generate new forms in new circumstances, and a portrait of the poet at the crossroads of past literary tradition and present lived experience.

I

Interpreting the dialectic between the poem's engagement with a culturally specific social and historical context and its participation in the codes and norms of an autonomous literary system has always been a crucial task of scholarship on *Paradise Lost*, and this holds true also for Milton's handling of supplication. The seventeenth century was a critical turning point in the history of communication, in which older forms like supplication underwent significant and durable changes, in part as a result of the interventions of

Milton and his revolution-minded contemporaries.[10] The paradigm of interaction involved in seventeenth century supplication had its roots in medieval political theory, where interactions between social unequals were modeled on the radically unequal relationship between human beings and God.[11] The suppliant's humble posture and self-abasing forms of address assimilated the language of prayer to social discourse, transferring the humility and abjection of the religious petitioner to the rhetoric of seeking favor in the political realm. Supplicatory gestures and utterances were an essential part of social intercourse well through the Tudor period, and it was only in the early decades of the seventeenth century that the petition began to shift in meaning from a mechanism for seeking favor into a way of asserting rights. Milton himself was a shaper of this process; as Annabel Patterson shows, Milton turned the structure of political petitioning on its head in his regicide pamphlets, helping to guide the process by which the petition "acquired a political and ideological force that caused it, through the new machinery of organized protest and more informed lobbies, to reverse its own semantics."[12] Political supplication, Milton writes in *Eikonoklastes*, should be a form by which "men require not favours only, but thir due" (YP 3:461).

At the same time that Milton was actively engaged in refashioning the language of social hierarchy—a discourse that poets such as Donne and Herbert had already transformed into a "poetics of supplication" in their devotional verse[13]—he also encountered in his classical reading the analogous and yet profoundly remote ancient practice of supplication. Here he found a trope directly keyed to the epic preoccupation of defining heroism. As Francis Blessington notes in the most substantial previous treatment of supplication in *Paradise Lost*, the suppliant in classical epic is "the defeated antithesis of the conquering warrior," "a foil for the hero in character, gesture, and idea," whose presence forces an internal conflict in the hero "between compassion for the enemy and pride in victory."[14] At the end of the *Iliad*, when Priam supplicates Achilles for the return of Hector's body for burial (*Iliad* 24.457–676), the hero's decision to accept the suppliant marks the end of the story of his wrath. The parallel scene in the *Aeneid* (12.930–1241) works in the opposite way: when Aeneas silently executes the suppliant Turnus in the heat of blind fury, his refusal to honor Turnus's supplication signals the triumph of anger over mercy.

Blessington's reading captures something of the ethical-aesthetic nature of classical suppliant scenes, but there remains much to be said about the larger cultural operations of supplication in classical literature in order to fully understand why this structure comes to matter to Milton. In recent work on supplication by classicists—both cultural historians and literary critics—the fundamental property of supplication is more accurately described as transition, the negotiation of a shift from one state of relationship, life situation, or emotion to another.[15] The Greek verb *hikō*, from which the words for suppliant (*hiketēs*), suppliant prayer (*hikesia*), and supplication (*hiketeia*) all derive, means "to approach" or "to come to," and this root captures the dynamism and movement at the heart of the suppliant situation.[16] A suppliant in the radical sense is someone who arrives, a newcomer whose entrance marks the beginning of an encounter. Depending on the nature of the suppliant, his arrival might be welcome or unwelcome, expected or startling, ominous or propitious. In any event, it precipitates an unsolicited meeting. The confrontation that ensues has high stakes (sometimes life or death, often safety or harm) and takes place under out-of-the-ordinary circumstances. As a normative paradigm for interaction, supplication gives formal structure to the process of negotiating relationships between high and low, inside and outside, powerful and powerless.

The transitional quality of supplication arises not only from the suppliant's status as an arriver, but also from the two main formal elements of a suppliant interaction: reciprocity and inequality. The instability of suppliant scenes, and their tendency to morph into other kinds of interactions, derives in part from the uneasy union of these two components. The reciprocal structure of the encounter arises from the fact that supplication involves a series of steps that requires the participation of both parties engaged in the scene, the suppliant, and the supplicatee. The suppliant initiates the interaction by arresting the attention of the supplicatee with a physical gesture of self-abasement, which is then followed by a plea. The gesture and the plea are designed to elicit a response from the supplicatee, who must decide whether to accept, reject, or defer the supplication. The action of the suppliant is not unilateral but, rather, depends for its completion on a corresponding action performed by the person to whom it is addressed.

This reciprocal structure, however, coexists with a radical inequality between the participants. The suppliant makes his request not as an equal partner, but from a posture of total powerlessness. In lowering his body and making a gesture of helpless vulnerability—whether crouching, raising up his hands, or clasping the knees of the person he supplicates—the suppliant signals that he places himself entirely in the power of the supplicatee. In the logic of the interaction, the gesture of subordination, with its abdication of autonomy on the part of the suppliant and corresponding elevation of the status of the recipient, constrains the supplicatee to accept the request. The suppliant gives up his own honor, prestige, or shame (ancient forms of selfhood) as advance payment for acceptance or protection. To refuse the request that accompanies this display of self-abasement would be to take the suppliant's honor without giving anything in return—in short, a theft. Sara Brill nicely sums up this aspect of the interaction: "Because payment has already been rendered, the host is inhibited by shame from refusing the request; such a refusal would be tantamount to stealing the honor the host had garnered from the suppliant."[17] The economy of power in the interaction, then, is remarkably complex. The gesture of self-abasement forces the supplicatee into a position of indebtedness, which effectively realigns the power structure between the two individuals. The powerless suppliant, by very virtue of his demonstration of vulnerability, gains an eerie power over the person supplicated, the ultimate purpose of which is to unwind or realign the hierarchical relationship between the two participants. At the end of a supplication interaction, if it is successful, the suppliant will make the transition from a position of vulnerability to a new, more integrated status vis-à-vis the supplicatee.

An example from the gallery of suppliant scenes in Homer will help to illustrate this process more clearly. In book 7 of the

Odyssey, Odysseus lands on the island of Scheria, shipwrecked and alone, with no food or shelter and no way to get home. When he arrives at the court of the Phaeacians, he enters the main hall and flings his arms around the knees of the queen Arete, begging her to show him mercy and give him safe transport back to his native land. Once he has made his plea, he retreats to the hearth and sits in the ashes to wait for a reply. One of the senior Phaeacian lords reprimands the king Alcinous for leaving Odysseus sitting on the ground: he must be raised up out of the hearth, given a seat of honor, and furnished with a generous meal—such is the appropriate treatment of suppliants "whose rights are sacred."[18] Alcinous does exactly as he is told: he raises Odysseus to his feet, sits him in the chair next to himself, displacing his own son, and orders large quantities of food and wine to be brought in by the servant women. According to the logic of the ceremony, every step of which is carefully delineated in this scene, Odysseus undergoes a careful process of social integration. By embracing Arete's knees, lowering himself into the hearth, and giving up the claims to honor that might naturally accrue to him as king of Ithaca and hero of the Trojan War, Odysseus constrains Alcinous to repay the honor that as a suppliant he has renounced. The result is that Odysseus moves from exigent beggar on the outside of the court to honored guest, seated adjacent to the king himself.

Not all supplication scenarios end so well. In Homer (and in the lineage of epic scenes that originate from the material of the Homeric poems), the rights of the suppliant are regularly violated, and requests of supplication frequently fail. This is not simply an instance of a ritual-based culture showing concern for the violations of its rituals; the persistence of rejected supplications in the Homeric poems points to the entanglement of supplication with larger issues of selfhood and identity. The notion of personhood that informs the argument for accepting the suppliant in the *Odyssey* scene—that the suppliant's honor is his most valuable asset and giving it up is an action of such significance that he deserves compensation—is, in fact, a central point of contention in the *Iliad*. A number of critics have observed that the *Iliad* is a drama of supplication with compositionally parallel suppliant scenes, from Agamemnon's refusal to honor the supplication of the priest Chryses for the restoration of his captive daughter to the final acceptance by Achilles of Priam's request for the return of Hector's corpse.

The reason these scenes serve as symbolically powerful bookends for the action of the poem is that the story of the *Iliad* is the story of Achilles' struggle (and failure) to replace the notion of selfhood that informs the act of supplication with an explanation of the value of human life that is not dependent on traditional ideas of heroic honor. Achilles refuses to see a human being in the honor-based terms required by supplication, and so he regularly flouts the rules of the game. This appears most vividly in Achilles' confrontation with Lycaon, where Achilles denies that any form of compensation—not the honor that Lycaon surrenders by clasping Achilles' knees, and not the ransom he offers as the material equivalent of his humiliated being—can make up for the loss of Patroclus. The value of a human life cannot be calculated in terms of conventional honor, whether it be martial prowess, the accumulation of wealth, or the everlasting renown that is the end of the warrior's existence. Supplication then is more than an isolated *agon* between the hero's compassion and desire for vengeance. It is both an organizing principle for the story of Achilles' struggle with the implications of his own mortality, and a microcosmic drama of the premises of the heroic code that Achilles subjects to relentless interrogation.[19]

Supplication is also the context for some of Homeric epic's most durable reflections on the nature of poetry. The moment of supplication precipitates a dramatic crisis in which the strategies of drama are imported into epic. Stella Revard develops this point by suggesting that supplication facilitates an unexpected change in narrative direction analogous to Aristotelian *peripeteia*. The crisis of supplication "reverses the action, and brings about closure."[20] When Achilles accepts Priam's supplication, the story of the *Iliad* undergoes a dramatic reversal, as anger suddenly gives way to peace. Homeric supplication events also tend to treat pity in aesthetic as well as ethical terms in ways that anticipate later affective views of poetry. As Kevin Crotty argues with regard to Priam's supplication of Achilles in *Iliad* 24, the pity that the suppliant aims to arouse in the person he supplicates—a feeling of generalized grief in response to individual suffering—is the same feeling that Homeric poetry aspires to cultivate in its audience. When Priam begs, "Honor then the gods, Achilleus, and take pity on me, remembering your father" (*Iliad* 24.503–04), he uses the Greek verb *eleeō*, based on the noun *eleos*, the virtually untranslatable term that describes the painful visceral reaction one would have in response to seeing someone in extreme distress. Aristotle will later use this term to describe the spectator's experience of tragic *katharsis*, and there are hints of this aestheticized meaning in Homer as well. Like Achilles' experience of *eleos* in response to Priam's supplication, the poem "offers an 'objective' experience of sorrow, in which the listener feels the characters' distress but in doing so learns about the kind of thing sorrow is, and its significance within human life."[21] In Priam's supplication in *Iliad* 24, the kind of pity the suppliant seeks to evoke by calling to mind the memory of a loved one's suffering has a strong affinity with the aestheticization of emotion in Aristotle's theory of audience response.

The suppliant scene, then, invokes a matrix of interconnected issues in the epic tradition. It acquires its poetic power both from its status as a ceremonialized form of reciprocity and from its tendency to assimilate adjacent discourses into itself. Situated at the juncture of religion, politics, and poetics, supplication has a special plasticity that allows it to fuse easily with other forms, and this plasticity is one of the features that appealed to Milton—so much so that he develops the suppliant scene into a master trope that pulls together his thinking on religious politics, the poetics of forgiveness, and the use of hierarchical forms to unravel inequality.

II

If supplication is a condensed archive of ethics, politics, religion, and poetics, with parallel instantiations in Milton's immediate cultural context and in the literary system in which his epic participates, how do the assumptions and logic of supplication shape the structures of *Paradise Lost*? In order to answer this question, let us return first to Satan's resistance to the "suppliant knee." When Satan considers his course of action in the aftermath of the war in heaven, the one possibility he categorically rejects is supplication. He arrives on the poem's stage as a figure of Homeric proportions, a towering classical warrior obsessed with the balance sheet of glory and shame. Satan will soon acquire other attributes of a would-be classical epic hero (gripping oratory, a voyage), but in the reader's first encounter with him Milton connects Satan to a classical lineage through his attitude to supplication.[22] What bothers Satan about the prospect of asking God for pardon is not that he thinks God will refuse (indeed, the logic of the gesture points to success), but that the lowering of the "suppliant knee" will increase God's prestige and diminish his own. Like his classical forebears, Satan believes that the act of supplication requires a confession of fundamental inferiority; but unlike Odysseus or Priam, he does not realize that vulnerability is the starting point for a reciprocal interaction that may lead to genuine transformation.

Milton does not leave Satan for long inside the ethical universe of classical epic; he soon adds another register to Satan's refusal to supplicate. The defeated leader of the rebel angels believes that bowing and kneeling in order to ask for God's pardon will "deify his power" (*PL* 1.112). The word "deify" leaps out from the otherwise martial vocabulary of the speech, and the scene of the Homeric battlefield jostles with the seventeenth century house of worship. There is evidently more at stake for Satan in the act of supplication than a warrior's shame of bowing in self-abasement; the physical gesture of suppliant kneeling takes on theological implications as well. By the end of the speech, the warrior's aversion to the "suppliant knee" bleeds into the nonconformist discourse of idolatry, in which kneeling is a form of adoration that elevates the object of supplication to the status of divinity.

In fact, Satan's objection to supplication both on heroic and nonconformist grounds turns out to be a main strand in the story of his fall. What appears to the reader at first to be a problem restricted to the postmartial context of book 1 is implicated in the rationale for the battle itself. As the poem moves backward in time, Homeric supplication is increasingly entangled with the issues of religious kneeling and political subjection; the metaphorics of Satan's original rejection of submission to the Son open into a nexus of liturgical and political ideas only hinted at in his postrebellion speech to Beelzebub. Satan's persistent objection to self-lowering, which begins at the chronological origin of the poem with his refusal to give "knee-tribute" to the newly anointed Son, taps into Milton's preoccupation with hierarchical structures in both civic and religious spheres. In book 5, faced with the revelation of the Son's new status as anointed king, Satan recoils from the physical homage owed to the "vicegerent" ruler of heaven, making explicit the link he perceives between supplication, political inequality, and idolatry.

> Thrones, dominations, princedoms, virtues, powers,
> If these magnific titles yet remain
> Not merely titular, since by decree
> Another now hath to himself engrossed
> All power, and us eclipsed under the name
> Of king anointed, for whom all this haste,
> Of midnight march, and hurried meeting here,
> This only to consult how we may best
> With what may be devised of honours new
> Receive him coming to receive from us
> Knee-tribute yet unpaid, prostration vile,
> Too much to one, but double how endured,
> To one and to his image now proclaimed? (*PL* 5.772–84)

The speech is a masterpiece of satanic rhetoric. Having gathered together his partisans under the pretext of discussing "the great reception of their king" (5.769), Satan shifts from the opening deliberative rhetoric of consultation to a passionate judicial argument for resistance to the Son's rule "too much" to be endured. The turn of thought and rhetorical genre occurs with the word "knee-tribute," which slides provocatively into the appositive phrase "prostration vile" and unleashes Satan's fiery protest on behalf of liberty and equality. Satan's refusal to pay "knee-tribute" is deeply connected to his belief in his own autonomy, in the idea that he is "self-begot, self-raised" (5.860) and that it is more appropriate for him to approach God's throne "besieging" rather than "beseeching"

(5.869). This notion of selfhood, which invokes the Homeric warrior's belief that personal honor (and its correlative, upright posture) is the ultimate measure of individual value, prevents him from performing any gesture that admits to vulnerability or dependency, or that places him in need of a reply to a request. Satan clings to the autonomy he believes he would give up if he were to approach God "by supplication" (5.867). His hatred of hierarchy excludes him from the supplicatory relationship of reciprocity.

The significance of kneeling in this passage continues to expand outward into larger spheres of meaning, as Satan conflates kneeling in supplication with kneeling in adoration. The economic metaphor implicit in "knee-tribute" casts the angels as subject polities of a domineering empire, whose liberty is constrained by a demand for physical as well as financial signs of submission. The political resonance that continues in "prostration vile," evokes classical *proskynesis,* the self-abasement before supreme royal power typical of Eastern monarchs. But if resistance to "knee-tribute" and "prostration vile" is a republican rally cry, "prostration" is also a religious term, which Patrick Hume, the author of the first full set of annotations to *Paradise Lost,* glosses as: "*Prostratio,* Lat. a lying flat on the Ground, of Prosternere, to lie along, to worship by falling flat on the Earth."[23] Hume's identification of prostration as term of worship points to the theological as well as political resonance of Satan's objection to physical self-lowering. If the object of the gesture is an "image," as Satan calls the Son, kneeling becomes one of the outward signs of worship that Milton on another occasion called "the new-vomited Paganisme of sensuall Idolatry" (*Of Reformation,* YP 1:520).

In book 5, kneeling in supplication becomes part of the same continuum as kneeling in adoration; one slips into the other, preserving the feature of inequality, but losing the reciprocity. In fact, Satan's complaint against paying "knee-tribute" to God's "image," might very well belong to the rhetoric of a theological treatise of the 1630s or 1640s on the unlawfulness of religious kneeling.[24] The stance he takes on giving "knee-tribute" to the Son corresponds more generally to the anticeremonialist rejection of any physical gesture of adoration, but his *in malo* interpretation of the Son as God's shadowy "image" draws specifically on the spirit of iconoclasm. For Satan, kneeling to any image presented for worship necessarily bestows upon the image a residue of adoration, and such adoration, regardless of the intention of the worshipper, has the effect of deifying a sign. But while Satan presents himself as a scrupulous Puritan in denying worship to an image, in the economy of *Paradise Lost* the "image" he refuses to kneel to is not a sign but the thing itself. The slippage between Satan's resistance to classical supplication and his anxiety about image worship suggests a certain hysteria about physical gestures of subordination, which Milton himself seems to have held back from endorsing. In *De doctrina Christiana* (1.4) he makes the case that kneeling is not a necessary form of worship, and that Scripture itself requires no particular style of prayer, but says nothing more (YP 6:168–202). The same lack of specificity reappears in prelapsarian Eden, where Adam and Eve say their evening prayer "unanimous" but "other rites / Observing none" (*PL* 4.736–37).

More importantly for my purposes, however, Milton distances himself from the satanic resistance to kneeling by directing attention to Satan's failure to understand supplication as a reciprocal rather than one-sided interaction. The history of Satan's increasing distance from heaven is told through his incomplete understanding of supplication as it functions in the classical epic world to which he partially belongs—namely, as a mechanism for unraveling the very hierarchical relationships to which he so vehemently objects. At the beginning of book 4, as he contemplates his happy, innocent Edenic victims, who know nothing of their future, Satan once again comes close to adopting the position of suppliant. Realizing that he cannot escape hell, but instead carries it with him wherever he goes, Satan brings himself to the point of despair from which repentance might be born:

> Oh then at last relent: is there no place
> Left for repentance, none for pardon left?
> None left but by submission; and that word
> Disdain forbids me, and my dread of shame.   (*PL* 4.79–82)

The suppliant role presents itself again for a flickering instant as Satan imagines repenting and asking for pardon. But submission, in book 5 a point of debate and instigation to rebellion, in book 1 a possible, though rejected, means of regaining God's favor after defeat, immediately pulls Satan up short. He can only imagine a submission that is "feigned" (4.96) and concludes, "This knows my punisher; therefore as far / From granting he, as I from begging peace" (4.103–04). The syntax of these lines shows how close and at the same time how remote Satan is from salvation; the correlatives "as far / From granting...as...from begging" suggest that Satan grasps the reciprocal relationship between granting and begging, but he reverses and inverts them so that his own decision not to beg is predicated on the assumption that God will not grant. This failure to embrace reciprocity leads Satan to the point of no return where he can say, "Evil be thou my good" (4.110). It also brings him to apply the same perverse reciprocity to Adam and Eve. Satan's conviction that his inability to repent hinges on God's inability to pardon persuades him to reject the possibility of sparing Adam and Eve.

> Happy, but for so happy ill secured
> Long to continue, and this high seat your heaven
> Ill fenced for heaven to keep out such a foe
> As now is entered: yet no purposed foe
> To you whom I could pity thus forlorn
> Though I unpitied.   (*PL* 4.370–75)

The innocent happiness Adam and Eve enjoy in the garden and the knowledge of its future destruction leads Satan to consider an act of preemptive pity. He imagines the human pair proleptically as "forlorn," seeking his mercy, and contrasts their situation, should he pity them, with his own unpitied isolation. He has the choice of the supplicatee in the epic tradition, to spare or to kill, to pardon or to avenge. His decision to reject his hypothetical suppliants connects him with a long epic lineage of supplication crises where reciprocity goes awry. Just as Achilles rejects Lycaon because no one spared Patroclus, and as Aeneas rejects Turnus because he killed Pallas, Satan applies the tit-for-tat logic of revenge to a situation that calls for the more positive reciprocity of supplication. As Satan is "unpitied," so Adam and Eve must be. This link between them perversely becomes the basis of the "mutual amity" (4.376) he seeks. Satan's partial and incomplete application of the reciprocal dynamics of supplication leads to his self-exclusion from a positive connection with the poem's human protagonists. As Satan moves between his roles as Homeric warrior, scrupulous Puritan, and isolated self-victimizer, the underlying thread is his hostility to supplication. When we leave Satan looking in on paradise, he now stands outside the reciprocal structure of supplication—a structure that, as we will see, becomes central to Milton's view of the slow process of reconciliation both on earth and in heaven.

III

Satan's rejection of the reciprocity of supplication tracks his unfolding distance from God and also anticipates in diabolical form the cluster of scenes involving the supplication gestures of Adam, Eve, and the Son. In the earthly and heavenly spheres of the poem, supplication becomes a key to understanding the dynamics of reconciliation after the Fall. In discussions of the reconciliation scene between Adam and Eve in book 10, Milton critics have rightly focused increasing attention on Eve's role in the process that restores the first couple to mutual sympathy. For Joseph Summers, Eve's speech begging Adam's forgiveness is "the turning point" of the poem.[25] More recently, William Shullenberger has made the case that after the Fall, "Eve breaks the grip of self-hatred and mutual accusation by subordinating herself, by pleading for Adam's forgiveness, and by offering her own life as a sacrifice out of her love for Adam."[26] But if scholars have pinpointed the pivotal role Eve plays in the book 10 reconciliation, less attention has been devoted to the narrative mechanisms through which that transformation unfolds.[27] I argue that Milton models the narrative form of Eve's petition and Adam's response to her plea on the structure of a Homeric supplication scene. Eve presents herself as a suppliant, performing the supplicatory gesture of clasping the knees, while Adam takes on the role of supplicatee who evaluates her petition and makes a judgment whether or not to accept it. The paradigm of supplication—with its emphasis on dynamic interaction, reciprocity, and process—provides Milton with the narrative mechanism to describe the physical and psychological steps that lead to reconciliation. As a narrative event, the supplication scene provides a formal structure of transition and a dramatic fluidity that allows Milton to show how reciprocity is reestablished out of hierarchical forms in postlapsarian Eden.

At the spiritual nadir of the poem, reconciliation seems entirely out of reach both psychologically and poetically. Adam and Eve, judged guilty by the Son and given a foretaste of their punishment, spiral downward into an abyss of mutual accusation and resentment. Their drama reaches its lowest point in Adam's bitter lament (*PL* 10.720–844) as he lies alone outstretched on the cold ground "in a troubled sea of passion tossed" (10.718), vacillating between contrition and despair. In an effort to purge himself of self-loathing, Adam tries to take all the blame for his sin and spare his descendants the effects of God's curse: "On me, me only, as the source and spring / Of all corruption, all the blame lights due; / So might the wrath" (10.832–34). But rather than extricating him from egocentrism, his "fond wish" (10.834) ironically plunges him deeper into the "abyss of fears / And horrors" (10.842–43) and further isolates him in his misery.[28] When Eve tries to console him, he responds with an outpouring of bitterness and misogyny: "Out of my sight, thou Serpent, that name best / Befits thee with him leagued, thyself as false / And hateful" (10.867–69).

Instead of responding in kind, Eve breaks through the psychological impasse by acknowledging her guilt and begging Adam's forgiveness. The narrator introduces the scene with the formal signals of supplication:

> but Eve
> Not so repulsed, with tears that ceased not flowing,
> And tresses all disordered, at his feet
> Fell humble, and embracing them, besought
> His peace, and thus proceeded in her plaint. (*PL* 10.909–13)

Alastair Fowler cites the "great contemporary icon" of the penitent Magdalene as an analogue for the narrator's description of Eve's tears and disordered tresses, linking Eve with the specific iconographic tradition of Titian's *St. Mary Magdalene*.[29] In offering Titian's painting as a point of comparison—a biblical portrait that depicts Mary Magdalene with a tearful expression of repentance—Fowler captures the highly visual nature of the scene, but misses the more important gesture of physical submission enacted in the embracing of Adam's feet. The narrator represents Eve not just as Mary Magdalene, who in the iconographic tradition of the *Noli me tangere* episode appears kneeling before Christ's feet, but as a classical supplicant, using the conventional gesture of embracing the feet or knees to make her plea. The gestural formula takes on further significance when Eve, picking up on the narrator's suggestion, explicitly describes herself as a supplicant:

> Forsake me not thus, Adam, witness heaven
> What love sincere, and reverence in my heart
> I bear thee, and unweeting have offended,
> Unhappily deceived; thy suppliant
> I beg, and clasp thy knees.   (*PL* 10.914–18)

Eve first identifies herself verbally as a supplicant, and then performs by speech-act the gesture of touching the knees. The knee clasp is a posture common to suppliants across classical literature, but Milton seems to have in mind a specifically Homeric version of the ritual: the phrase "clasp thy knees," a direct translation of the Greek word *gounomai*, appears only three times in seventeenth century literature, two of which are from Chapman's *The Whole Works of Homer* (1616).[30] Both instances of the phrase in Chapman occur in situations of successful supplication. In book 9 of the *Iliad*, Phoenix's mother repeatedly clasps his knees in order to persuade him to take vengeance on his father—which he ultimately does; and in book 22 of the *Odyssey*, the bard Phemius successfully petitions Odysseus to exempt him from the slaughter of the suitors.

The allusion to the formal structure of Homeric supplication primarily functions as a way of opening up a rhetorical space for Eve's petition. By initiating the interaction with the knee-clasp, she sets in motion the series of steps that give supplication its transformative and transitional power. As she clasps Adam's knees, Eve delivers a speech that complements her gesture in power and passion. She begins by begging him not to abandon her, casting her petition in terms of a plea for life: "bereave me not, / Whereon I live, thy gentle looks, thy aid, / Thy counsel in this uttermost distress, / My only strength and stay" (*PL* 10.918–21). Her life, she argues, depends on Adam's presence: "forlorn of thee / Whither shall I betake me, where subsist?" (10.921–22). To persuade him further, she offers a ransom: in exchange for Adam's forgiveness, she will ask God to transfer the blame for their transgression onto her alone so that she might be able to pay the debt she owes to regain Adam's favor.

> both have sinned, but thou
> Against God only, I against God and thee,
> And to the place of judgment will return,
> There with my cries importune heaven, that all
> The sentence from thy head removed may light
> On me, sole cause to thee of all this woe,
> Me, me only just object of his ire.   (*PL* 10.930–36)

The ideological content of Eve's supplication speech, though structurally analogous to its classical antecedents, takes a remarkable turn. She proposes a ransom, not (as in Homer) a gift of gold or silver that is commensurate with the value of the suppliant's life, but her life itself. Eve offers to take unilateral responsibility for a mutual act of disobedience, allowing Adam to escape the consequences of sin and remain alive, while accepting the punishment of death herself. Eve's supplication, then, amounts to the extreme form of self-abasement: she lowers herself to the point of extinction.

Just as the structural elements of supplication give Eve the poetic space to make her plea, so the contingency of the interaction provides Adam with a formal mechanism to reciprocate. The response of the supplicatee has a vexed history in the epic tradition, especially when the suppliant pleads for life and offers a ransom. As we have seen, in the *Iliad*, the rejection of the battlefield suppliant is one of the ways Achilles demonstrates his dissatisfaction with the notion of value that underlies the heroic code. But Milton uses the reciprocal structure of supplication to open possibilities rather than to foreclose them. Eve's supplication leaps away from earlier precedents in her offer of self-sacrifice, and allows Adam—unlike Satan in book 4—to escape the prewrittenness of earlier supplication scenes that fail. In the domestic context of postlapsarian Eden, the structure of supplication facilitates the unwinding rather than the tightening of conflict.

Adam's response is "commiseration" (*PL* 10.940), and Eve's petition succeeds. Her physical gesture of self-lowering and her self-immolating appeal arouse in Adam a compassion that reawakens his reason and inspires him to action. Adam's "commiseration," rather than blinding him with passion, allows him to see his course of action more clearly.[31] When confronted with Eve's argument for self-sacrifice, Adam recognizes the flaws in his own similar attempt to take on all the blame, and in describing Eve's unilateral offer as "unwary, and too desirous" (10.947), he implicitly rejects his own "fond wish" to expiate their sin alone.[32] He tells Eve to rise—the physical sign of an accepted supplication—and then, in a sequence that brings the steps of supplication to a conclusion, follows the physical gesture with a rhetorical turn away from the isolationist language of individual self-sacrifice toward a vocabulary of mutuality and restored dialogue:

> But rise, let us no more contend, nor blame
> Each other, blamed enough elsewhere, but strive
> In offices of love, how we may light'n
> Each other's burden in our share of woe. (*PL* 10.958–61)

Adam accepts Eve's request for forgiveness but refuses the terms on which she offered it, thereby rejecting the notion of unilateral self-sacrifice altogether. By putting aside the language of "I" and returning to "we," Adam erases their separate attempts to shoulder the burden of sin alone and insists on a mutual relationship of help and comfort.

The reciprocal process inherent in the structure of supplication allows Adam the rhetorical space to be moved and to move himself and Eve into new psychological terrain. But just as importantly, Adam's response also attempts to transcend the hierarchical structure inherent in the drama of supplication. He asserts the superior status of the supplicatee in accepting Eve's petition but then immediately relinquishes it, telling her to rise and acknowledging the inadequacy of both of their attempts to take on all the blame themselves. Instead, they both return to the place of judgment to offer their supplications—not to each other, but to God—and acquire perhaps the greatest degree of equality they have had as of yet in the poem.[33] In sharing the burden of sin, they arrive at a radical equality before God, mirrored in the collective language used to describe their prayers: "both confessed / Humbly their faults, and pardon begged" (*PL* 10.1100–01).

Eve's voluntary self-abasement in the form of supplication, then, initiates the psychological and poetic process by which the first couple moves out of contention and misery to a place of shared contrition and mutual subordination before God. The key concept in this move from hierarchy to equality, from despair to regeneration, is *process*. In the first human scene of reconciliation, Adam and Eve do not follow a ritual script. They invent the steps of future ritualized actions. From the outside perspective of the reader, it is easy to see the ceremonialized aspects of their interaction, but from the inside, their reconciliation is a precarious process, every stage of which is uncertain. Eve begs for pardon for the first time, inventing its language and gestures, not knowing what the outcome will be; Adam forgives her for the first time, still unsure of where his love for her will lead him. The structure of supplication, with its emphasis on the transformative power of physical gesture and the back-and-forth pattern of reciprocal action, emerges as a poetic device for expressing the unstable dynamics of the originary process of reconciliation. What is most remarkable is that Milton saw in the classical, and especially Homeric, ritual of supplication the poetic potential for articulating the instability and preritualized experience of the first human act of forgiveness.

This instability is felt nowhere more strongly than in Adam and Eve's petition to God at the end of book 10. In the process of their own reconciliation, they have come to recognize the power of supplicatory gesture, but they do not know what will happen if they initiate the same sequence of gestures with God. In the immediate aftermath of the Fall, with their future fate unknown, they begin to understand only gradually what the ominous word "death" means. Adam has an inkling that beseeching God's pardon might have a positive outcome when he remembers "with what mild / And gracious temper" (*PL* 10.1046–47) God sentenced the guilty pair. Instead of the expected "immediate dissolution" (10.1049), Adam recalls that Eve is sentenced to "pains only in child-bearing" (10.1051), and that instead of eating from the self-generating cornucopia of Eden, he must earn his bread with labor (10.1054–56). The mitigation of punishment—which they both expected to be instant annihilation—gives Adam hope that God will hear their petition. Even so, the resolution to seek God's pardon by returning to the place of judgment is a leap of faith. The future of supplication as a ceremonial practice in Christian worship is gently hinted at as Milton repeats verbatim, in Homeric fashion, the words of Adam's speech in the description of their prostration and petition, but ritualized petition is at first entirely experimental.[34] In book 10 supplication is a process, not yet fossilized, the outcome of which is unpredictable and unknown. In Adam and Eve's reconciliation, Milton cultivates a reciprocal relationship with the epic tradition; he takes from Homer, but gives back as well. From the vantage point of *Paradise Lost*, situated at the chronological origins of human time and civilization, Homer might have learned the narrative force of supplication from Adam and Eve.

IV

In the book 10 reconciliation scene, Milton relies on the dynamic structure of supplication to facilitate the resolution of conflict and an unraveling of hierarchy, building on his portrait of Satan's incomplete understanding of the reciprocal potential of supplication that binds him in those same hierarchical structures. But the patterning of Adam and Eve's interaction in book 10—descent, ascent, and finally the discovery of a shared equality before God—does more than perform Milton's indebtedness to classical epic even as he articulates his version of Christian ethics. It recapitulates in human and domestic terms the idiosyncratic metaphysics that underlies the theological core of *Paradise Lost*. In the parallel world of heaven, the Son's supplication on behalf of humankind becomes the cause of his subsequent exaltation and begins the process by which God intends to bring the created universe into a state where "God shall be all in all" (*PL* 3.341). In the heavenly narrative, Milton transposes the structures of supplication into a new configuration, crucially collapsing the distinction between suppliant and supplicatee so that the Son takes on both roles to effect another reconciliation, this time between creator and creation.

In the heavenly assembly in book 3, when God announces to the angelic host Satan's imminent arrival on earth and the corruption of human beings soon to follow, he claims that they will fall and be doomed to death unless they find a redeemer in heaven willing to take on the burden of sin and die in "rigid satisfaction" (*PL* 3.212) for their transgression. Faced with God's pronouncement of humanity's future fate, the Son, mirroring both structurally and verbally Eve's supplication in book 10, voluntarily offers to become human and pay the debt of death for humanity to live:

> Behold me then, me for him, life for life
> I offer, on me let thine anger fall;
> Account me man; I for his sake will leave
> Thy bosom, and this glory next to thee
> Freely put off, and for him lastly die
> Well pleased, on me let Death wreak all his rage. (*PL* 3.236–41)

The Son's offer to exchange his life for humanity's is presented not as an inevitable event but, like Eve's physical humiliation, as a transformative moment that suddenly breaks through an impasse. His petition "Account me man" generates the poetic energy to move forward out of a crisis moment, when the heavenly assembly stands silent and the fate of humanity hangs in the balance.

Initially it seems as though the Son intends to engage in a straightforward exchange; the grammatically parallel phrases "me for him" and "life for life" play out in formal terms the idea of an equal economic transaction of the Son's life for humankind's. However, it soon becomes clear that the Son's sacrifice is anything but a comparable exchange. In order to make the two sides of the equation "life for life" equivalent, the Son, continuing the economic metaphor, asks to be "accounted" human, to be allowed to give up his seat of glory next to God, and to abandon his divinity for humanity.

In the terms of Milton's materialist view of creation, the Son's voluntary self-humiliation implies a descent down the monist continuum of being.[35] The Son's offer to become human is neither a metaphor nor an ineffable mystery, but a material reality. Just as Raphael tells Adam that "Your bodies may at last turn all to spirit...If ye be found obedient" (*PL* 5.497, 501), the Son's promise to take on flesh means that he will adopt a denser form of material substance. The Son physically reduces himself, taking on a degree of corporeal being below his own. Only as a result of this descent can the terms of the exchange he envisions in "me for him" take place. Anticipating the structure of the book 10 reconciliation scene, the Son's physical humiliation—etymologically taking on the *humus* from which Adam was fashioned—is accepted. But the manner in which God accepts the Son's offer begins to suggest the fundamental difference between supplication on the human level and on the divine. It is not only that the Son is sinless and can function as a pure victim; he also enacts both sides of the reciprocal drama of supplication.

As we have seen, in the paradigmatic scene of supplication, the suppliant attempts to constrain the supplicatee to accept his request, to use his vulnerability to activate pity; the recipient of the suppliant's plea is either moved or not, either acts on his pity or not. In the case of the Son's supplication, however, God accepts the Son's petition without showing any such pitiful response; God expresses pleasure ("my sole complacence" [*PL* 3.276]) at the Son's self-lowering but does not pity him. Rather, it is the Son who pities humanity and persuades God to incline toward mercy. The pity that is part of an accepted supplication is transferred from supplicatee to suppliant: the Son takes on both roles. In fact, it is precisely the Son's pity and his willingness to become the object of pity that ensures God's acceptance of the petition and his decision to exalt the Son for his excess of self-reduction. For Milton, merit is determined by the willingness to fall. The Son becomes the Messiah not by birthright as God's offspring but because he lowers himself ontologically on humanity's behalf and accepts the punishment for a transgression not his own. God proclaims:

> Because thou hast, though throned in highest bliss
> Equal to God, and equally enjoying
> Godlike fruition, quitted all to save
> A world from utter loss, and hast been found
> By merit more than birthright Son of God,
>
> ....
>
> Therefore thy humiliation shall exalt
> With thee thy manhood also to this throne;
> Here shalt thou sit incarnate, here shalt reign
> Both God and man, Son of both God and man,
> Anointed universal king.   (PL 3.305–09, 313–17)

The union of God and man in the Son points to the collapse of the distinction between suppliant and supplicatee; as God, the Son's role is to hear petitions; as man he makes them.

Even more importantly, God's promise that "humiliation shall exalt" (PL 3.313) turns out to be a preface to his larger eschatological vision in which hierarchical distinctions like the Son's kingship become finally irrelevant. Indeed, this erasure of hierarchy seems to be God's intention from the beginning. When he first presents the newly begotten Son to the heavenly assembly in book 5, God's motivation in elevating the Son to "vicegerent reign"—a move Satan interprets as a tyrannical power-grab and forced submission to an apparent equal—appears to be the elimination of the very hierarchy and difference he seems to be imposing (5.609). He explains to the angels:

> This day I have begot whom I declare
> My only Son, and on this holy hill
> Him have anointed, whom ye now behold
> At my right hand; your head I him appoint;
> And by myself have sworn to him shall bow
> All knees in heaven, and shall confess him Lord:
> Under his great vicegerent reign abide
> United as one individual soul
> For ever happy: him who disobeys
> Me disobeys, breaks union, and that day
> Cast out from God and blessed vision, falls
> Into utter darkness, deep engulfed, his place
> Ordained without redemption, without end.   (PL 5.603-15)

Amid the blitz of imperatives, assertions of autonomous action, and threats of punishment, Satan might perhaps be forgiven for missing God's altruistic goal for the angels to "abide / United as one individual soul / For ever happy." But the meaning of God's commandment is unpacked later by Abdiel, who responds to Satan's rebellious demagoguery with a more generous view of God's intention. Abdiel looks through God's imperialistic rhetoric and sees beneath it a hidden desire for unity. He intimates that the Son's apparent elevation to "vicegerent reign" is, like his subsequent promise to become man, a form of physical reduction. The angels, therefore, are not

> by his reign obscured,
> But more illustrious made, since he the head
> One of our number thus reduced becomes,
> His laws our laws, all honour to him done
> Returns our own.   (PL 5.841-45)

By becoming head of the angels, the Messiah is actually lowered from his position as God's Son, and the angels in turn are raised by his sharing of their nature. Raising and lowering are interdependent.

The ultimate purpose of this paradoxical humiliation as exaltation is articulated in two parallel passages that gloss God's original proclamation that the angels be "United as one individual soul."

On his way to do battle with the rebel angels, the Son describes what seems to be the *telos* of his action: "Sceptre and power, thy giving, I assume, / And gladlier shall resign, when in the end / Thou shalt be all in all, and I in thee / For ever, and in me all whom thou lov'st" (*PL* 6.730–33). The Son proleptically refers to the moment the reader has already experienced when God prophesies the coming of a new heaven and earth: "thou thy regal sceptre shalt lay by / For regal scepter then no more shall need, / God shall be all in all" (3.339–41).

In eschatological terms, the humiliation of the Son aims to abolish all hierarchical distinction between levels of being.[36] In structural terms, God's vision of a universe in which creator and creation are ultimately brought together in a relationship of radical equality mirrors the resolution of the reconciliation scene, when Eve's self-humiliation and Adam's assertion of temporary authority result in the dissolution of the hierarchical relationship they just enacted. The goal of all of God's actions appears to be to bring other beings closer to him. He ultimately aims to offer a kind of divine mercy that is not negatively implicated in the power structure of a superior offering pardon to an inferior; God uses hierarchical forms primarily in the interest of abandoning them.[37]

The most important aspect of God's eschatological plan is that the mechanism by which ultimate equality is to be accomplished is the dual nature of the Son, as suppliant and supplicatee, pitier and pitied, man and God. In both theological and rhetorical terms, the conventional way to articulate this union of God and man was the Crucifixion. Other Christian epicists rely on the Crucifixion for this purpose; as Colin Burrow observes, "the crucifixion is the ultimate moment on which to center a transvaluation of pity into divinely incarnate sympathy: it manifests both an extreme of active pity, since it represents God pitying man enough to die for him, and an unsurpassable form of passive pity, as God himself becomes the object of pity."[38] But unlike previous writers of biblical epic, and unlike many (even Puritan) theologians, Milton notoriously shies away from an aesthetic representation of the Passion, both in his early poetry and in *Paradise Lost*.[39] Instead, the means by which Milton expresses the fulfillment of the Son's role in effecting reconciliation between God and humanity is another transposition of the suppliant scene.

At the beginning of book 11, Adam and Eve continue their humble prayers, which fly up to heaven (*PL* 11.15) and find their way to God's throne. However, instead of being directly received by God, the prayers are presented to God by the Son:

> See Father, what first fruits on earth are sprung
> From thy implanted grace in man, these sighs
> And prayers, which in this golden censer, mixed
> With incense, I thy priest before thee bring,
>
> ....
>
> Now therefore bend thine ear
> To supplication, hear his sighs though mute;
> Unskilful with what words to pray, let me
> Interpret for him, me his advocate
> And propitiation, all his works on me
> Good or not good engraft, my merit those
> Shall perfect, and for these my death shall pay.
> (*PL* 11.22–25, 30–36)

This scene is a heterodox Miltonic invention: the Son fulfills his role as Messiah in the poem not in a representation of the Crucifixion, but in a preincarnate act of priestly mediation.[40] Milton situates the full articulation of the Son's action of atonement ("for these my death shall pay") in a scene that involves an intercessory supplication. It is only when God accepts the Son's request to receive Adam and Eve's prayers, perfected by the Son's merit, that the atonement promised in book 3 finally takes place. In his role as intercessor for Adam and Eve's supplication, the Son reimagines the classical suppliant drama that has become so crucial for the poem's negotiation of hierarchical relationships. The intercessor that functions as both suppliant and supplicatee breaks through the opposition implied in the structure of the interaction, crucially unburdening the participants on either side of some of the risk and vulnerability involved in their encounter. In this final supplication crisis, Milton performs the transvaluation of classical into Christian, positing the Son as the missing term that guarantees the success of supplication and erases its unpredictability. With the Son's help, Adam and Eve make the precarious transition back into God's grace. Even more importantly, God becomes involved in the reciprocity of supplication. As the Son lifts up the prayers of Adam and Eve, he asks God to "bend thine ear," to follow the same pattern of downward movement and self-lowering that the Son himself has taken. Descent is again interwoven with ascent, and God participates in the poem's inversion of high and low.

Given Milton's aversion to "bowings and cringings" and his sensitivity to gestural manifestations of hierarchy, the prominence of supplication in the literary theology of *Paradise Lost* may come as something of a surprise in its hint of conservatism (YP 7:425). Instead of looking for a radically novel structure of interaction to describe his vision of cosmic equality, Milton returns repeatedly to classical supplication as a poetic mechanism for dramatizing the negotiation of hierarchy. Ancient hierarchical forms turn out to be useful insofar as they provide a mechanism for explaining how unequal relationships might be unraveled. In *Paradise Lost*, in fact, supplicating is never the wrong approach. Satan's refusal to supplicate is the result of a misevaluation of the possibilities of the suppliant exchange, of failing to understand the poem's paradox that humiliation can exalt. As Adam and Eve grapple their way to reconciliation, they unknowingly but auspiciously act out in their gestures this core principle of Miltonic theology, which finds its full articulation in the Son's self-lowering and subsequent elevation. It is their gesture that becomes the last chapter in the poem's story of descent as ascent, as they leave paradise on newly equal terms, "hand in hand" (*PL* 12.648).

Harvard University

Notes

1. William Empson, *Milton's God* (London, 1961), 44–45, adding, "our recent pious critics, eager to catch Satan out on a technicality all the time, must be unable to read his speeches aloud." C. S. Lewis, *A Preface to "Paradise Lost"* (Oxford, 1961), 46, praises the turn of the speech, whose

"complex syntax...has enabled you to feel, even within these few lines, the enormous onward pressure of the great stream on which you are embarked."

2. The return of historicist inquiry in Milton scholarship has led to a productive reopening of the "Satan controversy," with many critics linking Satan to Milton's own political engagement. See esp. Joan S. Bennett, *Reviving Liberty: Radical Christian Humanism in Milton's Great Poems* (Cambridge, Mass., 1989); Laura Lunger Knoppers, *Historicizing Milton: Spectacle, Power, and Poetry in Restoration England* (Athens, Ga., 1994); Sharon Achinstein, *Milton and the Revolutionary Reader* (Princeton, N.J., 1994); David Armitage, Armand Himy, and Quentin Skinner, eds., *Milton and Republicanism* (Cambridge, 1995); David Norbrook, *Writing the English Republic: Poetry, Rhetoric, and Politics, 1627–1660* (Cambridge, 1999); Barbara Lewalski, "*Paradise Lost* and Milton's Politics," in *Milton Studies*, vol. 38, ed. Albert C. Labriola and Michael Lieb, 141–68 (Pittsburgh, 2000); Nigel Smith, "*Paradise Lost* from Civil War to Restoration," in *The Cambridge Companion to Writing of the English Revolution*, ed. N. H. Keeble, 251–67 (Cambridge, 2001); David Loewenstein, *Representing Revolution: Religion, Politics, and Polemics in Radical Puritanism* (Cambridge, 2001) and "The Radical Religious Politics of *Paradise Lost*," in *A Companion to Milton*, ed. Thomas N. Corns, 348–62 (Malden, Mass., 2001); Martin Dzelzainis, "The Politics of *Paradise Lost*," in *The Oxford Companion to Milton*, ed. Nicholas MacDowell and Nigel Smith, 547–68 (Oxford, 2009). Blair Worden, "Milton's Republicanism and the Tyranny of Heaven," in *Machiavelli and Republicanism*, ed. Gisela Bock, Quentin Skinner, and Maurizio Viroli, 141–68 (Cambridge, 1990), argues ultimately for Milton's retreat away from the political arena and the writing "of the left hand," but generates an indispensable catalogue of republican and antimonarchical language in *Paradise Lost*. Roger Lejosne, "Milton, Satan, Salmasius, and Abdiel," in *Milton and Republicanism*, 106–17, assembles a helpful list of satanic arguments that also appear in Milton's prose.

3. All quotations of *Paradise Lost* are taken from John Milton, *Paradise Lost*, ed. Alastair Fowler (Harlow, 2007); hereafter cited in the text.

4. *Eikonoklastes*, in *Complete Prose Works of John Milton*, 8 vols., ed. Don M. Wolfe et al. (New Haven, Conn., 1953–82), 3:344. All citations from Milton's prose are to this edition, hereafter cited parenthetically in the text as YP.

5. The case against reading Satan as a stand-in for any particular historical figure is made persuasively by Loewenstein, *Representing Revolution*, 203–26.

6. Ibid., 203.

7. For Milton's theory of accommodation, see *De doctrina Christiana* (YP 6:133). Christopher Ricks, *Milton's Grand Style* (Oxford, 1967), 149–50, makes a case for the deliberate misreadability of *Paradise Lost*, arguing that "Milton writes at his very best when something prevents

him from writing with total directness." Armand Himy, "*Paradise Lost* as a Republican 'tractatus theologico-politicus,'" in Armitage, Himy, and Skinner, *Milton and Republicanism*, 118–34, points to the "flexibility" of Milton's strategy of accommodation in which "theology and literature, poetic and political style, are all involved at once" (119).

8. The most complete treatment of classical supplication in *Paradise Lost* to date is Francis Blessington, "*Paradise Lost* and the Apotheosis of the Suppliant," *Arion* 6 (1998): 83–97. Stella Revard, "Milton, Homer, and the Anger of Adam," in *Milton Studies*, vol. 41, ed. Albert C. Labriola, 18–37 (Pittsburgh, 2002), also identifies supplication as part of Milton's Homeric borrowings.

9. Two major exceptions are Norbrook, *Writing the English Republic*, 438–67, and David Quint, *Epic and Empire: Politics and Generic Form from Virgil to Milton* (Princeton, N.J., 1993), 41–46, 268–325. Both of these critics see Milton's classical heritage, especially his appropriation of the republican literary strategies in Lucan's *Pharsalia*, as crucial to the political speech-act of *Paradise Lost*.

10. For the shift in forms of political and social communication in the seventeenth century, see David Zaret, *Origins of Democratic Culture: Printing, Petitions, and the Public Sphere in Early Modern England* (Princeton, N.J., 2000); Annabel Patterson, "A Petitioning Society," *Reading between the Lines* (Madison, Wis., 1993), 57–79.

11. For the intertwined political and religious history of medieval supplication, see Geoffrey Koziol, *Begging Pardon and Favor: Ritual and Political Order in Early Medieval France* (Ithaca, N.Y., 1992).

12. Patterson, "A Petitioning Society," 77.

13. See Michael Schoenfeldt, "The Poetics of Supplication: Toward a Cultural Poetics of the Religious Lyric," in *New Perspectives on the Seventeenth-Century English Religious Lyric*, ed. John R. Roberts, 75–104 (Columbia, Mo., 1994).

14. Blessington, "Apotheosis of the Suppliant," 84, 85, 87, 88.

15. The classic study remains John Gould, "Hiketeia," *Journal of Hellenic Studies* 33 (1973): 74–103. Gould sees supplication as a social and religious institution that appears both in literary texts and in the direct historical record in Greek culture from Homer to the fifth century and beyond. For an alternative view of supplication as a quasi-legal practice in the Greco-Roman world, see F. S. Naiden, *Ancient Supplication* (Oxford, 2006). Naiden pursues the role of suppliants and supplication in ancient practices of sacrifice in *Smoke Signals for the Gods: Ancient Greek Sacrifice from the Archaic through Roman Periods* (Oxford, 2013), 123–24, 169. Literary approaches include G. Whitfield, "The Restored Relation: The Suppliant Theme in the *Iliad*" (Ph.D. diss., Columbia University, 1967); Agathe Thornton, *Homer's "Iliad": Its Composition and the Motif of Supplication* (Göttingen, 1984); Michael Lynn-George, *Epos: Word, Narrative, and the "Iliad"* (Basingstoke, 1988); and Kevin Crotty, *The Poetics of Supplication: Homer's "Iliad" and "Odyssey"* (Ithaca, N.Y., 1994).

16. Henry George Liddell, Robert Scott, and Henry Stuart Jones, *A Greek-English Lexicon*, 9th ed. (1940), with revised *Supplement*, ed. P. G. W. Glare et al. (Oxford, 1996), s.v. *hikō*. See also Naiden, *Ancient Supplication*, 30–41.

17. Sara Brill, "Violence and Vulnerability in Aeschylus's *Suppliants*," in *Logos and Muthos: Philosophical Essays in Greek Literature*, ed. William Wians (Albany, N.Y., 2009), 165.

18. Homer, *Odyssey*, 7.165. I use the translation in *The Odyssey of Homer*, trans. Richmond Lattimore (New York, 2007).

19. For a nuanced account of the heroic warrior ethic represented in the *Iliad*, see James M. Redfield, *Nature and Culture in the Iliad: The Tragedy of Hector* (Durham, N.C., 1994).

20. Revard, "Milton, Homer," 33.

21. Crotty, *Poetics of Supplication*, 69.

22. For Satan's classical genealogy, see John M. Steadman, *Milton and the Renaissance Hero* (Oxford, 1967); Francis Blessington, *"Paradise Lost" and the Classical Epic* (Boston, 1979); Charles Martindale, *John Milton and the Transformation of Ancient Epic*, 2nd ed. (1986; repr., Bristol, 2002); Colin Burrow, *Epic Romance from Homer to Milton* (Oxford, 1993), 250–75; Norbrook, *Writing the English Republic*, 438–67; Katherine Calloway, "Beyond Parody: Satan as Aeneas in *Paradise Lost*," *Milton Quarterly* 39 (2005): 82–92.

23. Patrick Hume, *Annotations on Milton's "Paradise Lost"* (London, 1695), note to 5.782.

24. For the history of the debate over the intersecting issues of religious and political kneeling, see Lori Anne Ferrell, *Government by Polemic* (Stanford, Calif., 1998), esp. chap. 5, "Kneeling and the Body Politic," 140–66.

25. Joseph Summers, *The Muse's Method: An Introduction to "Paradise Lost"* (London, 1962), 44.

26. William Shullenberger, "Wrestling with the Angel: *Paradise Lost* and Feminist Criticism," *Milton Quarterly* 20 (1986): 76. Barbara Lewalski, *"Paradise Lost" and the Rhetoric of Literary Forms* (Princeton, N.J., 1985), expresses a similar view: "[Eve's] eloquent psalmic prayer begging forgiveness of Adam begins her redemptive role as type of the Second Eve whose Seed is the Messiah" (250). John C. Ulreich, "'Argument Not Less but More Heroic": Eve as the Hero of *Paradise Lost*," in *"All in All": Unity, Diversity, and the Miltonic Perspective*, ed. Charles W. Durham and Kristin A. Pruitt, 67–82 (Selinsgrove, Pa., 1999), makes the case that Eve's embodiment of the bard's argument for "the better fortitude / Of patience and heroic martyrdom" (*PL* 9.31–32) earns her the elusive status of the poem's true hero.

27. An exception is Jun Harada, "The Mechanism of Human Reconciliation in *Paradise Lost*," *Philological Quarterly* 50 (1971): 543–52, who approaches the reconciliation scene from a psychoanalytic perspective, identifying the mechanism of restoration as a form of mirroring.

28. John B. Broadbent, *Some Graver Subject: An Essay on "Paradise Lost"* (London, 1960), argues that the verbal link between Adam's speech and the Son's offer of self-sacrifice functions as the first step toward Adam's regeneration.

29. John Milton, *Paradise Lost*, ed. Alastair Fowler (Longman, 1997), note to 5.910–12. For this image, see Johannes Wilde, *Venetian Art from Bellini to Titian* (Oxford, 1981), 122–24, plate 102.

30. George Chapman, *Chapman's Homer: The Iliad*, ed. Allardyce Nicoll (Princeton, N.J., 1998), 192: "she...still would claspe my knee / To do her will" (*Iliad* 9.431–32); George Chapman, *Chapman's Homer: The Odyssey*, ed. Allardyce Nicoll (Princeton, N.J., 1998), 385: "venture to Ulysses, claspe his knee / And pray for ruth" (*Odyssey* 22.444–45). The other instance of the phrase appears in a dramatization of an epic moment that also ultimately derives from classical sources: Sophonisba's successful supplication to Massinissa in John Marston's *The Wonder of Women; or, The Tragedie of Sophonisba* (1606), 5.3.20–23: "Therefore with teares that wash thy feet, with hands / Vnusde to beg I claspe thy manlie knees, / O saue me from their fetters and contempt, / Their proud insultes, and more then insolence."

31. Christopher Tilmouth, *Reason's Triumph over Passion: A History of the Moral Imagination from Spenser to Rochester* (Oxford, 2007), points to this passage as part of his argument that Milton follows a number of seventeenth century theorists of the emotions in seeking to replace the dualistic model of an inner battle between reason and passion with an Aristotelian view of the passions in the service of virtue. Other scholars have similarly argued that the passions, especially pity, were increasingly accepted in early modern ethics as catalysts for virtue that should be cultivated and moderated rather than extirpated. See especially the essays in *Reading the Early Modern Passions: Essays in the Cultural History of Emotion*, ed. Gail Kern Paster, Katherine Rowe, and Mary Floyd-Wilson (Philadelphia, 2004).

32. Harada, "Mechanism of Human Reconciliation," observes that Adam first blames and then corrects his own faults in Eve.

33. Richard Strier, "Milton against Humility," in *Religion and Culture in Renaissance England*, ed. Claire McEachern and Debora Shuger, 258–86 (Cambridge, 1997), argues that in this scene Adam reasserts the "intellectual clarity and leadership" that he failed to exercise in book 9 and thus reassumes his divinely ordained superiority over Eve (273). Similarly, Norbrook, *Writing the English Republic*, suggests that after the Fall, "the limits between masculine and feminine spheres become firmer" (489). The reinforcement of hierarchy is certainly suggested by the Son's judgment of the pair at the beginning of book 10, but it is significantly altered by the outcome of the reconciliation scene.

34. See *PL* 10.1087–92, repeated at 1099–1104. This device is typical of Homeric narrative and is echoed by Vergil, most notably in *Georgics* 4,

where Aristeus receives instructions on how to expiate his sin, and the narrator then describes him performing the sacrifices in precisely the language in which they were prescribed.

35. For the development of Milton's materialist metaphysics, see Stephen M. Fallon, *Milton among the Philosophers: Poetry and Materialism in Seventeenth-Century England* (Ithaca, N.Y., 1991). For Milton's monism as partial, temporary, or rhetorical, see John Rogers, *The Matter of Revolution: Science, Poetry, and Politics in the Age of Milton* (Ithaca, N.Y., 1996); Gordon Teskey, *Delirious Milton* (Cambridge, Mass., 2006), esp. chap. 5, "God's Body"; and most recently, N. K. Sugimura, *The Matter of Glorious Trial: Spiritual and Material Substance in "Paradise Lost"* (New Haven, Conn., 2009).

36. Loewenstein, *Representing Revolution,* nicely evokes in political terms the paradox Milton creates: "Milton invites readers to envision a future time when the metaphor of kingship and its potent symbols will not only be reformed but ultimately abandoned" (231). See also William Empson's observations on this point in *Milton's God* (London, 1961), 123–45.

37. For two superb articulations of this argument, see Burrow, *Epic Romance,* 256–63, and Norbrook, *Writing the English Republic,* 467–80.

38. Burrow, *Epic Romance,* 275.

39. His youthful poem "The Passion" breaks off with the note, "This Subject the Author finding to be above the yeers he had, when he wrote it, and nothing satisfi'd with what was begun, left it unfinisht." See John Milton, *Complete Shorter Poems,* ed. Stella P. Revard (Malden, Mass., 2009), 34.

40. John Rogers, "Milton and the Heretical Priesthood of Christ," in *Heresy, Literature, and Politics in Early Modern English Culture,* ed. David Loewenstein and John Marshall, 203–20 (Cambridge, 2006).

Striking a Miltonic Pose: William Jackson's *Lycidas* and National Musical Identity

John Luke Rodrigue

Introduction: A Memorial De-Memorialized

On November 4, 1767, *Lycidas,* adapted and composed by William Jackson (1730–1803), debuted in London. The last full-length musical adaptation of John Milton's poetry in the eighteenth century, the elegy followed a performance of Nicholas Rowe's *Tamerlane* (1701) at Covent Garden and was designed to honor the recently deceased Prince Edward Augustus, Duke of Albany and York, brother of George III, and onetime heir presumptive. Unfortunately for Jackson (and for the memory of Prince Edward), *Lycidas* was a commercial and critical flop. The November 4 performance was its only one in the metropolis, and the *Monthly Review* had nothing kind to say about it: "Milton's Lycidas is here applied to the late breach made in the Royal Family, by the death of the Duke of York. The design was absurd, and the performance was treated as such a piece of impertinence deserved."[1]

Nonetheless, Jackson soon put the poor London showing behind him. A few weeks later, he took his unappreciated work to the friendlier environs of Bath, where it fared slightly better. Concrete evidence for additional performances in Bath or elsewhere is lacking, but, regardless of whether *Lycidas* truly did better commercially at Bath than at London, it at least found one ardent admirer in the former city. Thomas Underwood penned "The Grateful Tribute" "upon hearing the Lycidas of Milton perform'd...Thursday, Nov. 26, 1767." Perhaps letting his enthusiasm run ahead of his judgment, Underwood proclaims that the "fire" of Frederick Handel has been revived in Jackson and fervently enrolls the singers in the "List of Fame." He does not mention the original occasion for Jackson's *Lycidas* (i.e., Edward's death), but Underwood does allude to its lackluster reception in London, referring to the audience's "Roast-Beef Ears" and explaining that "This piece was but indifferently receiv'd at Covent-Garden."[2] Apparently, Londoners did not know a good thing when they heard it.

Beauty may be in the ear of the auditor, but the difference of opinion between Underwood and the *Monthly Review* bespeaks something more than a simple matter of taste. The elegy's uninspiring showing at Covent Garden reveals Jackson's poor decision making in yoking the debut to an event to which the work was not originally connected, for Jackson did not adapt *Lycidas* as an actual memorial. Trapped in Exeter for most of his career and already working on this adaptation, he seized the opportunity to attract a wealthy or aristocratic patron by attaching *Lycidas* to "the late breach...in the Royal Family" and maneuvering his "memorial" onto the London stage the day after Edward's funeral. When this gambit failed, Jackson reverted to his original and far more ambitious plans for the piece and took *Lycidas* to Bath, where he had intended to introduce it in the first place.

In London, *Lycidas* mourned the dead; in Bath, it heralded the philosophical concerns of the living. Much as Milton's *Lycidas* is less about the death of his friend, Edward King, than about Milton's own poetic vocation, so is Jackson's *Lycidas* about his own career goals in music.[3] Even though its success was less than spectacular, the choice was most fitting, for Jackson revered Milton as a creator of a national poetic idiom and hoped to do the same for

English music. Like Milton's rejection of modish rhyme in the 1660s, Jackson's vocal compositions of the 1760s dismiss cosmopolitan fashions for a more native idiom, and his writings express a passionate desire to preserve clear words in music and to revive England's "national melody"—a program related to Milton's own musical theories and to his reclamation of "ancient liberty" through blank verse. A trailblazing artist in his own right, Jackson molded *Lycidas* into a poignant expression of his musical philosophy and thereby identified himself with Milton as a stout defender of "Englishness" who uses art as his weapon.

Nationalism, Milton, and the English Literary and Musical Canons

Jackson's decision to adapt *Lycidas* shows that he was a man of his time, but also slightly out of joint with it. As Carter Revard eloquently states, "In the late seventeenth and early eighteenth century it became possible for English poets to amplify their voices by using Milton's lion-skin as an echo chamber." "English poets," especially the Romantics, Revard explains, later "came to think of themselves as *like* Milton—antiestablishment, marginalized midwives to the future, rather than guardians of the past."[4] Prior to Shelley and Keats, however, Milton was co-opted by English poets (and musicians) for less radical ends. As literary criticism matured throughout the eighteenth century and formed a coherent understanding of England's literary history, Milton was appropriately celebrated as a leading poetic light. Excluding his own youthful boast in *The Reason of Church-Government* (1642) that, in imitation of Virgil, he "would leave something so written to aftertimes, as they should not willingly let it die," comparisons to the archetypal epic poets, Homer and Virgil, began with the prefatory matter to *Paradise Lost*, such as Samuel Barrow's tribute in the second edition in 1674 and Dryden's epigram for the fourth edition in 1688.[5] The comparison was also central to Joseph Addison's 1712 *Spectator* papers on *Paradise Lost*, which set the tone for much Milton criticism that followed. Whether Milton still followed Virgil's path as a national epic poet once he finally composed *Paradise Lost* is debatable. This made virtually no difference to later generations who were determined to make the comparison themselves.

A healthy (and often unhealthy) strain of nationalism runs through eighteenth century Milton criticism and through the formation of the English literary canon as a whole. Many critics and poets associated the achievements of pre-Restoration poets (especially Chaucer, Spenser, Shakespeare, and Milton) with freedom from neoclassical strictures imported from France. Given that England (and after 1707, Great Britain) was almost constantly at war with France from the late seventeenth century until the end of the Napoleonic Wars in the early nineteenth century, the comparison is far from politically innocent.[6] From the 1740s on, the desire for artistic liberation from French influence drove Thomas and Joseph Warton to construct the "school of Milton" in defiance of the neoclassical "school of Pope." As the former name suggests, Milton played a significant role in midcentury English poets' understanding of their national literary history. "At a time when English poetry seemed to have settled for competing with the French on their own neoclassical terms," says David Fairer, "Milton offered poets a confident voice and an unfettered style that could colonize new subjects." Indeed, poets like Thomas Gray, William Collins, Mark Akenside, and the Wartons sought to recover a past they felt had been buried beneath the refined façade of French neoclassicism, and one of their major vehicles for doing so was Miltonic blank verse.[7]

Jackson's own contributions to literary criticism late in his career indicate he was well acquainted with what his eighteenth century contemporaries were saying about Milton, and like those who engaged in discussions of England's literary canon he, too, thought in nationalistic terms that compared English poetry to that of France and, to a lesser degree, Italy. Jackson was no starry-eyed admirer of Milton's verse and certainly did not view him as the epitome of civility and artistry, but he did consider Milton an immensely vital poet in England's artistic development. This is especially evident in the cult of genius that revolved around Milton and into which Jackson initiated himself. In "Letter 23" ("On Taste") in *Thirty Letters on Various Subjects* (1792), he asserts that the English writers of 150 years prior did not have the refined taste of the present age but had ample genius to make up for that lack. "Shakespeare and Milton had not taste," he claims, "the finest passages of these great poets are very superior to any that a writer of a polished age *can* produce; but they are such as no writer of a polished age *would* produce: for taste equally tends to abate extreme beauties, and great faults." Jackson also expresses an odd reverence for the poets of pre-Restoration England: "As a barbarous age is not the period for taste, so a refined state of society is not the area of genius. An epic poem can never be again produced, possessing the true characteristics of that species of composition.... Had not the civil wars interrupted the refinement that was dawning in the beginning of the reign of Charles the first, the *Paradise Lost* would not have been so grand—would not have been so mean."[8] Apparently, Jackson believed in his era's self-image as a more genteel and refined time than earlier, "barbarous" ages. However, his attitude toward this assumption is ambivalent. Though proud of England's artistic development, Jackson places a high premium on originality and genius. When comparing Tasso's *Jerusalem Delivered* (1581) to *Paradise Lost*, for instance, he explains that taste "had advanced much further in Italy" in the sixteenth century than it had in England a century later; thus, *Paradise Lost* "has great faults and transcendent beauties—[whereas *Jerusalem Delivered*] seldom rises much above mediocrity, but never sinks below it." This may sound like tepid praise, if praise at all, yet Jackson consistently links refined taste with a paralysis of genius (something he later applied to music as well as to poetry). For example, he states that France's refinement, rather than its lack of genius, "has long incapacitated every poet of that country for any epic production" and rendered it "impossible to produce a work whose characteristic is fire and sublimity."[9] For all the faults that Jackson found with Milton's verse (including calling one section of *A Maske* "disgusting"), he apparently subscribed to the popular idea that Milton was England's Virgil and stood as a national symbol of the freedom of English poetry from the constrictions of Francophile neoclassicism.

In trying his hand at literary criticism, Jackson, a career musician and composer, was not crossing an impenetrable border; the English literary canon had its counterpart in music. Music historian William Weber remarks that the literary and musical canons often took different trajectories, with the former playing out in "nationalistic" and the latter in "cosmopolitan" terms and often lagging behind. Nevertheless, discussions of the musical canon were not devoid of nationalistic fervor. According to musicologist Richard McGrady, the English "were searching for a musical figure whom, in the face of the dominance of foreign musicians, they could revere in the way they revered Shakespeare. Much ink was being spilt by writers trying to define a national character for English music to complement other national idioms."[10] Some thought Henry Purcell (1656–95) best fit the role of music's Shakespeare; others put forth Handel (1685–1759), despite his German birth, as a distinctly English (or British) composer.[11] But no matter whom they considered for the part, those writing about the national musical canon did so in terms closely related to those used in literary criticism. Charles Burney's influential *General History of Music* (1776–89), for example, observes a developmental line for English music extending from Purcell to Jackson's immediate predecessors, Handel and Thomas Augustine Arne (1710–78). This musical lineage resembles the one that eighteenth century critics used to forge a link between Chaucer (the "father" of English poetry) and his poetic "sons"—Spenser, Shakespeare, and, of course, Milton.

Moreover, England's music may have been more cosmopolitan than its poetry, but the nationalistic elements of both arts regularly coalesced around Milton. Patriotic eighteenth century musicians often made use of Milton as a symbol of "Englishness" (or "Britishness") by adapting his poetry to new purposes. Arne, for example, was remarkably adept at attaching his name to Milton's in order to present a devoutly patriotic image to the public. In 1740, he published the score for the immensely popular *Comus* (1738) and dubbed it his "opera prima" (op. 1), and, according to

Suzanne Aspden, "thereby stamped his career with initial success, and associated it, of course, with the national canonical figure of its author, John Milton. It was a deliberate act of image manipulation, for Arne's first composition—a resetting of Joseph Addison's *Rosamond*—had been written some eight years earlier."[12] In 1743, Handel and librettist Newburgh Hamilton adapted *Samson Agonistes* (1671) into the oratorio *Samson* and diverted Milton's polemical animus toward new targets, from domestic corruption and internal divisions to an external enemy, the Philistines representing Catholic Spain. They did so at least partially to aid Prince Frederick (Prince Edward's father) in drumming up support for a war against the Spanish. That the vitriol of Milton's closet drama fell more on the English than on any outside threat seems to have caused no embarrassment to anyone and illustrates the extent to which Milton was exalted as a figurehead of enthusiastic, and sometimes even outright militant, nationalism.[13]

Ancient Liberty Recovered, Ancient Melody Preserved

As the appearances of *Comus* and *Samson* on the stage indicate, by the late 1760s, musical appropriation of Milton for nationalistic aims was nothing new. And as the successes of both imply, doing so could prove lucrative.[14] In adapting *Lycidas*, Jackson followed an established template but put new touches on it. While Burney and others argued about the importance of individual musicians to the national canon, Jackson identified himself with Milton in order to secure his own place in it.

It is thus as an expression of musical philosophy and artistic nationalism, rather than as a memorial piece, that Jackson hoped *Lycidas* would resonate, first, with Bath audiences and, eventually, with the English people as a whole. Jackson's expressed intent for his other compositions of the 1760s suggests he planned to introduce *Lycidas* not in London but in Bath, for the western city was particularly receptive to his innovations and ideas. In the late eighteenth century, Bath had become a cultural center for English music, in contrast to the cosmopolitan capital: "Although, as in

London, the exotic excitements of Italian opera, or the thrills of the new symphonic music, did not pass unnoticed by Bath audiences, there was a place in these concerts for English music, which found it much more difficult to get a hearing in the major London concerts."[15] That Bath was Jackson's intended venue is further evidenced by the fact that, despite the explicitly different purposes of the two performances, the Bath and London librettos are virtually the same. There are only nine textual deviations between the two, of which seven are changes in spelling and capitalization. The other two are minor word changes. Whatever Jackson felt doomed *Lycidas* in London, the libretto was apparently not to blame. One must conclude that the composition was also not the problem from Jackson's perspective, although this cannot be determined with absolute certainty. The music for *Lycidas* no longer exists, but given the short turnaround (about three weeks) between the first performance in London and the second in Bath, any musical changes to *Lycidas* were probably as minimal as the textual ones.[16] Instead, Jackson determined that his adaptation needed only a change of location and context to thrive. In other words, he needed to "de-memorialize" (so to speak) *Lycidas*. As a result, the Bath libretto displays textual differences from the London one that dissociate the elegy from Prince Edward and from Covent Garden. The title of the libretto, for instance, sheds light on a different performance context: "The Lycidas of Milton; / and, Wharton's Ode to Fancy / Altered and set to music by William Jackson." First, Jackson's compositions are the feature pieces, instead of the afterpiece. Second, in the London libretto, the title contained the phrase (perhaps something of a boast) "As it is performed in the Theatre Royal in Covent Garden"; Jackson wisely removes this from the Bath libretto. The second time around, he intended the elegy to be an entertainment in its own right wholly untethered from the Covent Garden debacle.

Jackson had enjoyed some success in Bath prior to *Lycidas*, and he probably envisioned Milton's elegy as a central piece in his catalogue of musical elegies, perhaps even as the chief example of the philosophy they embodied. In 1760 and 1765, he had organized performances and published music books for *Elegies* (op. 3) and *Twelve Songs* (op. 4), respectively. Both were sets of interconnected musical "elegies," a genre Jackson and Bath musician Thomas Linley the elder (1733–95) pioneered and that the former explains in the preface to *Elegies* and in his autobiography. In these works, Jackson sought to restore clear language and sober sense to English music. To help forward his task, he turned to *Lycidas* and implicitly linked himself with Milton, England's blank verse innovator and poetic reformer.

Jackson's aversion to excessive ornamentation in music leagues him philosophically with Milton, who believed modern rhyme no "true Ornament" to verse. "If it should become fashionable to perform Music as plain and unadorned, as what is now offered to the Public,... perhaps our Tastes might at last settle in a proper Medium," Jackson proclaims in the preface to *Elegies*. "The easier to attain this End," he continues:

> in some Pieces I have endeavored to unite the Air of the Moderns, to the plain substantial Harmony of the Ancients. In others, the Melody, as well as the Harmony is rather antique: And in some Passages, the modern Improvements in respect to the Management and Succession of Discord, are introduced, and, I hope, with Effect. As this is the only real Improvement in Harmony of late, it is a Pity it is not solely applied to the Effect it seems so admirably to produce, *viz.* to excite the Ideas of Pain, Terror, &c. for surely the contrary can never be produced from the most discordant Sounds that can be combined, where Art has any Share in the combination.[17]

McGrady explains that Jackson's negotiation between "ancient" and "modern" made him a provocative figure in the world of late eighteenth century English music. Essentially, the controversy revolves around the use of harmonic "division" (or "ornamentation") and its effects on the audience's ability to understand the words in vocal music and thereby respond to their emotional content. Elsewhere in the preface to *Elegies,* for instance, Jackson upbraids Purcell and his imitators for "false Ornaments" that exploit the musical potential of words at the expense of their meaning: "[Purcell's] imitating the Sounds of the Words, rather than expressing the Thoughts of the Sentence, his frequent Repetitions of the same Word, Divisions numberless, and some almost endless, were taken up by the Composers of the Times, who not having Genius enough to imitate his excellences, took the easier Task of copying his Faults."[18]

This mild denunciation of the revered Purcell marks Jackson as something of an apostate, and his compositions and convictions further set him apart as a composer. Jackson's creative period in the 1760s coincided with a heady transitional period in English music that compelled composers to choose from various approaches. The lush, symphonic "classical" style of Germany was making headway in Great Britain, slowly displacing Italianate opera and rococo-style compositions like those of the London pleasure gardens. Along with the shift in modern styles, the ever-present reverence for "ancient music" further complicated matters. Unlike in literature, where "ancient" generally meant pre-Christian Greek and Roman letters or biblical verse like the book of Job or the Psalms, in the field of eighteenth century music, "ancient" normally referred to the more recent and more local past, such as the choral works of English composers (like Purcell) in the sixteenth and seventeenth centuries. More than simply an escape or diversion from current fashions, explains McGrady, ancient music served as a critique of contemporary music and taste: "In 1760...the gulf between the two approaches [the rococo and the classical] was wide. Older or more conservative composers retained the merits of contrapuntal methods and generally eschewed the newer devices associated with the music being brought in largely from Germany. In England, the cult of 'ancient music' focused attention on the gulf between the two styles." In attempting a synthesis of new and old styles, Jackson adopted no single style and distinguished himself by his pursuit of clarity and simplicity. As McGrady notes, Jackson's attempts to include the new style in his music and his attempts to create a unique idiom in his vocal compositions made him an atypical composer in the late eighteenth century. His distinct approach allowed him to "create an individual voice in all his secular vocal music" that frequently displayed his "ability to choose poetry of distinction."[19]

To underscore his distinct innovations, Jackson branded his experimental works of the 1760s with their own name—elegies. At first, he admits, he called them madrigals but feared "that from the Name it might be apprehended I had adopted the Taste of the Times when the Madrigal flourished [i.e., Elizabethan and early Stuart England], which was never my Intention."[20] Instead, he chose a new name to spell out the "verbal and musical implications, affecting not only the choice of texts but the musical treatment too." Thus, the preface to *Elegies*, one of Jackson's earliest articulations of his musical philosophy, "develops what was to become a recurring theme of all his writings and one which reflects the sensibility behind his composition—the weaknesses of music which attempted to imitate natural sounds rather than exploring the nature of feelings and emotions."[21]

As his contributions to literary criticism suggest, Jackson was well acquainted with Milton's poetry, and his reading must have led him to believe that he and the poet were of one mind on vocal composition. In "At a Solemn Musick," Milton addresses the "Blest pair of *Sirens*, pledges of Heav'ns joy, / Sphear-born, harmonious Sisters, Voice, and Vers" (1–2), and in *Ad Patrem*, Milton speaks to his father (an accomplished musician in his own time) about the importance of clear words to vocal music: "And now, to sum it all up, what pleasure is there in the inane modulation of the voice without words and meaning and rhythmic eloquence?"[22] Jackson would have agreed; he based his search for a national musical idiom upon the kind of vocal clarity that Milton called for in music and that he believed blank verse could convey in poetry. Furthermore, Jackson perhaps saw himself as like Milton because of the latter's strong profession of his links to the past. Jackson's self-appointed quest to preserve national melody in and restore clear words and sense to English music resembles Milton's assertion that the blank verse of *Paradise Lost* should "be esteem'd an example set, the first in English, of ancient liberty recover'd to heroic Poem from the troublesom and modern bondage of Rimeing" ("The Verse," 250).[23] Although Jackson attempted to synthesize old and new in his elegies, his reverence for ancient music and his initial decision to call his elegies "madrigals" indicate that he considered himself the latest in a line of English musicians stretching to before the Interregnum—that is, before neoclassical art gained a strong foothold in England at the return of Charles II and his court from exile in France. Again, McGrady is extremely helpful: "[Thomas] Linley [the elder] and Jackson had 'steadfastly adhered to style of their own' and that this style owed much to an English tradition—'the melodies of our best old English masters.'"[24] Jackson's unique style did not make him old-fashioned, as his approach to elegies contained as much of the new as of the old, but the attempted synthesis and his refusal to fully embrace new styles made him less continental and more "English" than his contemporaries and also made him, perhaps not old fashioned, but certainly unfashionable.

In fact, Jackson's *Observations on the Present State of Music, in London* (1791)—written more than a decade after the elegies of the mid-1760s—shows a man falling further out of step with the times and with his country's international tastes: "But later Composers, to be grand and original, have poured in such floods of nonsense, under the sublime idea of being inspired, that the present Symphony bears the same relation to Good Music, as the ravings of a Bedlamite do to sober sense."[25] Jackson's attitude toward contemporary music grew more acerbic as he aged, but his aversion to dominant musical fashions was a lifelong contention. He had always considered himself a strong proponent of native, sober music standing against the enervating tastes for "false Ornaments." Before he openly denounced Germanic symphony, Jackson strove to distinguish himself from the rococo style of the middle and late century, which the nascent classical style would soon displace. As McGrady states, "By attempting to come to terms with the emotional content of his texts, Jackson's music at its best rises above the genial suavity and tuneful emptiness of much of the pleasure-garden song-writing of his contemporaries."[26] Jackson would be immensely pleased with this assessment, as he regularly heralded his differences from his fellow composers.

In pursuing a clearer understanding of the words in vocal music, Jackson wanted to spark no less than a national artistic revolution:

> This Species of Composition appears to me very difficult to succeed in, for I imagine its Characteristic to be Elegant Simplicity. The Subject should be tender and pathetic—The Air chaste and affecting—The melody easy—The Harmony full—The Disposition of the parts learned, but not formal; and from the Union of the whole, must be produced the Effect, the ultimate End of Music. Tho' perhaps I am making Laws for my own Condemnation, yet it is esteemed laudable even to fail in attempting great things; and whatever may be the Fate of these Pieces, *I shall think my Time in composing them well bestowed, if they should prove a Hint to some better Artist to do something more effectual towards the Reformation of our present Taste.*[27]

Again, much like Milton, Jackson's proposed artistic reform breaks with the present for the sake of reconnecting to the past. In his autobiography (written in 1800–01 but not published until 1882), Jackson recounts the immense success of his first collection, *Twelve Songs* (op. 1), in 1755 (not be confused with 1765 *Twelve Songs*, op. 4). Since this work more than any other made his musical character most known to the nation, he feels compelled to explain its significance: "Our national melody is peculiar to ourselves; it bears no resemblance to the Italian, German, French, or even the Scottish. What this *was* was almost forgotten.... We were losing our national melody apace when my songs appeared. I depended upon tune as their principal support, to this I added expression (hitherto not much attended to), and choice of words, which had never before been considered as essential to the effect of vocal music. I had the satisfaction to find my principle applauded, from which I have never departed." Jackson also likens this collection to his approach in *Elegies:* "In 1760, my elegies came out, which having as musical compositions a new title, and combining with harmony a more elegant melody in the construction of the parts, together with an expression of passion in such poetry as was worth being expressed—those circumstances occasioned the elegies to become much noticed, which consequently were profitable to me. As these elegies are in the general style I have just mentioned [in 1755 *Twelve Songs*], they are still as much in fashion as ever."[28]

One can speak of Jackson's search for a national idiom as a three-pronged approach. Clarity and simplicity were the first two points, and melody the third and most vital. Melody most linked him to the past and, to his chagrin, he found melody most absent in contemporary English music. In addition to his self-assessments in his autobiography, he also devotes much of the 30-page *Observations on the Present State of Music, in London* to bemoaning the disappearance of melody. "Though not absolutely unknown," he says, "Melody was in a barbarous state until the last hundred years. It long continued improving, but now seems, in this country at least, to be in a fair way of shortly losing it's [sic] existence."[29]

Jackson's frustration with the dominant artistic modes of his time and his railing against the bedlamite composers of the symphony sound very much like Milton's railing against the Restoration fashion for rhyme as "no necessary Adjunct or true Ornament of Poem or good Verse...but the Invention of a barbarous Age, to set off wretched matter and lame Meeter...as a thing of itself, to all judicious ears, triveal, and of no true musical delight; which consists onely in apt Numbers, fit quantity of Syllables, and the sense variously drawn out from one Verse into another, not in the jingling sound of like endings" ("The Verse," 249–50). Like the mid-eighteenth-century poets who imitated Milton and used his blank verse as a liberation, Jackson took up Milton's task of reclaiming "ancient liberty" by reviving "national melody" with musical and textual "sense variously drawn out" against the ravings of current musical fashions. Like Milton, he presented himself as an artist rebelling against corrupt and corrupting modern styles and believed himself poised to rejuvenate English art by tapping into its glorious past. For Milton, the past meant ancient Greek and Roman literature and the best of English tragedy; for Jackson, the past meant the best melodies from the previous 100 years of English music.

Jackson the Swain and Lycidas Jackson

Unlike Arne or Handel's adaptations of Milton, Jackson intended his to be more than just another appropriation of Milton for patriotic (and commercial) ends. Jackson had something far more grandiose in mind. Apparently, the success of *Elegies* and *Twelve Songs* emboldened him and left him feeling sufficiently confident to strike a Miltonic pose in *Lycidas*. Unfortunately, the elegy did not have the desired effect. Perhaps registering his disappointment by his silence, Jackson, who never tired of explaining the importance of his compositions, makes absolutely no mention of *Lycidas* in his prose. As such, one can only speculate as to what he thought would be the significance of this work if it turned out to be as successful as he had envisioned.

Sadly, the music for *Lycidas* is now lost, so what it sounded like may never be known; however, it most probably resembled Jackson's other 1760s elegies. The proximity of time between them and *Lycidas* (seven years for *Elegies*, two for *Twelve Songs*) makes a similar approach quite plausible. The success of these collections also suggests that Jackson hoped to produce a rousing encore in the genre by adapting the work of one of the most treasured and frequently adapted poets in the century.[30] Additionally, Underwood's tribute offers a hint of the musical dimensions of the performance that help partially to fill the void of the missing composition. A footnote to Underwood's poem identifies the singers in Bath as "Miss [Elizabeth Ann] Linley.—Master [Thomas] Linley [the younger].—[and] Mr. [Thomas] Linley [the elder]." It seems *Lycidas* required only three singers; in the preface to *Elegies*, Jackson describes the ideal manner of performing the latter as "three voices singing moderately soft, and accompanied with any Bass instrument that may have the effect of an accompaniment only."[31] Lastly, like *Twelve Songs* and *Elegies*, Milton's poem presents a shepherd-poet singing his sorrow in a pastoral landscape, so all three partake of the fashionable pastoral milieu of the late eighteenth century. Such was the common mode for the so-called poets of sensibility—the very same who used Milton's blank verse to rebel against the neoclassical "school of Pope."

In *Lycidas*, Jackson found a text ready-made to express his philosophical convictions, and, in Milton, he had a representative of English genius—a national trait he valued highly and strove to exhibit himself. Indeed, Jackson spoke of Milton in such a manner almost 20 years after *Lycidas*. Despite some censures of Milton's verse in *Thirty Letters*, the final letter of the collection ("On

Genius") speaks extremely well of him and shows that Milton's alleged obscurity in his own lifetime resonated with Jackson. The letter complains that "the rubs and difficulties which the public throw in the way of genius at its first appearance, are often too great to be surmounted." Rather than achieving recognition and prosperity, geniuses and originals too often toil in hopeless obscurity. (From this discussion, he omits Virgil and Pope because "they were not original.") As for Shakespeare and Milton, although both were financially well off by the end of their careers, explains Jackson, the former gained his living more from acting than writing, and the latter lived "in tolerable circumstances," but if he had had to rely on "the finest poem in the world" to earn his bread, "he must have been starved." As the letter and the collection come to a close, Jackson rises to a sentimental crescendo. He pictures himself entering a library, where he sees rows of books, and, perhaps recalling Thomas Gray's "Elegy Written in a Country Churchyard," he is struck upon beholding "a vast collection of monuments to trouble and unrewarded merit." "The author's first ideas undoubtedly are present rewards," continues Jackson, "but he soon finds, that though death seems not essential to reputation, yet that life is too short to establish it. Impressed with these melancholy ideas, he exclaims with the Poet—

> But the fair guerdon when we hope to find,
> And think to burst out into sudden blaze,
> Comes the blind fury with th' abhorred shears,
> And slits the thin spun life."[32]

Thus, Jackson closes the volume as a whole with a rumination upon genius that leaves behind the echo of none other than *Lycidas*.

Although containing some truth, the myth of Milton as a neglected genius appreciated only after his death was largely forged by late seventeenth and early eighteenth century biographies. Milton himself provided the kernel for this idea by referring to himself as "On evil dayes...fall'n, and evil tongues; / In darkness, with dangers compast round, / And solitude" (*PL* 7.26–28)—a picture early biographers embellished into a vision of the isolated poet-genius.[33] English musicians were not immune to this alluring depiction; one encounters it, for instance, in the Prologue to John Dalton and Arne's opera, *Comus:*

> Our steadfast bard, to his own genius true,
> Still bade his muse, fit audience find, tho' few.
> Scorning the judgment of a trifling age,
> To choicer spirits he bequeath'd his page.
> He too was scorn'd, and to Britannia's shame,
> She scarce for half an age knew Milton's name.[34]

This popular conception of Milton struck home with many eighteenth century readers, and to this list one must add Jackson. Thus, at the end of *Elegies* when Jackson invites a later composer to complete his reformation of "present Taste," his modesty conceals a monumental conceit. In "On Genius," he opines that genius and originality rarely get more than posthumous praise; such was Milton's fate, eighteenth century biography had determined, and just so might be his own, thought Jackson.

And just as the swain in *Lycidas* is Milton contemplating his career, so the swain in Jackson's *Lycidas* presents the composer contemplating his. Such an appropriation necessitated a few significant alterations; nevertheless, the libretto by and large does not differ radically from the source. Jackson takes a light touch, preserving most of Milton's wording and prosody. Where he does not cut lines, he merely tinkers with meter, spelling, and punctuation, and his changes do not alter the poem's grief and its agonizing deliberation of the poetic vocation. The recitatives, sung in a way that amounted to musical speaking, preserve the pentameter, but the airs and choruses, where one might reasonably expect greater musical virtuosity (vibratos, elongated notes, repeated words and syllables, etc.) are shortened to tetrameter. For instance, Jackson's recitatives retain almost wholly the thought and the expression of the original when Milton questions the value of being a poet (Milton's original spelling and punctuation in brackets):

> Alas! What boots it with incessant [uncessant] care
> To tend the homely slighted shepherd's [Shepherds] trade,
> And strictly meditate the thankless muse?
> Were it not better done as others use,

> To sport with Amaryllis in the shade,
> Or with the tangles of Neæra's hair?
> Fame is the spur that the clear spirit doth raise
> (That last Infirmity of noble mind)
> To scorn delights, and live laborious days;
> But the fair guerdon when we hope to find,
> And think to burst out into sudden blaze,
> Comes the blind Fury with th' abhorred shears,
> And slits the thin-spun life.[35]

Elsewhere, Jackson is more heavy-handed. When the swain recalls his happy days with Lycidas, Jackson makes the passage more amenable to the type of singing employed for an air or chorus (Jackson's omissions struck through, other alterations and additions in brackets):

> Together ~~both,~~ ere the ~~high~~ Lawns appear'd
> Under the ~~opening~~ eyelids of the morn,
> We drove afield~~, and both~~ together heard
> ~~What time~~ [T]he Gray-fly winds ~~her~~ [his] sultry horn,
> ~~Batt'ning our flocks with the fresh dews of night,~~
> ~~Oft till the Star that rose, at Ev'ning, bright~~
> ~~Toward Heav'ns descent had slop'd his westering wheel.~~
> ~~Mean while~~ [T]he Rural ditties were not mute,
> [Attemper'd] ~~Temper'd~~ to th[e] Oaten Flute,
> ~~Rough~~ Satyrs ~~danc'd,~~ and Fauns with clov'n heel,
> ~~From the glad sound would not be absent long,~~
> ~~And old Damœtas lov'd to hear our song.~~
> [The influence of our strains would feel,
> To the glad sound would listen long
> And hang enraptured on our song!]   (Jackson, *Lycidas*, 2–3)

Jackson deletes words and even whole lines and phrases, but the general picture remains the same. Even without old Damœtas, one sees, as one would in Milton's original, a vision of fleeting pastoral happiness as two young shepherds sing to a circle of pleased auditors.

Although the above represents Jackson's usual method of redaction, he makes more substantial changes to three sections: Saint Peter's speech, Lycidas's resurrection, and the famous eight-line conclusion of the poem that surprises readers with a dizzying shift in perspective. Some of these redactions have practical musical reasons, but they also reveal Jackson attempting to claim as much of the poem as possible for himself in order to identify not only with the swain/Milton but also with Lycidas.

For some passages, Jackson did not need to alter much in order to appropriate Milton's poem for his national musical philosophy. Simply by taking *Lycidas* as the basis for his libretto, he recodifies a number of the poem's allusions; the meditations become his (instead of Milton's) and contemplate music (rather than poetry). For instance, in Milton's poem, the stock pastoral characters Neæra and Amaryllis could refer to mirthful sports that distract one from "laborious days," or they could evoke the fashionable cavalier poetry of Caroline England that Milton did not wish to imitate (Milton, *Lycidas*, 72). In Jackson's *Lycidas*, these imaginary revels with gamesome shepherdesses stand in for the cosmopolitan music of London—Italian operas; symphonic compositions in the new classical style; and the sprightly, rococo songs of the pleasure gardens. More than 20 years later, in *Observations on the Present State of Music, in London,* Jackson would express his position as a man apart, and it appears that in *Lycidas* he hoped to present this image to the public in a more dramatic fashion.

A similar allusive shift applies to Camus's complaint, which Jackson redacts from Saint Peter's address. In Milton's poem, Saint Peter's screed is a polemical tour de force against the English church that bears repeating if only to compare it to Jackson's startling alterations:

> How well could I have spar'd for thee, young swain,
> Anow of such as for thir bellies sake
> Creep and intrude, and climb into the fold?
> Of other care they little reckning make,
> Then how to scramble at the shearers feast,
> And shove away the worthy bidden guest.
> Blind mouths! that scarse themselves know how to hold
> A sheephook, or have learn't ought els the least
> That to the faithfull herdmans art belongs!
> What recks it them? What need they? They are sped;
> And when they list, thir lean and flashy songs

> Grate on thir scrannel pipes of wretched straw,
> The hungry sheep look up, and are not fed,
> But swoln with wind, and the rank mist they draw,
> Rot inwardly, and foul contagion spred:
> Besides what the grim wolf with privy paw
> Daily devours apace, and little sed,
> But that two-handed engine at the dore,
> Stands ready to smite once and smite no more.
> (Milton, *Lycidas*, 108–31)

Jackson reduces this nineteen-line speech to a mere eight lines and attributes them, not to Peter, but to the personification of the River Cam:

> How well could I have spar'd thee [for?]
> The swains who [whose?] lean and flashy songs
> Grate on their pipes of wretched straw?
> The sheep look up and are not fed,
> But swoln with the rank mist they draw,
> Rot and foul contagion spread—
> Not so thy flocks, O shepherd dear;
> Not so thy songs, O muse most rare! (Jackson, *Lycidas*, 8)

Expunging Milton's nascent but already virulent antiprelatism, Jackson writes his own satire onto *Lycidas*. Ironically, he does so by imposing a far more explicit meaning onto these lines than Milton intended. In 1638, the swains in question were the clergymen of the Church of England, and their lean and flashy songs were their poorly and lazily crafted sermons. In 1767, the swains are eighteenth century musicians, and their lean and flashy songs are, quite literally, their lean and flashy songs. Indeed, the essential complaint of these lines echoes through Jackson's later observations on music, in which he worries about the manner of pleasure audiences gain from contemporary compositions. "As perhaps, the purest and most enchanting pleasure which the mind can feel arises from Music...surely any attempt to heighten that pleasure is laudable," Jackson proclaims, but "if, by some awkward and unfortunate circumstances, our present pleasure is derived from polluted sources, it cannot be amiss to shew that they are so; and point out others which, being more pure, are undoubtedly capable of producing that exquisite sensation which it is the exclusive property of Music to bestow."[36] In Camus's complaint, immortal souls may not be at stake as they are in Saint Peter's, but the topic of musical pleasure was one Jackson saw as a holy undertaking of sorts. Thus, both the uncouth swain and Lycidas in the above passage represent Jackson, for the "shepherd dear" and "muse most rare" refer to Jackson and his songs—which he hoped distinguished him from his "flashy" contemporaries.

Jackson's next-largest change relates to Lycidas's ascension to heaven (lines 165–85 in Milton's poem), which Jackson converts to an air and a chorus that conclude his musical elegy. Lines 172–85, which Jackson places in the chorus, are especially altered (omissions again struck through and additions and other changes in brackets):

Air
Weep no more, woful Shepherds weep no more,
For [LYCIDAS] ~~Lycidas~~ your [S]orrow is not dead,
Sunk ~~though~~ tho' he be beneath the ~~watery floar~~ [wat'ry floar],
So sinks the [D]ay-[S]tar in the Ocean[-]bed,
And yet anon repairs his drooping [H]ead,
And tricks his [B]eams, and with new-spangled Ore,
Flames in the [F]orehead of the [M]orning sky ~~Sky~~:
Chorus
[Woful Shepherds weep no more,
He is the Genius of the Shore,
He is ascended from the Waves]
~~So Lycidas sunk low, but mounted high,~~
~~Through the dear might of him that walk'd the waves,~~
~~Where other groves, and other streams along,~~
With Nectar pure his ~~oozy Lock's~~ [Locks] he laves,
And hears the ~~unexpressive nuptiall~~ Song,
~~In the blest Kingdoms meek~~ of [J]oy and [L]ove.
~~There entertain him all the Saints above,~~
~~In~~ [From] solemn [T]roops~~, and sweet Societies~~ [amid the skies],
[Who] ~~That sing, and~~ singing in their glory move,
And wipe the tears for ever from his [E]yes[!]
~~Now Lycidas the Shepherds weep no more,~~

> ~~Hence forth thou art the Genius of the shore,~~
> ~~In thy large recompense, and shalt be good~~
> ~~To all that wander in that perilous flood.~~
>
> (Jackson, *Lycidas*, 10–12)

In Jackson's elegy, Lycidas makes it to heaven, but unlike in Milton's poem, one can almost miss his apotheosis, as it happens so relatively quickly and subtly:

> Woful Shepherds weep no more,
> He is the Genius of the Shore,
> He is ascended from the Waves.
> With Nectar pure his Locks he laves,
> And hears the Song of Joy and Love.
> From solemn Troops, amid the skies,
> Who singing in their glory move,
> And wipe the tears for ever from his Eyes!
>
> (Jackson, *Lycidas*, 10–12)

The alterations give the impression that the shepherd rises from his watery grave but proceeds no further. Instead of soaring to the "Blest Kingdoms" to join the "Saints," Lycidas seems to arrest his ascent in order to listen to the heavenly choir who meet him halfway, "amid the skies." Perhaps Jackson is implying that the heavenly music that comforts Lycidas is the music of *Lycidas* itself. Such self-referentiality would not be out of character, for elsewhere Jackson associates himself not only with the swain but also with Lycidas. As previously stated, when Camus bursts out, "Not so, thy flocks, O shepherd dear! / Not so, thy songs, O muse most rare!" it is difficult to tell if he is addressing the departed Lycidas or the swain. Similarly in this case, there is no reason to weep, for Lycidas is Jackson, and he is most certainly "not dead."

Indeed, even though *Lycidas* required three singers, Jackson helps audiences associate the elegy as a whole with the single voice of the uncouth swain. He removes Milton's eight-line closing from his libretto, a change that constitutes his third-largest alteration after the removal of Saint Peter and the redactions to Lycidas's ascension, yet the prefatory matter to the libretto restores the perspectival shift of the poem's conclusion. For both the London and

Bath performances, the title page contains an epigram taken from the deleted conclusion: "Thus sings the uncouth Swain, / With eager Note warbling his Doric lay." The elegy may necessitate three voices, and the funeral within the text may contain even more than that, but Jackson reinstates a single overarching voice and perspective to *Lycidas*. In just about every way he could, he fuses his identity as a musician with that of the swain/Milton and with that of Lycidas in a perfect circle of self-reference. Had *Lycidas* been well received, the work would have been a most spectacular announcement of Jackson's "arrival" as a pathbreaking artistic reformer. As a matter of fact, by the late 1760s, Jackson had already arrived, musically speaking, in "fresh Woods, and Pastures new." More's the pity that his declaration of this fact largely fell on deaf (or at least unappreciative) ears.

Like many before him and many to come, Jackson sought to cloak himself in the majesty of Milton's soaring reputation and identify himself with the poet as a reformer striving to turn English art away from its "polluted sources" into purer, native streams. Whether Jackson's art actually resembles Milton's is irrelevant. It does not. His compositions (which he likens to William Hogarth's illustrations in the preface to *Elegies*) share more in common with the "tidy" refinements of Dryden and Pope than with the perceived "roughness" of Chaucer, Spenser, or Milton. On a stylistic level, comparing Jackson's music to Milton's poetry yields dubious fruit. But when considering their philosophical and cultural aims, relation stands. More importantly, Jackson *believed* that his music resembled both Milton's reformation of English verse and his embodiment of untamed English genius, for his adaptation presents another in a long line of instances of Milton being posthumously made to take up, yet once more, his old role as a defender of the English people. In his lifetime and with the whole of Europe as his audience, Milton proudly stepped into this part when he battled Salmasius in the Latin defenses. Indeed, he saw the community of European humanists as his primary audience and his colleagues. Given that Jackson's primary targets in *Lycidas* were the cosmopolitan and continental musical influences he believed had debased England's national melody, the reprisal of such a part for "John Milton, Englishman," is paradoxically appropriate and rather misplaced all at once. Yet for a man whose reputation in the eighteenth century veered between full-throated praise as a national literary hero and a "grand Whig" and revilement as a religious rebel and a proponent of regicide, the paradox is also apt.

American University in Bulgaria

Notes

1. "Art. 17. *Lycidas: A Musical Entertainment,*" *Monthly Review; or, Literary Journal: By Several Hands* 37 (London, 1767): 393.

2. Thomas Underwood, "The Grateful Tribute," *Poems &C. by T. Underwood, Late of St. Peter's College, Cambridge* (Bath, 1768), 139–40. Only a few months after Jackson's death, Thomas Busby, "Memoirs of William Jackson of Exeter," *Monthly Magazine* 16 (London, 1803), hinted at additional performances of *Lycidas:* "A piece called the 'Fairy Fantasies,' Milton's 'May Morning,' 'Lycidas,' an elegy, and other vocal works of Mr. Jackson's in manuscript, are spoken of with such high commendation, that it is to be hoped they will ere long find their way to the public ear; and add to that praise which every real judge of fine composition cannot but allow him" (141). By whom and when *Lycidas* and these other works received "high commendation" are unknown, but if the elegy was sufficiently known to warrant such praise, one may reasonably assume it enjoyed more than two performances. Unfortunately, the lack of more concrete evidence does not allow this conjecture to be verified.

3. E. M. W. Tillyard, *Milton* (New York, 1930), 79–80, defends Milton against charges of artificiality (e.g., Samuel Johnson's *Life of Milton*). One must not, he argues, mistake the nominal subject, King, for the real one, Milton. The latter could not help but see the similarities between himself and the former, for both planned to take holy orders and both had literary ambitions. Like King, Milton was also about to embark on a sea voyage. Tillyard thus reverses the charges of insincerity and calls *Lycidas* one of Milton's most "personal" poems. J. Martin Evans, "Lycidas (1638)," in *The Cambridge Companion to Milton,* ed. Dennis Danielson, 40–41(Cambridge, 1999), similarly contends that the poem's conventional, occasional, and imitative nature does not negate the possibility of intense, personal concerns.

4. Carter Revard, "Milton as Muse for Keats, Shelley, and Frost," in *Milton Studies,* vol. 53, ed. Laura L. Knoppers, 205–34 (Pittsburgh, 2012), 205.

5. John Milton, *The Reason of Church-Government*, in *Complete Prose Works of John Milton*, 8 vols., ed. Don M. Wolfe et al. (New Haven, Conn., 1953–82), 1:810.

6. Linda Colley's landmark study, *Britons: Forging a Nation, 1707–1837* (New Haven, Conn., 1992), 6, names Catholic France as the primary Other against which Protestant Great Britain forged its self-identity in the eighteenth and early nineteenth century.

7. David Fairer, "Creating a National Poetry: The Tradition of Spenser and Milton," in *The Cambridge Companion to Eighteenth-Century Poetry*, ed. John Sitter, 177–201 (Cambridge, 2001), 179, 187. For earlier and less affirmative views of Milton's impact on eighteenth century poetry, see Walter Jackson Bate, *The Burden of the Past and the English Poet* (Cambridge, Mass., 1970), and Harold Bloom, *The Anxiety of Influence: A Theory of Poetry* (Oxford, 1972), both of whom Fairer challenges. For additional commentary on Milton's reputation in the eighteenth century, see Dustin Griffin's *Regaining Paradise: Milton and the Eighteenth Century* (Cambridge, 1986), and G. F. Sensabaugh's *That Grand Whig, Milton* (Stanford, Calif., 1952).

8. William Jackson, *Thirty Letters on Various Subjects* (London, 1792), 168–69.

9. Ibid., 170–71.

10. Richard McGrady, "The Elegies of William Jackson and Thomas Linley the Elder," *Music and Letters* 77 (1996): 210.

11. William Weber, "The Intellectual Origins of Musical Canon in Eighteenth-Century England," *Journal of the American Musicological Society* 47 (1994): 501–03.

12. Suzanne Aspden, "Arne's Paradox: National Opera in Eighteenth-Century Britain," *Word and Music Studies* 4 (2002): 200.

13. For the political use of *Samson Agonistes*, see Stella Revard, "Restoring the Political Context to *Samson Agonistes:* Milton, Handel, and Saint-Saëns," in *Milton, Rights and Liberties*, ed. Christophe Tournu and Neil Forsyth, 379–95 (Bern, Germany, 2007), and Ruth Smith's *Handel's Oratorios and Eighteenth-Century Thought* (Cambridge, 1995). For discussions of similarly patriotic use of *A Maske*, see Don-John Dugas, "'Such heav'n taught Numbers should be more than read': *Comus* and Milton's Reputation in Mid-Eighteenth-Century England," in *Milton Studies*, vol. 34, ed. Albert C. Labriola, 137–57 (Pittsburgh, 1997), and Berta Joncus, "Handel at Drury Lane: Ballad Opera and the Production of Kitty Clive," *Journal of the Royal Musical Association* 131 (2006): 179–226, and "'His spirit is in action seen': Milton, Mrs. Clive and the Simulacra of the Pastoral in *Comus*," *Eighteenth-Century Music* 2 (2005): 7–40.

14. The commercial success of *Comus* is staggering. Dugas counts 387 performances between its debut in 1738 and 1800 ("'Such heav'n taught Numbers," 154). Both the opera-length adaptation and George Colman's shortened version of 1772 appeared regularly in print in England and

Ireland for the rest of the century. *Samson* was one of the successes of the 1742–43 season with seven performances. The royal family even attended the fourth performance of the season (March 2, 1743), at which it was remarked that the oratorio "has been performed four times to more crouded audiences than ever were seen"; see Arthur H. Scouten, *The London Stage, 1660–1800: A Calendar of Plays, Entertainment, and Afterpieces Together with Casts, Box-Receipts, and Contemporary Comment* (Carbondale, Ill., 1961), 1038.

15. McGrady, "Elegies of William Jackson," 216. Not coincidentally, Jackson titled his essay *Observations on the Present State of Music, in London* (London, 1791). At times, he speaks broadly about the development and the loss of melody "in this country" (10); at others, he insists that "It is the general state of Music in this metropolis, it's defects [sic], and it's [sic] excellencies, which have been the subject of this short and imperfect sketch" (33).

16. The *Monthly Review*'s reference to "design" could mean that negative reactions related to an inferior composition, a poor performance, or an ill-conceived libretto. It is probable that Jackson's unique musical style and the doomed associations of Lycidas with Prince Edward may also account for the work being "indifferently received." In many ways, Edward fell short of the praise the swain lavishes on Lycidas, and considering the libretto as an actual elegy exposes some carelessness in design. For instance, if he wished to fit *Lycidas* to the circumstance, Jackson would have done well to omit such lines as "Ah me! Whilst thee the shores and founding seas / Wash far away; where e'er thy bones are hurled" (Jackson, *Lycidas* 11). The inclusion of these two lines might have caused some embarrassment seeing as the prince was interred at Westminster on November 3, 1767, the day before *Lycidas* was performed. Edward may have died abroad like King/Lycidas, but unlike the latter, those mourning him knew exactly where his body lay.

17. William Jackson, *Elegies Compos'd by William Jackson of Exeter* (London, 1760), iv.

18. Ibid., iii.

19. McGrady, "Elegies of William Jackson," 215, 225.

20. Jackson, *Elegies*, v.

21. McGrady, "Elegies of William Jackson," 214–15.

22. All citations of Milton's poetry are from John Shawcross, *The Complete Poetry of John Milton* (New York, 1971); hereafter cited in the text.

23. Ironically, Jackson did not agree with Milton's claim that rhyme is barbarous, nor did he praise Milton's poetry uncritically. In *The Four Ages; Together with Essays on Various Subjects* (London, 1798), Jackson includes a brief essay titled "On Rhyme." Much as he does in his musical compositions, he finds a middle way, this time between Milton's dismissal

of rhyme and Samuel Johnson's assertion that poetry cannot subsist without it. Jackson instead argues that "Possessing so much exquisite poetry in rhyme, let us not call rhyme barbarous; and when reading Shakespeare and Milton, can we say that rhyme is essential to poetry?" (311–12).

24. McGrady, "Elegies of William Jackson," 226.

25. William Jackson, *Observations on the Present State of Music, in London* (London, 1791), 16.

26. McGrady, "Elegies of William Jackson," 225.

27. Jackson, *Elegies*, v; emphasis added.

28. William Jackson, "William Jackson, of Exeter, Musician: An Autobiography," *The Leisure Hour* (London, 1882), 275–76. Jackson associates England's national melody most strongly with songs from John Gay's *The Beggar's Opera*, Henry Carey's ballad operas, and the more "elegant" forms of Maurice Greene, Thomas Arne, and William Boyce.

29. Jackson, *Observations*, 10.

30. Adaptations of and borrowings from Milton's poems appeared regularly on the musical stage in eighteenth century Britain. Six of his works—*A Maske Presented at Ludlow Castle*, *L'Allegro* and *Il Penseroso* (combined into one), *Samson Agonistes*, *Paradise Lost*, and *Lycidas*—enjoyed the privilege of full-length presentations in London as well as in Scotland, Ireland, and the English provinces. Parts from a number of others ("At a Solemn Musick," "Ode on the Morning of Christ's Nativity," "On Time," and some of his Psalms translations) as well as various excerpts from the longer poems also figured into musical works and miscellanies. Such treatment by no means made Milton unique. Dustin Griffin names Homer, Virgil, Chaucer, Spenser, Donne, Shakespeare, and Dryden as poets whose works were also regularly adapted; however, he singles out Milton adaptations for "their variety and frequency" (62).

31. Underwood, "The Grateful Tribute," 40; Jackson, *Elegies*, v.

32. Jackson, *Thirty Letters*, 231, 234–36.

33. The myth of the isolated poet-genius manifests itself in early biographers' belief that Samuel Simmons hoodwinked Milton in the contract for *Paradise Lost*. For instance, Elijah Fenton, "The Life of Mr. Milton," in John Milton, *Paradise Lost: A Poem in Twelve Books* (London, 1730), xxiii, looked upon the contract as an example of a naïve poet selling his talents cheap. Contemporary scholarship has dispelled this myth. Peter Lindenbaum, "Milton's Contract," *Cardozo Arts and Entertainment Law Journal* 10 (1992), points out that the 1,500-copy limit for each impression of *Paradise Lost* ensured "that Simmons' profits would not increase inordinately in relation to the amounts Milton would receive." "This is not," he concludes, "the off-hand agreement of someone affecting to be an amateur or a gentleman-poet, anxious to avoid the stigma of print, or a figure using poetry for advancement in some other, non-literary, realm" (443–44). Kerry MacLennan, "John Milton's Contract for *Paradise Lost*:

A Commercial Reading," *Milton Quarterly* 44 (2010), further proposes "that Milton was the architect, indeed, the author, of the contract for *Paradise Lost*, as much as he was the creator of its poetry" and believes the contract shows "that the inheritance of Milton's father's professional skills as a scrivener may have directed him how to anticipate, and circumvent, contractual loopholes and trapdoors" (227). On the more general topic of Milton's early biographers, Edward Jones, "'Ere Half My Days': Milton's Life, 1608–1640," *The Oxford Handbook of Milton*, ed. Nicholas McDowell and Nigel Smith, 3–25 (Oxford, 2008), reminds us that the early lives of Milton contain little evidence that can be verified and corroborated, and Thomas Corns and Gordon Campbell, *John Milton: Life, Work, and Thought* (Oxford, 2008), offer a discerning view of Milton's entire life that refuses to take the poet at his word, as many of his earliest biographers did.

34. John Dalton, Prologue to *Comus, a Maske*, 4th ed. (London, 1738), n.p.

35. Jackson, *Lycidas: A Musical Entertainment. As it is performed at the Theatre Royal in Covent Garden. The Words altered from Milton* (London, 1767), 5. Additional citations of Jackson's *Lycidas* appear parenthetically in the text by page number.

36. Jackson, *Observations*, 8–9.

History, Politics, and Poetics

Satan's Pardon: The Forms of Judicial Mercy in *Paradise Lost*

Alison A. Chapman

God's willingness to pardon is a mainspring of *Paradise Lost*, one that transforms the epic from bleak to hopeful. The opening lines express John Milton's trust that the Son—the "greater Man"—will one day "Restore" fallen men and women, and the merciful restoration planned in God the Father and the Son's conversation in book 3 is initiated in book 10 when Adam and Eve, their hearts softened, fall prostrate and beg pardon in "sorrow unfeign'd and humiliation meek."[1] Milton also gives a surprising amount of attention to the possibility of Satan's pardon. Chronologically speaking, the earliest reference appears in book 5 when Abdiel urges Satan to "hast'n to appease / Th'incensed Father, and th'incensed Son, / While Pardon may be found in time besought" (5.846–48). In book 1, Satan entertains the hypothetical idea of mercy even as he refuses "To bow and sue for grace / With suppliant knee" (1.111–12), and Mammon revisits this subject during the epic debate when he allows that even if God were to "relent / And publish Grace to all, on promise made / Of new Subjection" (2.237–39), the fallen angels would refuse to rejoin heaven's polity. In book 3, we see this issue from heaven's point of view, for God proclaims that the fallen angels are not eligible for mercy because they are "Self-tempted, self-deprav'd" (3.130). Finally, the idea of pardon centrally occupies Satan during his soliloquy at the beginning of book 4. Reflecting on his own rebellion and punishment, he asks, "is there no place / Left for Repentance, none for Pardon left?" (4.79–80), and he wonders whether he "could repent and could obtain / By Act of Grace my former state" (4.93–94).

Milton scholars have thoroughly examined the theological dimensions of Adam and Eve's pardon, showing how Milton's treatment of mercy reflects his broadly Protestant and specifically Arminian view of salvation.[2] Satan's pardon has received similarly theological treatment. Harry F. Robins and C. A. Patrides both discuss it in relationship to the doctrine of *apocatastasis*, or universal salvation, widely credited to Origen of Alexandria, and Patrides concludes that while *apocatastasis* interested Milton for its dramatic possibilities, it was not a position he ultimately endorsed.[3] While illuminating on their own terms, such theological examinations capture only part of how Milton depicts pardons in *Paradise Lost*. Specifically, the use of juridical pardons was soaring in the seventeenth century. As England's Bloody Code got bloodier, as measured by the rising number of capital statutes, more and more pardons were issued by the crown to avoid overusing the scaffold.[4] Given the early modern period's religious and political tumults, an increasing number of men and women had had a brush with the law, and, as social historians such as Krista Kesselring and Natalie Zemon Davis show, they were remarkably well versed in pardoning procedures and protocols.[5]

Pardons acquired a further visibility during the second half of the seventeenth century. Although in theory mercy was the sole prerogative of the monarch, Parliament increasingly claimed the right to determine who should and should not receive mercy, and by the late 1670s pardons had become a politically supercharged symbol of the struggle over executive privilege.[6] Milton indisputably knew the contested nature of the monarch's right to pardon, for he writes about it in both *Eikonoklastes* and *Observations upon the Articles of Peace*. And he had a personal familiarity with the workings of judicial mercy, having received two separate pardons in the months following the Restoration.

In this essay, I argue that when he describes pardons, Milton is not only thinking theologically; he is also thinking judicially, socially, and politically, and the scenes of pardon in *Paradise Lost* are as much influenced by the forms of mercy he saw around him as by the writings of Saint Paul, Saint Augustine, and John Calvin.[7] As an essentially extralegal phenomenon that occurred after the law had done its work, pardons have very little place in the official legal writings of the period. But despite this lack of formal codification, pardoning had developed into an elaborate cultural discourse with its own forms of address, assumptions, gestures, procedures, preconditions, and contingencies.[8] *Paradise Lost* shows this same cultural discourse at work.

When Milton's God issues an act of grace, it has elements that closely resemble those in the collective pardoning acts so common in Tudor and Stuart political culture. When Satan wonders in book 4 if he could still be pardoned, his language and actions suggest that Milton thinks of mercy as a series of specific, culturally determined procedures rather than as just a divine yes or no option. And when Adam and Eve seek a pardon, they spontaneously follow the same protocols that led to successful appeals for mercy in the wake of legal convictions. For instance, early modern social practice held that pardons should, whenever possible, be sought in the same place where the accused had been judged or, alternatively, where the crime had been committed, and care in choosing one's pardoning ground was seen as an important indicator of penitence. Milton takes pains to show Adam and Eve observing this feature of contemporary pardoning practice.[9] Eve says that she will return "to the place of judgment" (10.932) to ask pardon; Adam says they should beg pardon at "the place /...where he judg'd us" (10.1086–87); and Milton's narrator describes Adam and Eve's actions in the same terms: they "forthwith to the place / Repairing where he judg'd them prostrate fell / Before him reverent" (10.1098–1100).

Speaking of the traces of ceremonial devotion evident in *Paradise Lost*, Achsah Guibbory argues that while Milton rejected the elaborate rituals of the Laudian church, he also wanted to "engage body as well as soul" in religious devotion.[10] We see a similar effort to involve the whole person—body and soul—in the work of seeking pardon. When Satan wonders in book 4 if he could regain "by Act of Grace my former state"—in effect, "Am I eligible for pardon and if so, what could I do to bring that pardon about?"—he is not only raising a theological question about the nature of forgiveness; he is also wondering about the same kinds of pardoning protocols that preoccupied so many of those who ran afoul of the law in the seventeenth century, Milton included. In thinking about the workings of judicial mercy in his own world, Milton was examining God's ways from a different angle than those provided by theology. As he writes in *The Tenure of Kings and Magistrates*, "justice and Religion are from the same God, and works of justice [are] ofttimes more acceptable."[11]

Milton's Pardon

Broadly speaking, there were two different kinds of pardons available in early modern England: the individual or special pardon and the collective pardon, which was also called an "Act of Grace." The individual or special pardon was, as its name indicates, granted to a single person or small group of persons who had offended against the law and toward whom the king, through his good pleasure, chose to show mercy. In contrast, collective pardons were more impersonal, usually aimed at whole classes of offenders, and were motivated by broadly social and political concerns. For instance, Henry VIII and Elizabeth I issued Acts of Grace as often as every four to six years for a variety of reasons. Sometimes prison overcrowding had reached the critical point, and so these blanket pardons were used to ease the strain on a literally crumbling judicial system. At times Acts of Grace were issued in tacit recompense to Parliament for having levied new taxes.[12] Sometimes Acts of Grace targeted perceived inequities in the law. For instance, the seventeenth century witnessed a rising imprisonment for debt, and the rogue John Hall, in his lurid description of Newgate prison, describes debtors who talk "altogether of an *Act of Grace,*" hoping for a royal pardon that would protect them from their creditors.¹³ Other times Acts of Grace seemed simply intended to foster improved relations between sovereign and people. In April 1582, the Elizabethan justice of the peace William Lambarde wrote that the queen issued "her general and free pardon, thereby not only forgiving us the most part of our offenses that are past but also giving us great cause to use better obedience for the time that is to come."¹⁴ In Lambarde's view, collective pardons helped to mend small tears in the social fabric.

Milton was the beneficiary of both types of pardon. As his early biographers stress, Milton was included in the general 1660 Act of Indemnity and Oblivion, a collective pardon drafted by Parliament and ratified by Charles II in the wake of the Restoration. Writing near the beginning of the eighteenth century, Jonathan Richardson notes that with Charles II's return, Milton's writings "were Now Accounted Criminal, Every One of Them," but Milton had "very Powerful Friends at That Time," indicating that Milton had firsthand experience with the importance of intercessors in the pardoning process. As a result, Milton was "Screen'd from being Excepted in the General Pardon," and "Secur'd by Pardon [he] Appear'd again in Publick."¹⁵ Edward Phillips, arguably a more reliable biographer, describes Milton going into hiding at "a Friends house in *Bartholomew Close* where he liv'd till the Act of Oblivion came forth." This act "prov'd as favourable to [Milton] as could be hop'd or expected," and he took a house in Holborn "not long before his Pardon having pass'd the Seal."¹⁶

Milton also received a special pardon that same year. During the period of his concealment, the House of Commons had directed the attorney general to send for Milton "in Custody, by the Serjeant at Arms" in order to answer an indictment about his antimonarchical books.¹⁷ Because this second order was never rescinded, Milton was taken into custody after he emerged from hiding and was imprisoned in the Tower, probably in October or November 1660. Sometime around mid-December, Milton received a special pardon from Parliament remitting this particular offense, although the sergeant still charged him for his jail expenses. The text of this special pardon is not extant, but two contemporary accounts speak briefly of it. A Dutch report notes that Milton was "freed through good promises," and Cyriack Skinner writes that Milton "early sued out his Pardon; and by means of that when the Serjeant of the House of Commons had officiously seisd him, was quickly set at liberty."[18] Milton had to make "good promises," and he "sued out" his pardon (suggesting that he had to "plead, appeal or supplicate"), indicating that he observed the typical forms and protocols of pardon that are described in more detail below.[19] He likely made his submission and trusted to an intercessor to speak eloquently on his behalf. And in the manner of so many early modern pardon seekers, he likely offered solemn vows of his future obedience and good behavior.

This image of Milton begging pardon is hard to reconcile with his outspoken and principled antiroyalist stance. Indeed, Milton's decision to sue for pardon is starkly at odds with claims that he himself made 11 years earlier in *Eikonoklastes*. In *Eikon Basilike*, Charles I had congratulated himself on offering "Acts of Indempnity, and Oblivion, to so great a latitude, as may include all, that can but suspect themselves to be any way obnoxious to the Laws."[20] Milton retorts in *Eikonoklastes* that good people will spurn such forms of pardon, for they would never seek to be pardoned for the very actions "which may be justly attributed to thir immortal praise." Accepting a pardon was an admission of guilt, and Milton argues that a just person would not "assent ever to the guilty blotting out of those actions before men, by which thir Faith assures *them they chiefly stand approv'd, and are had in remembrance before the throne of God*" (YP 3:577). But when he "early sued out his Pardon" in 1660, Milton did precisely this "guilty blotting" of his earlier actions. We can only speculate about the reasons for Milton's change of heart. Perhaps this bitter pill was eased by the fact that both the Act of Oblivion and the indictment against him were at least nominally issued by Parliament and not the king, and so Milton was submitting to a governing body whose authority he accepted. Perhaps long experience and political disillusionment had led him to conclude that it was better to accept a spurious pardon than to face criminal prosecution. Those exempted from the Act of Oblivion were gruesomely drawn and quartered, as Milton knew well.[21] Although we cannot know precisely what Milton's punishment would have been for the lesser indictment for writing against the king, the case of Alexander Leighton, convicted in 1630 for writing a pamphlet against prelacy, provides a possible point of comparison. Leighton was pilloried, whipped, pilloried again, had one ear cut off and then one nostril slit, had his forehead branded with "SS" (for "Sower of Sedition"), pilloried again, whipped again, had the other nostril slit and the other ear cut off, and then was imprisoned for life.[22] Perhaps Milton concluded that begging a pardon, however noxious to his principles, would, in effect, allow him to live to fight another day—in this case, to write a work like *Paradise Lost*, which offers a tacit critique of human mercy by showing how it falls short of the divine ideal.

Collective Acts of Grace

Satan's soliloquy at the beginning of book 4 of *Paradise Lost* revolves centrally around whether he would be eligible for an "Act of Grace" that might allow him to escape the punishment of hell and regain "[his] former state" (4.94). In seventeenth century terms, he has two valid reasons to be asking himself this question. First, collective pardons were commonly issued at the beginning of reigns (witness the 1660 Act of Oblivion), and they played an especially important symbolic role in coronation processions.[23] For instance, in 1603 the new James I pardoned liberally on his journey south from Edinburgh as a way to signal that his reign would be marked by peace and clemency (in fact, London experienced a crime wave as the king neared the city, for the felonious saw an ideal opportunity to commit crimes and escape penalty).[24] In France, coronation pardons were so customary that fugitives from the law often surrendered themselves to prisons on the new monarch's processional route.[25] Given this general expectation that the installation of a new ruler would be followed by a celebratory Act of Grace, it is hardly surprising that Satan thinks in book 4 about his chances of a pardon. The Son's "great Vice-gerent Reign" (5.609) has only recently begun, and earlier Satan imagines that the Son will "pass triumphant" on a coronation procession through heaven "and give Laws" (5.693). Now a defeated rebel who has been sentenced to a place Milton calls his "Prison ordain'd / In utter darkness" (1.71–72), Satan is in much the same position as those criminals who listened from jail to the ecstatic ringing of London's coronation bells and wondered to what degree the new monarch would remit old offenses.

In a second, related usage, English monarchs often issued Acts of Grace in the wake of war or insurrection, and since armed rebellion often broke out during the transition from one ruler to the next, inaugural Acts of Grace frequently included rebels who had submitted. In 1651 at the beginning of the Commonwealth, Parliament "Acquitted, Pardoned, Released and Discharged" all offenses "made, committed, suffered or done before the Third day of September, in the year One thousand six hundred fifty one."[26] Similarly, in 1660 at the beginning of Charles II's reign, the Act of Oblivion pardoned combatants on both sides of the war, exempting from penalty "all Acts of Hostilitie and Injuries, whether between the late King, and the Lords and Commons then in Parliament assembled, or between any of the People of this Nation...by reason of the late Troubles or in the late Warrs."[27] As the leader of an insurrection, Satan has "Against the Throne and Monarchy of God / Rais'd impious War," so when he wonders if he could regain his former position "By Act of Grace," he imagines God as acting like the commonwealth Parliament or Charles II, letting bygones be bygones in order to heal the polity of heaven (PL 1.42–44). From Satan's standpoint, the collective pardon has another great advantage: recipients did not have to petition for it. Instead, the Act of Grace was proclaimed by the sovereign and its provisions printed in broadside and distributed. Those who wished to avail themselves of the pardon's clemency simply paid a court fee to have their pardons ratified. Given that Satan refuses to "bow and sue for grace / With suppliant knee" (1.111–12), the impersonal mercy characteristic of the Act of Grace has a definite appeal. In imagining a pardon without personal abjection, Satan tacitly echoes a moment from book 2 in which Belial speculates that in time God will "much remit / His anger" (2.210–11) and "Not mind us not offending, satisfi'd / With what is punish't" (2.212–13). Like Satan, Belial hopes that the fallen angels might be the passive beneficiaries of a distant mercy and receive a pardon without having to ask for it.

In one sense, Satan is right: God *does* issue a formal act of grace in the "judicial oration" of book 3.[28] After the Son quells the military threat to his new rule, he and God consider those criminals who have already disobeyed the law (the fallen angels) and those who will do so shortly (Adam and Eve). God lays out the conditions of the pardon, conditions that exempt Satan and his crew: "The first sort by thir own suggestion fell, / Self-tempted, self-deprav'd: Man falls deceiv'd / By the other first: Man therefore shall find grace, / The other none" (*PL* 3.129–32). The mixture of "Mercy and Justice both" (3.132) in this act of grace matched widespread assumptions about the proper use of the collective pardon. Although Satan's exclusion from grace has disturbed many modern readers, it is a typical feature of Acts of Grace, for monarchs routinely stipulated that certain more heinous offenses were not open to clemency.[29] For instance, upon entering into Newcastle, the new James I pardoned all city prisoners "except those that lay for treason, murther, and Papistrie."[30] Such exemptions from pardon were frequently made for those who had been the ringleaders of rebellion. While the Act of Oblivion pardoned not only those who had fought against the king but also "all manner of Treasons, Misprisions of Treason, Murthers, Felonies, Offences, Crimes, Contempts, and Misdemeanors," it also stipulated that this general pardon was not extended to "the persons hereafter by name Excepted," primarily those who had been directly instrumental in the trial and execution of Charles I.[31]

God's careful attention to motive in *Paradise Lost* also reflects early modern ideas about the proper use of the pardon. While a consideration of motive is indispensable in modern trials and crime dramas, it was only just beginning to have a formal role in sixteenth and seventeenth century courts. Trials for homicide illustrate this fact clearly: all killings were technically capital offenses in the eyes of the law, whether the accused was a hired assassin or had killed by accident or in self-defense. But while an assessment of motive had little place at the trial stage, it was crucial at the pardoning stage. As Richard Hooker wrote, "who knoweth not, that harme advisedly done is naturally lesse pardonable, and therefore worthie of the sharper punishment?"[32] Accordingly, early modern Acts of Grace routinely discriminated on the basis of motive, as when the new James I, in his general pardon issued for York, pointedly excluded "willfull murtherers" from mercy.[33]

Milton's God performs a similar calculus of intent when he declares that those who are "Self-tempted, self-deprav'd" cannot find mercy. Although Adam and Eve will commit substantively the same treasonous offense as Satan (in book 10, Adam will admit that he is "To *Satan* only like [in] both crime and doom" [*PL* 10.841]), they are pardonable because they were seduced by another. In one sixteenth century pardon document, an anonymous judge recommends that the crown offer clemency to the accused who, "being young, were persuaded by others to commit the offenses whereof they stand indicted."[34] By showing God granting a pardon in *Paradise Lost* for a similar reason, Milton suggests that a sober assessment of motive is an important part of mercy both in heaven and on earth. He also seems aware that, for hardened offenders, pardons just paved the way to renewed crimes. In *The Tenure of Kings and Magistrates*, Milton argues that mercy, if extended to one who has shown himself to be a tyrant, is really just a form of cruelty, particularly since such spurious expressions of mercy hazard "the welfare of a whole Nation" on behalf of a few offenders (YP 3:193). Satan effectively admits as much when he allows that even if God were to grant an Act of Grace, his nature would lead him to "a worse relapse / And heavier fall" (*PL* 4.100–01), one that would bring renewed disorder and division to the heavenly commonwealth.

But while Milton establishes points of continuity between the Acts of Grace in heaven and those on earth, he also highlights a crucial difference between the two: God's general pardon does not arise from political considerations, and it is not a "tool of state formation" in the manner of most Stuart pardons.[35] One preliminary qualification is in order here, since Milton shows that God's proclamation of mercy in book 3 works to consolidate the polity of heaven. In a sense, it even *creates* the polity of heaven since Milton first refers to the collective body of angels immediately after his account of God's prophetic proclamation of grace. God declares that "Mercy first and last shall brightest shine" (*PL* 3.134), and this edict "in the blessed Spirits elect / Sense of new joy ineffable diffus'd" (3.136–37), narratively speaking, Milton's first description of the angelic hosts.

Although the proclamation of mercy results in increased unity and obedience among the good angels, it is not primarily motivated by political expediency. Under the Tudors and the Stuarts, in contrast, Acts of Grace often depended on careful assessments of power and advantage. In his *Eikon Basilike*, King Charles frankly admits as much when he comments that while pardons are acts of "Christian charitie and choice," they are also "Act[s] of State-policie and necessitie."[36] Charles had issued a series of pardons during the civil war, such as his 1642 "A Proclamation of His Majesties Grace, Favour, and Pardon, to the Inhabitants of His County of Dorsett," which promised a pardon to the men of Dorset provided that they laid down their arms and took certain key offenders into custody. The king's discussion of the death of Sir John Hotham and his son shows a similarly calculated awareness of the advantages of mercy. Although Hotham had initially fought for Parliament and had held Hull, with its valuable munitions depot, against royalist forces, he later conspired with his son to surrender the city to the king. Commenting on Parliament's subsequent execution of the Hothams as traitors, Charles regrets that they were "so unhappie as to fall into the hands of their Justice and not my mercie."[37] Milton takes up this claim in *Eikonoklastes,* asserting that since Charles had not pardoned others who had similarly opposed him, the hypothetical postmortem mercy extended to the Hothams is merely a political gambit intended to refurbish the king's image (YP 3:432).

Indeed, judging from discussions in *Eikonoklastes* and *Observations upon the Articles of Peace,* Milton despised the way in which pardons had become bargaining chips in a larger political game. In *Eikon Basilike,* lamenting the armies raised against him, King Charles exclaims, "Is this the reward and thanks that I am to receive for those many acts of Grace I have lately passed?"[38] In response, Milton scoffs, "He twitts them with *his Acts of grace;* proud, and unself-knowing words in the mouth of any King.... For if they were unjust acts, why did he grant them as of grace? If just, it was not of grace, but of his duty and his Oath to grant them" (YP 3:435). Milton here argues that by congratulating himself on his Acts of Grace and expecting gratitude for them, the king reveals that he granted pardons merely to consolidate his own hold on power. Similarly, when Charles says that the "Tumults" occasioned by Parliament "threatned to abuse all Acts of Grace, and turne them into wantonnesse" (in Miltonic terms, to turn liberty into license),[39] Milton retorts that the king is merely using the Pauline language of grace to cover his own political use of mercy (YP 3:404).

In his *Observations upon the Articles of Peace,* Milton cites item 18 of the Articles, which was an extensive Act of Oblivion remitting the offenses of the Irish rebels and punishing instead "any person or persons that will not obey and submit unto the peace concluded and agreed on by these Articles."[40] Milton claims that with this politically motivated Act of Grace, Charles I "sold away that justice so oft demanded" in order "to be aveng'd" on his opponents in England (YP 3:308). In *Paradise Lost,* however, Milton is careful to show that God, unlike Charles I, practices a disinterested form of mercy. In book 10, the Son promises to "temper so / Justice with Mercie" (*PL* 10.77–78), a phrase that alludes to the English coronation oath in which the monarch swore to "cause Law and Justice, in Mercy, to be executed" in all judgments.[41] But whereas Tudor and Stuart monarchs frequently reaped political and financial rewards from the exercise of mercy, Milton specifies that the Son has nothing to gain.[42] As the Son reminds the Father, "I go to judge / On Earth these thy transgressors, but thou knowst, / Whoever judg'd, the worst on mee must light" (10.71–73).

Milton also specifies that the judicial proceedings in *Paradise Lost* are private affairs, thereby offering a powerful contrast to the way in which early modern pardons and legal proceedings had become forms of political theater.⁴³ In answer to his own rhetorical question, "But whom shall I send to judge them?," God says, "whom but thee / Vicegerent Son" (*PL* 10.55–56). Milton here likens the Son to one of the England's assize judges. Given the rural, remote nature of most of England, only a small percentage of court cases were heard in London. Instead, officials of the King's Bench traveled a circuit through towns (hence the term "circuit court"), trying those cases deemed too serious for the county quarter sessions. For most early modern men and women, justice was symbolized not by some imposing central courthouse as in the modern world but, rather, by the quarterly arrival of these justices on the outskirts of town. Milton was clearly familiar with the assizes. In *Doctrine and Discipline of Divorce,* he likens those who condone injustice to "some wretched itinerary Judge" who fears to pronounce an impartial verdict lest those convicted "break his head" (YP 2:323). His image of the Son as God's traveling judge is more akin to his complimentary description in *The History of Britain* of King Edgar, who often "rode the Circuit as a Judge Itinerant through all his Provinces, to see justice well administered" (YP 5:322). Several features of this scene in *Paradise Lost* strengthen the association with early modern assize practices. God tells the Son, "to thee I have transferr'd / All Judgement" (*PL* 10.56–57), a phrase that recalls the way in which the assize judges were formally invested with the commission of jail delivery and *oyer et terminer* (literally, "to hear and determine"). After the trial, the Son leaves paradise "with swift ascent" (10.224), a speed that resembles that of the assize judges, who "arrived, presided, and then immediately departed," a procedure that "lent an air of mystery and finality" to the assize proceedings.⁴⁴ And once he returns to God's "blissful bosom" (10.225), the Son relates what has happened ("what had past with Man / [He] Recounted" [10.227–28]), a detail reminiscent of the postcircuit reports that each assize judge made to the king or lord keeper.

But having likened the Son to an English assize judge, Milton also calls attention to the differences between them. When the Son states firmly that "Attendance none shall need, nor Train"

(*PL* 10.80), Milton repudiates the pageantry typical of the assizes, particularly the ceremonial processions that escorted the judges through town.[45] Furthermore, the Son specifies that the judgment of Adam and Eve will have no witnesses, for "none / Are to behold the Judgment, but the judg'd, / Those two" (10.80–82). This stress on the absence of a public hearing contrasts starkly with the assize courtrooms, which were notorious for their noise and chaos. At a trial in 1582, one onlooker described the judges elbowing their way through the crowds "like ushers," and in 1684, a courtroom floor in East Grimstead collapsed under the weight of the assembled spectators.[46] The simplicity and directness of the Son's legal proceedings in *Paradise Lost* also contrast markedly with the elaborate rituals of the assize court proceedings, as when the judge in a capital case solemnly draped a square of black fabric over his head before pronouncing a guilty verdict. (In *Doctrine and Discipline of Divorce*, Milton expresses his aversion to public courtrooms when he argues that one reason to make divorce a private matter is to prevent the "unseemly affront" of having wives "aggravated in open Court" by lawyers, whom he calls "those hir'd maisters of tongue-fence" [YP 2:347].) In a 1617 speech to assize judges, Francis Bacon likened the assize circuits to "rivers in Paradise that go to water the whole kingdom."[47] Milton would have agreed—but only up to a certain point. His image of the Son as heaven's version of the assize judge partially endorses Bacon's idealized vision, but he simultaneously draws attention to how much human justice falls short of the divine model.

It is worth pausing here to note a related way in which this scene in *Paradise Lost* mirrors early modern judicial practice, for Adam and Eve actually have time to ask for pardon. In the first part of the judgment scene, Milton stresses the speed of events. Once the Son hears their confessions, "without delay / To Judgement he proceeded on th'accused" (*PL* 10.163–64), and he leaves with equal rapidity. But although Adam and Eve are left with judgment ringing in their ears, they see no immediate evidence of their sentence being enacted. Milton even emphasizes the delay. Oppressed by his deferred sentence, Adam laments, "why delayes / His hand to execute what his Decree / Fixd on this Day?" (10.771–73). While Milton here reflects theological consensus about why Adam and Eve did not die on the day of their sin, he also nods toward contemporary judicial practice. In previous centuries, convicted criminals were taken straight from the courtroom to the scaffold, stocks, or whipping post.

The case of Arnold Cosby, convicted in 1591 for the fatal stabbing of Lord Burke, speaks to this common practice. Hearing the pronouncement of his death sentence, Cosby asked that he "might not bee executed that present daie, but that he might have that daies respite, and a Preacher appointed to comfort him," a request that the judge allowed.[48] By Milton's day, this gap between sentencing and punishment had become a matter of course. After the trial, the convict was returned to jail, and penalties were not enacted until the end of the quarter sessions or assizes, a delay that sometimes stretched for weeks. In the words of one historian, "The reason [for the delay] was neither to allow the judge time to reflect nor the prisoner to squirm, but to allow time to secure pardon or prepare a motion in arrest of judgment."[49] This is precisely how the delay works for Adam. As he tells Eve, "wee expected / Immediate dissolution" (10.1048–49), but the deferral of sentence and the Son's mildness as a judge embolden Adam to think of begging a pardon.

Adam and Eve's pardon in book 11 is as private as their judgment in book 10, and we see here another instance of what Guibbory calls "Milton's distaste for a culture addicted to external shows."[50] When the Son brings Adam and Eve's penitent prayers into the throne room of God, Milton is careful to show that the conversation is a private one. Indeed, it is arguably the only private conversation that God and the Son have in the epic. Having conceded to his Son's petition for mercy, God then says, "But let us call to Synod all the Blest / Through Heav'ns wide bounds" (*PL* 11.67–68), and the Son "gave signal high / To the bright minister that watchd" (11.72–73). Milton specifies that only this one attendant angel has heard the Son's intercession and the Father's merciful assent. The "bright minister" blows his trumpet, and the hosts of heaven come flocking in: "the Sons of Light / Hasted, resorting to the Summons high, / And took thir Seats" (11.80–82). As with the earlier act of grace in book 3, God shares his merciful decree with his angels. He says, "from them I will not hide / My judgments" (11.68–70), and he knows that because of this administrative transparency, the good angels "in thir state, though firm, stood more confirmd" (11.71). But there is a crucial difference between a public pronouncement of pardon and the public theater of pardon.

Over and over again under the Tudors and Stuarts, pardons had become forms of state-sanctioned spectacle. For instance, in the aftermath of the 1603 Bye Plot, James I carefully stage-managed the last-minute pardons he dispensed. The accused men were painstakingly put through the pre-execution ceremonies on the scaffold only to be told that the hanging would be delayed several hours, and one observer, noting the king's care "to prevent all...colour of suspicion" that a pardon was forthcoming, called the whole affair a "well-acted comedy."[51] Theatrical themselves, pardons also made for good stage material, as attested by the pardons that Prospero hands out at the end of *The Tempest* and the pardon that Shylock receives in *The Merchant of Venice*. But while both the Globe audience and the onstage audience watched as Shylock was told, "Down, therefore, and beg mercy of the Duke," Milton allows for no such drama.[52] When the good angels arrive in response to the "Summons high" (*PL* 11.82), Milton specifies that they "took thir Seats" (11.81), a detail that suggests a legal arena like Westminster Hall. By invoking the image of a quasi-judicial building, the seats all filled with attentive angels, Milton tacitly draws more attention to the fact that there are no abject pardon petitioners on the arena's floor.

Special Pardons

The collective pardon was not the only form of human mercy that Milton alludes to in *Paradise Lost*, for Satan seems to be considering also the possibility of a special or individual pardon when, having asked, "Is there no place /...for Pardon left?" (*PL* 4.79–80), he answers himself, "None left but by submission" (4.81). As historian Krista Kesselring notes, the single most important criterion in special pardon petitions was the "simple, abject submission" of the convicted man or woman.[53] The need for unreserved submission is made spectacularly clear in a 1602 letter from Hugh O'Neill, the Earl of Tyrone and the defeated leader of the Irish rebellion, to Lord Mountjoy, who was acting as Queen Elizabeth's proxy in Tyrone's ongoing pardon negotiations. Tyrone laments that Mountjoy has rejected his earlier petition on the grounds that he "did not make therein an absolute submission." Accordingly, Tyrone remedies the lapse: "without standing upon any terms or conditions I do hereby both simply and absolutely submit myself to her Majesties mercy."[54] Early modern pardoning protocols held that these acts of submission were best performed in person, as Queen Elizabeth stipulated in another letter to Mountjoy: "First, our pleasure is upon no consideration to give him our pardon unless he do come personally where you shall assign him to receive it."[55]

Given these contexts, Satan accurately understands that a pardon would require him to come before God and "bow and sue for grace / With suppliant knee" (*PL* 1.111–12). Although such personal professions of submission might seem the *sine qua non* of all pardons, this was not uniformly the case. As Zemon Davis demonstrates, early modern French offenders had to craft a pardon narrative that made their offense look excusable by law, and while a humble demeanor was certainly helpful, petitioners needed more to make a convincing claim to innocence (or, at least, to strongly mitigating circumstances). Indeed, an overly profuse submission could be counterproductive since it could verge on an admission of guilt.[56] As a result, Satan reasons specifically like an early modern Englishman when he admits that his only route to clemency would involve coming before God and abjecting himself. Milton invites us to contrast Satan's obduracy with Adam and Eve's willingness to perform all the right gestures of penitence: they "prostrate fell / ... and both confess'd / Humbly thir faults, and pardon beg'd, with tears / Watering the ground, and with thir sighs the Air / Frequenting" (10.1099–1103).

While such physical forms of submission were important in early modern special pardons, they needed to be supplemented by the active efforts of an intercessor. Historian Douglas Hay argues that the role of elite intercessors made pardons into an important part of the "currency of patronage" in the eighteenth century, and Kesselring shows that the phenomenon Hay traces in the eighteenth century was equally prevalent in the sixteenth and seventeenth: "In a polity predicated upon personal relationships and hierarchical ties of obligation, it should come as no surprise that the receipt of a pardon often relied upon the favor and support of those better situated within the social hierarchy."[57] As a result, "Mediators were not just important in bringing cases to the Crown's attention—they did not just remedy a gap in bureaucratic procedures. Rather, their intervention and humble requests formed part of the cultural protocol for pardon."[58]

To give just one example of many, in an attempt to get his brother pardoned, a late-sixteenth-century man named Michael Shafto wrote to Sir Henry Percy, who in turn wrote to the Earl of Sussex, who in turn presented Shafto's request to Queen Elizabeth.[59] So when Satan wonders if there is room for pardon, seventeenth century readers accustomed to the contemporary protocols in pardoning would likely have understood that this question raised a related one: who would intercede on his behalf? The situation that Zemon Davis identifies in early modern France applied equally well to those seeking pardon in England: "The obstacle to asking for the king's pardon was not so much poverty by itself, but isolation."[60] Satan, however, has isolated himself from all society; as he tells Uriel, he has come "Alone thus wandring" (*PL* 3.667). Furthermore, since Satan was once one of heaven's elites, he has few potential patrons who outrank him. Realistically, the only available intercessor should he sue for pardon would be the Son. The fact that Satan speaks to the Sun with "no friendly voice" (4.36) when he should instead be speaking to the Son indicates that he is simultaneously aware of and yet unwilling to follow the approved channels of intercession. And without such intercession, no pardon can happen.

The Son performs precisely this intercessory function on behalf of Adam and Eve. When he writes in book 3 that the Son will act as a "Patron or Intercessor" (*PL* 3.219) for humanity, Milton draws on a specifically legal meaning of "patron" as a "defender or advocate before a court of justice."[61] In book 11, the Son's chosen role as the "Patron or Intercessor" enables the success of Adam and Eve's pardon petition, for the prayers of Adam and Eve fly up "through Heav'nly dores" (11.17), where they are "clad / With incense" by "thir great Intercessor" (11.17–19). The Son then brings these petitions with him into the presence of God: "Before the Fathers Throne: Them the glad Son / Presenting, thus to intercede began" (11.20–21). In this passage, Milton alludes to Hebrews 7:25–28 where Jesus is the priest of God, offering up sacrifices on behalf of a fallen humanity. However, by showing the Son coming into a throne room and bearing the petitions of those guilty specifically of "Treason," Milton also echoes contemporary pardon requests (*PL* 3.207). The Son's language recalls that used by early modern patrons as they sought to procure pardons for their clients: "Now therefore bend thine eare / To supplication, heare his sighs though mute; / Unskilful with what words to pray, let mee / Interpret for him" (11.30–33). According to the unwritten rules of early modern pardoning, the role of the convicted man or woman was humbly to perform an array of sighs, tears, and other postures indicative of sorrow and submission, as when the imprisoned Duke of Norfolk mended his own hose as a mute testament to his abjection.[62] The tacit role of the intercessor was to put these penitent gestures into words before the monarch, literally to translate on behalf of the client. Thus, the Son acts precisely like a good patron should when he understands that since Adam is "Unskilful with what words to pray" and can only heave "mute" sighs, he must "Interpret for him."

To some degree, the intercession that the Son performs on behalf of Adam and Eve is enabled by the intercession that Adam and Eve offer to perform for each other. Eve expresses her hope that, if she begs pardon for Adam, "The sentence from thy head remov'd may light / On me sole cause to thee of all this woe" (*PL* 10.934–35). Adam replies in kind, imagining himself requesting a pardon for her. He says that he would ask "That on my head all might be visited, / Thy frailtie and infirmer Sex forgiv'n, / To me committed and by me expos'd" (10.955–57). Milton invites us to contrast such moments of altruism with Satan's self-interested reflections in book 4. When he wonders, "Is there no place / Left for Repentance, none for Pardon left?" (4.79–80), Satan is thinking about a strictly individual form of remission. In effect, he is asking, "Am *I* eligible for pardon?," and not "Are *we?*"

Satan's focus on his own options conflicts with a whole set of early modern ideas of hierarchy and the proper actions of social superiors. Particularly in the case of pardons sought after treason and armed insurrections, the paternalistic assumptions of the day held that leaders should first and foremost seek forgiveness for those who followed them. For example, in another letter to Mountjoy, Queen Elizabeth allows that while Tyrone can negotiate a pardon for himself "and his own natural followers of Tyrone," he may not seek pardon for "all others." These men must "make their own suits for themselves." Elizabeth accepts that in seeking pardon for himself, Tyrone was also duly seeking a pardon for his "natural followers," those Irishmen from County Tyrone who owed him loyalty.[63] The fact that Elizabeth so carefully limits the extent of Tyrone's suit for pardon—and accepts automatically that pardoning him entails also pardoning some portion of his followers—indicates the degree to which leaders seeking pardons were assumed to be simultaneously acting on behalf of their subordinates. Since Milton has pointedly said that the rebel angels are not "The fellows of [Satan's] crime" but "the followers rather" (*PL* 1.606), Satan should by rights be considering a pardon for all of them. Indeed, Abdiel's reprimand of Satan in book 5 stresses that Satan bears the obligation to intercede on behalf of others. Abdiel tells Satan, "Cease then this impious rage, / And tempt not these; but hast'n to appease / Th'incensed Father, and th'incensed Son, / While Pardon may be found in time besought" (5.845–48). The implication is that in abandoning his planned attack and seeking a pardon from God, Satan would be working to protect the angels loyally ranged at his back. But although he earlier wept at the sight of "Millions of Spirits for his fault amerc't" (1.609), Satan is not considering in his book 4 soliloquy how his own hypothetical plea for pardon might benefit his subordinates.

When Satan muses, "Say I could repent and could obtain / By Act of Grace my former state" (*PL* 4.93–94), he is entertaining a wildly inaccurate idea of the results of a special pardon. In short, virtually none of them came without strings attached or restored the offender to his or her previous position. (Such unconditional pardons were bestowed only when the accused had clearly been the target of unfair accusation and had powerful and disinterested friends.)[64] For instance, in a letter to a friend about the pardon that the Earl of Somerset (King James's favorite, who had been convicted of the Overbury murder) finally received in 1622, John Chamberlain writes, "Somersetts pardon was sealed on Thursday in as ample a manner as could be devised, and he hath taken a house at Cheswicke, but with promise not to looke towarde the court."[65] Although Somerset's pardon was seen as "ample," there was no question of his resuming his former position at court, and he was confined to a three-mile radius around his Cheswick property.[66] Similarly, after years of negotiations, Lionel Cranfield, the impeached Earl of Middlesex, wrote jubilantly that his impending pardon would finally give him "liberty, *quietus est*, absolute pardon, and be made a child new born." The irony is that what Middlesex calls an "absolute pardon" entailed the loss of his offices (including surveyor-general of Customs, master of the Court of Wards and Liveries, and chief commissioner of the navy) and a ban on ever holding office again.[67] In addition to specific forfeitures and penalties, those who received a pardon understood that they faced generally tighter restrictions than before and that small lapses in loyalty and obedience would result in swift penalties. In *Paradise Lost*, Mammon seems aware of this fact when he rejects the idea of a divine pardon on the grounds that the fallen angels could not bear to "Stand in [God's] presence humble, and receive / Strict Laws impos'd" (2.240–41). Where Mammon understands that a pardon would result in "Strict Laws" that would bind the pardoned angels more tightly than their unfallen peers, Satan unrealistically imagines himself regaining his "former state" and returning to his wonted "highth" (4.94, 95).

Adam has a better grasp than Satan on the fact that a pardon would not mean the erasure of all penalties, and, unlike Satan, he understands that his "former state" is lost to him. In the discussion leading up to their decision to seek pardon, Adam recalls to Eve the sentence of work laid upon him, and he notes that the Son has already provided them with clothes as a shield against the elements. Adam imagines that penitent prayers might move the Son to further teach them to bear their situation:

> How much more, if we pray him, will his ear
> Be open, and his heart to pitie incline,
> And teach us further by what means to shun
> Th' inclement Seasons, Rain, Ice, Hail and Snow,
> Which now the Skie with various Face begins
> To shew us in this Mountain, while the Winds
> Blow moist and keen, shattering the graceful locks
> Of these fair spreading Trees. (*PL* 10.1060–67)

Legally speaking, Adam here hopes for a commutation of sentence, in which the offender remains guilty of the crime but the penalty is lessened. Instead of fantasizing a complete release from all punishment, Adam more realistically imagines that they can find means of "remedie or cure / To evils which our own misdeeds have wrought" (10.1079–80), and he knows that these forms of remission will come from God: "Hee will instruct us praying" (10.1081). Rather than expecting God's pardon to reinstall them in their former life of bliss, Adam holds out the more modest idea that a pardon will allow them "To pass commodiously this life" (10.1083) that now lies before them.

What Adam does not understand, however, is that the pardon granted to him still entails the forfeiture of his land. In book 11, on the heels of their penitent prayers, Adam and Eve both receive a consoling sense of God's mercy. Adam has seen a vision of God as "placable and mild" (*PL* 11.151), and Eve sees him as "infinite in pardon" (11.167). They mistakenly assume that such a pardon will allow them to keep their home. As Adam says, "Here let us live, though in fall'n state, content" (11.180). Adam misunderstands, however, the way the law works since, as God says, Adam "shall find / Forbearance no acquittance" (10.52–53). Milton here echoes contemporary judicial practice since those pardoned from a crime still faced forfeiture of goods.[68] For instance, although the Earl of Middlesex got his long-sought "absolute pardon," he had to surrender his beloved Chelsea House and other properties. As a result, Milton's God follows the outlines of English law in exacting the forfeiture of a place that he has termed Adam's "Mansion" (8.296). Like the Earl of Middlesex, Adam can be pardoned, but he cannot be pardoned *and* keep his estate.

Exiled from their homelands because of their crimes, the fallen angels and Adam and Eve are in much the same situation as those many early modern convicts who were transported to work in the colonies. As J. Martin Evans points out in *Milton's Imperial Epic*, hell looks very much like one of the seventeenth century penal colonies—a place populated by rebellious malcontents who have been banished from their homeland and sent to do forced labor under miserable conditions.[69] Beelzebub suspects that despite their apparent freedom in hell, the fallen angels remain God's "thralls" (*PL* 1.149) and are doomed "Here in the heart of Hell to work in Fire" (1.151). Adam likewise receives "sad Sentence" (11.109) of "Perpetual banishment" (11.108), and he must go to labor in another land among "Thorns also and Thistles" (10.203). English courts had begun experimenting with transportation near the beginning of the seventeenth century, and by Milton's day, transportation was emerging as a viable solution to the nation's growing crime problem.[70]

The crucial point is that in early modern England no one was sentenced to transportation. Rather, those convicted of crimes were sentenced to death, and the sentence was then indefinitely reprieved (a deferral reminiscent of the Son's judgment, which "th'instant stroke of Death denounc't that day / Remov'd farr off" [*PL* 10.210–11]). In short, those who were transported had received a form of conditional pardon, the condition being their willingness to leave England and to serve out the stated period of overseas labor.[71] From this standpoint, it is not quite accurate to say that Satan has not received a pardon. Rather, he does not like the kind of pardon he has gotten and instead wants another that offers him more freedom. Indeed, an important difference between Satan and

Adam is in how they react to the penalty laid upon them. Whereas Satan repudiates the idea of working as God's thrall, Adam considers his sentence of work and tells Eve "Idleness had bin worse" (10.1055). Because Adam can see and appreciate the mercy extended to him in the midst of justice, he has the chance to create a new inner paradise.

Milton had firsthand experience with how pardons might and might not entail forfeitures. During his months in hiding in Bartholomew Close, Milton was waiting to hear not only if his life was forfeit but also if his goods and lands were to be seized by the state. In the event, the Act of Oblivion declared that all "Penalties, Escheats, and Forfeitures" were "hereby Declared and Enacted to be from henceforth Null and void" and that those to whom the pardon applied could retain "their Lands, Tenements and Hereditaments, Good, Chattels, and other things For cited."[72] As a result, Milton was able to emerge from hiding, albeit with his estate diminished, and he took a house first in Holborn and then in Jewin Street. But while the collective pardon forgave forfeitures, Milton's special pardon may well have been proved more expensive. Although he secured a pardon from Parliament for the offense of writing against the king, Milton was still obliged to pay the arresting sergeant the exorbitant sum of 150 pounds for his lodgings in the Tower.[73] Campbell and Corns suggest that the Dutch record of Milton's special pardon, indicating that he "was freed through good promises," may explain why Milton remained silent when rebuttals of his earlier controversial prose continued to appear in print. Having made pledges of reformed behavior, Milton was honoring those. Unlike Satan, who fantasizes that "Act of Grace" might restore him to his "former place," and unlike Adam, who is stunned to realize that a pardon also entails eviction from the garden, Milton understood clearly that his former place was lost to him, and he seems to have contented himself with his reduced life in his Jewin Street house and perhaps a quiet sense of "suffering for Truths sake" (12.569).

University of Alabama at Birmingham

Notes

This article has benefited greatly from suggestions made by Mary C. Fenton and by the anonymous reader at *Milton Studies*. My thanks go to both of them. This essay is part of a larger study on *Paradise Lost* and the early modern law. I am grateful to those scholars who have demonstrated Milton's awareness of the law: Elliott Visconsi, *Lines of Equity: Literature and the Origins of Law in Later Stuart England* (Ithaca, N.Y., 2008), 75–113; Mary C. Fenton, "Hope, Land Ownership, and Milton's 'Paradise Within,'" *Studies in English Literature, 1500–1900* 43 (2003): 151–80; John T. Shawcross, *The Development of Milton's Thought: Law, Government, and Religion* (Pittsburgh, 2008); Lynne Greenberg, "Law," in *Milton in Context*, ed. Stephen B. Dobranski, 192–218 (Cambridge, 2010); and Lynne A. Greenberg, "Paradise Enclosed and the *Feme Covert*," in *Milton and the Grounds of Contention*, ed. Mark R. Kelley, Michael Lieb, and John Shawcross, 150–73 (Pittsburgh, 2003).

1. John Milton, *Paradise Lost*, in *The Riverside Milton*, ed. Roy Flannagan (Boston, 1998), 1.4, 5; 10.1104. All subsequent references to Milton's poetry are from this edition and are supplied parenthetically in the text.

2. The classic treatments of Milton's Arminian views are provided by Maurice Kelley, *This Great Argument: A Study of Milton's "De Doctrina Christiana" as a Gloss upon "Paradise Lost"* (Princeton, N.J., 1941), and Dennis Danielson, *Milton's Good God: A Study in Literary Theodicy* (Cambridge, 1982). See also Stephen M. Fallon, "Milton's Arminianism and the Authorship of *De Doctrina Christiana*," *Texas Studies in Literature and Language* 41 (1999): 103–27.

3. See Harry F. Robins, *If This Be Heresy: A Study of Milton and Origen* (Urbana, Ill., 1963); and C. A. Patrides, "The Salvation of Satan," *Journal of the History of Ideas* 28 (1967): 467–78.

4. More detailed treatment of this change can be found in J. M. Beattie, *Crime and the Courts in England, 1660–1800* (Oxford, 1986); Cynthia Herrup, *The Common Peace: Participation and the Criminal Law in Seventeenth-Century England* (Cambridge, 1987); Harry Potter, *Hanging in Judgment: Religion and the Death Penalty in England* (New York, 1993); J. A. Sharpe, *Crime in Early Modern England, 1550–1750* (London, 1984); and Thomas Andrew Green, *Verdict according to Conscience: Perspectives on the English Criminal Trial Jury 1200–1800* (Chicago, 1985).

5. Krista J. Kesselring, *Mercy and Authority in the Tudor State* (Cambridge, 2003); and Natalie Zemon Davis, *Fiction in the Archives: Pardon Tales and Their Tellers in Sixteenth-Century France* (Stanford, Calif., 1987).

6. One of the only legal texts of the period that considers the extent of the king's pardoning authority is Sir Edward Coke's chapter, "Of Pardons."

Coke carefully spells out the limits on the royal prerogative: "the lawes of his Realm have in some sort limited and bounded the kings mercy, as shall appear hereafter." Injured individuals have a right to see justice done under the law, and so in the case of crimes like rape or homicide, the monarch cannot pardon in such a way that the accused or the accused's family do not receive satisfaction. Similarly, if an individual has a duty to perform a public service (such as maintain a bridge) and defaults, the king cannot use a pardon to prevent the offender from making amends (i.e., repair the neglected bridge) since this would harm the commonwealth. See Edward Coke, *The Third Part of the Institutes of the Laws of England* (London, 1644), 233. The monarch's pardoning prerogative erupted into a truly national debate in 1679. Parliament impeached the Earl of Danby for treason, and in response, James II offered him a special pardon. The heat of this debate can be gauged by works like John Brydall's *A New-Years-Gift for the Anti-Prerogative Men; or, A Lawyers Opinion in Defence of His Majesties Power-Royal, of Granting Pardons as He Pleases*. Jacquelyn Janelle Renfrow, "Tudor and Stuart Theories of Kingship: The Dispensing Power and the Royal Discretionary Authority in Sixteenth and Seventeenth Century England" (Ph.D. diss., University of Michigan, 1970), 380–94, provides a detailed discussion of the Danby impeachment and the many issues it raised.

7. For a discussion of how Milton uses early modern pardoning practices in *Samson Agonistes*, see Lynne Greenberg, "Dalila's 'Feminine Assaults': The Gendering and Engendering of Crime in *Samson Agonistes*," in *Altering Eyes: New Perspectives of "Samson Agonistes,"* ed. Mark R. Kelley and Joseph Wittreich, 192–218 (Newark, Del., 2002). Jillisa Brittan and Richard A. Posner glance very briefly at pardons in their "Penal Theory in *Paradise Lost*," *Michigan Law Review* 105 (2007): 1049–66. I am broadly indebted to those who have examined Milton's work in context of seventeenth century society. Particularly helpful examples include Laura Lunger Knoppers, *Historicizing Milton: Spectacle, Power, and Pageantry in Restoration England* (Athens, Ga., 1994); N. H. Keeble, *The Literary Culture of Nonconformity in Later Seventeenth-Century England* (Athens, Ga., 1987); Sharon Achinstein, *Literature and Dissent in Milton's England* (Cambridge, 2003); Stephen B. Dobranski, *Milton, Authorship, and the Book Trade* (Cambridge, 1999); and Thomas Fulton, *Historical Milton: Manuscript, Print, and Political Culture in Revolutionary England* (Amherst, 2010).

8. For the highly symbolic nature of medieval pardons, see Geoffrey Koziol, *Begging Pardon and Favor: Ritual and Political Order in Early Medieval France* (Ithaca, N.Y., 1992). Early modern pardon petitions indicate that many of the core features of this quasi-ritualized social discourse remained the same.

9. For instance, men and women who had been convicted in Star Chamber often waited until the next time that the king was present there

before coming in and begging for mercy. There are many instances of this attention to what we might call the symbolic geography of pardons. For example, in 1579 Thomas Appletree was standing on the banks of the Thames showing off his new gun to a friend when he sportively pulled the trigger. The bullet narrowly missed Queen Elizabeth and the French ambassador, who happened to be traveling by in the royal barge, and hit one of her bargemen in the leg. Authorities expended some effort to erect a gibbet for Appletree's execution on the precise place "betwixt Detforde and Greenwitch" where the crime had been committed; see *A Brief Discourse of the Most Haynous and Traytorlike Fact of Thomas Appeltree* (London, 1579), A2v. As a result, when a last-minute pardon arrived from the queen as Appletree stood with the noose around his neck, the place of the crime, the place of the execution, and the place of the pardon were all in perfect alignment.

10. Achsah Guibbory, *Ceremony and Community from Herbert to Milton: Literature, Religion, and Cultural Conflict in Seventeenth-Century England* (Cambridge, 1998), 205.

11. John Milton, *The Tenure of Kings and Magistrates*, in *Complete Prose Works of John Milton*, 8 vols., ed. Don M. Wolfe et al. (New Haven, Conn., 1953–82), 3:222. All citations from Milton's prose are to this edition, hereafter cited as YP.

12. Kesselring provides a general survey of Acts of Grace in *Mercy and Authority* 57–73. On parliamentary involvement in these Acts of Grace, see David Dean, *Law-Making and Society in Late Elizabethan England: The Parliament of England, 1584–1601* (Cambridge, 1996), 55–62.

13. John Hall, *Memoirs of the Right Villainous John Hall, the Late Famous and Notorious Robber* (London, 1714), 14.

14. William Lambarde, *William Lambarde and Local Government: His "Ephemeris" and Twenty-Nine Charges to Juries and Commissions*, ed. Conyers Read (Ithaca, N.Y., 1962), 71.

15. Helen Darbishire, ed., *The Early Lives of Milton* (New York, 1932), 271–75.

16. Ibid., 73–74.

17. This discussion is generally drawn from Gordon Campbell and Thomas Corns's fine biography, *John Milton: Life, Work, and Thought* (Oxford, 2008), 313–17.

18. Darbishire, *Early Lives*, 32. As Campbell and Corns point out, Skinner's account does not clarify matters since it is remains uncertain whether Milton was here claiming pardon under the Act of Oblivion or whether he had already negotiated a special pardon related to the parliamentary indictment (*John Milton*, 317).

19. "Sue," v. def. 22a, *OED Online*, June 2014, Oxford University Press, www.oed.com/view/Entry/193501?rskey=HyFPld&result=2 (accessed June 24, 2014).

20. Charles I, *Eikon Basilike* (London, 1649), 224.

21. On Milton's familiarity with the execution of the regicides, see Knoppers, *Historicizing Milton*, 42–51.

22. Donald Veall, *The Popular Movement for Law Reform, 1640–1660* (Oxford, 1970), 10.

23. Kesselring, *Mercy and Authority*, 90.

24. For a description of the king's procession south, including Acts of Grace pronounced for towns like Newcastle and York, see T. M., *The True Narration of the Entertainment of His Royall Majestie, from the Time of His Departure from Edenbrough; Till His Receiving at London* (London, 1603), E2. On the London spike in theft, see Kesselring, *Mercy and Authority*, 67.

25. Davis, *Fiction in the Archives*, 20.

26. *An Act of General Pardon and Oblivion* (London, 1652), 1546–47. For a pro-Parliament account of Cavaliers switching their allegiances at this news, see *The Cavaliers Jubilee; or, Long Look'd For Come at Last: Viz. the General Pardon* (London, 1652).

27. *Anno Regni Caroli II*, 1660, A4v.

28. Barbara Lewalski, *"Paradise Lost" and the Rhetoric of Literary Forms* (Princeton, N.J., 1982), 120, also notes similar judicial and forensic elements in Satan's Mt. Niphates speech (99).

29. As Kesselring notes, over the course of the sixteenth century the tendency was for more and more offenses to be excluded from the Act of Grace (*Mercy and Authority*, 73).

30. T. M., *The True Narration*, C4v.

31. *Anno Regni Caroli II*, A2.

32. Richard Hooker, *Of the Laws of Ecclesiastical Polity*, ed. Georges Edelen (Cambridge, Mass., 1977), 1:104.

33. T. M., *The True Narration*, D4v.

34. Quoted in Kesselring, *Mercy and Authority*, 108.

35. Kesselring, *Mercy and Authority*, 3.

36. Charles I, *Eikon Basilike*, 244.

37. Ibid., 50.

38. Ibid., 54.

39. Ibid., 29.

40. Ireland, Lord Lieutenant, *Articles of Peace Made and Concluded with the Irish Rebels and Papists by James Earle of Ormond* (London, 1649), 19.

41. Percy Schramm, *A History of the English Coronation*, trans. Leopold Legg (Oxford, 1937), 225.

42. As David Loades demonstrates, when King Philip came to the throne of England through marriage to Mary, he actively awarded pardons in order to create a clientage network loyal to him. See David Loades, "Philip II and the Government of England," in *Law and Government under the Tudors*, ed. Claire Cross, David Loades, and J. J. Scarisbrick (Cambridge, 1988), 181. Sometimes pardon requests degenerated into

purely financial transactions, as when Anthony Bacon frankly asked for 100 pounds and a bond for 500 pounds more in return for his intercession on behalf of Robert Booth (Kesselring, *Mercy and Authority*, 130).

43. On the ways in which seventeenth century trials were conducted like stage plays, see Elizabeth Sauer, *"Paper Contestations" and Textual Communities in England, 1640–1675* (Toronto, 2005).

44. Herrup, *Common Peace*, 51.

45. One later French visitor described "bells ringing and trumpets playing" and the judge as "preceded by the sheriff's men, to the number of twelve or twenty, in full dress, armed with javelins" (Beattie, *Crime and the Courts*, 317). On the awesome splendor of the assizes, see also Douglas Hay, "Property, Authority, and the Criminal Law," in *Albion's Fatal Tree: Crime and Society in Eighteenth-Century England*, ed. Douglas Hay (New York, 1976), 27.

46. J. S. Cockburn, *A History of English Assizes, 1558–1714* (Cambridge, 1972), 110.

47. Francis Bacon, *The Letters and the Life of Francis Bacon*, ed. James Spedding (London, 1868), 6:303. Bacon's metaphor was a centralizing one, intended to indicate how justices—and judges—are derivative of the king, hardly a position Milton would have supported. On Bacon's speech in context of the Stuart undermining of judicial independence, see Cockburn, *Assizes*, 230.

48. Henry Carey, Baron Hunsdon, *The Araignment, Examination, Confession and Judgement of Arnold Cosbye: Who Wilfully Murdered the Lord Burke, Neere the Towne of Wanswoorth* (London, 1591), B4.

49. J. H. Baker, "Criminal Courts and Procedure at Common Law, 1550–1800," in *Crime in England, 1550–1800*, ed. J. S. Cockburn (Princeton, N.J., 1977), 40.

50. Guibbory, *Ceremony and Community*, 187. See also Knoppers's account of how Milton "not only challenges but redefines the appropriate spectacles of state in Restoration England" (*Historicizing Milton*, 11).

51. Janet Spenser discusses this pardon and provides the quotes in "Staging Pardon Scenes: Variations of Tragicomedy," *Renaissance Drama* 21 (1990): 78–81. On the theatricality of pardons, see also Richard Wilson, "The Quality of Mercy: Discipline and Punishment in Shakespearean Comedy," *Seventeenth Century* 5 (1990): 1–42.

52. William Shakespeare, "The Merchant of Venice," in *The Norton Shakespeare Based on the Oxford Edition*, ed. Stephen Greenblatt et al. (New York, 1997), 4.1.358.

53. Kesselring, *Mercy and Authority*, 116–17.

54. Charles McNeil, ed., *The Tanner Letters: Original Documents and Notices of Irish Affairs in the Sixteenth and Seventeenth Centuries* (Dublin, 1943), 52.

55. Ibid., 57.

56. Davis, *Fiction in the Archives*, 60–61, 74–75.

57. Hay, "Property, Authority," 45.
58. Kesselring, *Mercy and Authority*, 120, 133.
59. Ibid., 124.
60. Davis, *Fiction in the Archives*, 10.
61. "Patron" n., defs. 2b and 4a, *OED Online*, June 2014, Oxford University Press, www.oed.com/view/Entry/138929?rskey=idCW6F&result=1 (accessed June 24, 2014).
62. Kesselring, *Mercy and Authority*, 116–17.
63. McNeil, *Tanner Letters*, 57.
64. Baker, "Criminal Courts," 44.
65. John Chamberlain, *The Letters of John Chamberlain*, ed. Norman Egbert McClure (Philadelphia, 1939), 2:582.
66. David Matthew, *James I* (Tuscaloosa, Ala., 1968), 218.
67. Menna Prestwich, *Cranfield: Politics and Profits under the Early Stuarts, the Career of Lionel Cranfield, Earl of Middlesex* (Oxford, 1966), 475.
68. Veall, *Popular Movement*, 1–3, explains that since felonies were still regarded legally as a breach of the feudal bonds, lands and goods reverted back to the felon's lord.
69. J. Martin Evans, *Milton's Imperial Vision: "Paradise Lost" and the Discourses of Colonialism* (Ithaca, N.Y., 1996), 33–40. I am grateful to Mary C. Fenton for suggesting that Adam and Eve have also been transported.
70. On the rise of transportation as a judicial option, see Christopher Harding et al., *Imprisonment in England and Wales: A Concise History* (London, 1985), 63–65. Beattie demonstrates that the Transportation Act of 1718 was the culmination of decades of thought on and experiment with penal sanctions (Beattie, *Crime and the Courts*, 468–519).
71. Cynthia Herrup, "Punishing Pardon: Some Thoughts on the Origins of Transportation," in *Penal Practice and Culture, 1500–1900: Punishing the English*, ed. Simon Devereaux and Paul Griffiths (New York, 2004), 121–37.
72. *Anno Regni Caroli II*, A1–A1v.
73. Milton protested the amount in Parliament, but the outcome of the complaint is not known (Campbell and Corns, *John Milton*, 317).

Foreign Policy and the Feast Day: Milton's Poetic Nativity

Andrea Walkden

In the spring of 1627, John Milton wrote a verse epistle to his former tutor Thomas Young, chaplain to the English merchants in Hamburg. Published in the 1645 *Poems* as "Elegia quarta," and likely accompanied by a prose letter to Young apologizing for a three-year delay in writing, the epistle anticipates its happy intrusion upon one of several scenes of quietude: a domestic Young surrounded by his wife and children, a contemplative Young in private communion with Scripture and the writings of the church fathers, or a pastoral Young in devoted attendance on his flock.[1] The occasion for these imagined epistolary intrusions is, as the elegy goes on to make clear, the threat of intrusion on a different scale and of a less welcome sort: "A faithful hand sends you these from the English shore, if there is time for the soft Muses amid the battles. Accept a sincere greeting, though it is late" (Haec tibi, si teneris vacat inter praelia Musis / Mittit ab Angliaco littore fida manus. / Accipe sinceram, quamvis sit sera, salutem) (51–53). The battles to which Milton refers were, in fact, never to reach Hamburg, although their plausible proximity provides the dramatic impetus for the verse letter: "For now busy Rumor reports—alas, true messenger of evils!—that wars arise in the areas near you, and you and your city are encircled by a fierce army, and the Saxon lords have already prepared for war" (Nam vaga Fama refert, heu nuntia vera malorum! / In tibi finitimis bella tumere locis, / Teque tuamque urbem truculento milite cingi, / Et iam Saxonicos arma parasse duces) (71–74). These mobilized Saxon lords are likely the dukes of Saxe-Weimar who had allied themselves to the Protestant military campaign of Christian IV of Denmark, financed by subsidies from England and the Dutch Republic. By the spring of 1627, the army of this international anti-Hapsburg coalition had been forced to retreat northward as the imperial armies of Tilly and Wallenstein overran Lower Saxony and, harrying the Danish army out of northwest Germany, moved to within 100 miles of the port city of Hamburg.[2]

As has long been recognized, Milton models "Elegia quarta" on Ovid's *Tristia* 3.7, inverting the respective positions of speaker and recipient so that the letter addresses the exile rather than being written by him. Estelle Haan explains how this inversion takes the form of a compliment, aligning Young with the exiled Ovid, and Milton with Ovid's stepdaughter and pupil, Perilla, whose literary education the *Tristia* elegy fondly recounts.[3] Haan notes also how Milton expands Ovid's single opening imperative ("Vade") into four distinct exhortations: "Run quickly" (Curre...subito); "go" (I); "seek" (pete); "Break off lazy delays" (Segnes rumpe moras) ("Elegia quarta," 1–3), an expansion that continues with the speaker's wish that his letter might co-opt the dragon-drawn chariots of Medea and Triptolemus in order to arrive all the sooner at its destination ("Elegia quarta," 9–12).[4] But "Elegia quarta" is doing rather more than simply inverting and elaborating the scenario of *Tristia* 3.7. Its opening imperatives carry an occasional urgency and historical specificity not found in the Ovidian original, dramatizing the letter's unaccompanied European journey in the context of the precarious military situation. Instructed to outpace the advancing Catholic armies, the letter must acknowledge its own tardiness, but also atone for it by arriving first; this poetics of priority we recognize from the first of the young poet's religious "feast day" poems, the "Ode on the Morning of Christ's Nativity" that Milton would write two and a half years later. In the proem to the Nativity ode, the poet instructs the "Heav'nly Muse" to arrive with her gift before the hastening kings: "O run, prevent them with thy humble ode, / And lay it lowly at his blessèd feet; / Have thou the honor first, thy Lord to greet" ("Nativity," 24–26). Staged shortly before dawn, the race between the "Heav'nly Muse" (15) and the "star-led wizards" (23) recasts the race already run between the poet's Ovidian verse epistle and the Catholic troops advancing across northern Europe.

"Elegia quarta" is one of three neo-Latin poems that the young Milton wrote during his second year at Cambridge that address themselves to the events of what would come to be known as the Thirty Years' War. Joined by "Elegia tertia," commemorating the death of Lancelot Andrewes, Bishop of Winchester, and, I shall here argue, by the miniature Gunpowder Plot epic "In quintum Novembris" ("On the fifth of November"), the verse epistle to Young ends a six-month span, from November 1626 to May 1627, in which Milton occupies his imagination with European affairs and escalating English involvement with them. The war itself had begun some eight years previously with the Calvinist rebellion in Bohemia in 1618 and, in reprisal, the 1621 Hapsburg-sponsored invasion of the Palatinate, the lands of James's daughter Elizabeth and son-in-law Frederick, by Maximilian of Bavaria. From its outset, the war was the subject of heated debate in England with calls for an evangelical alliance to defend the cause of international Protestantism. Acceding to the throne in 1625, Charles I, together with his favorite, the Duke of Buckingham, initially adopted a more aggressive, interventionist approach to foreign policy, the main outcome of which were the naval expeditions against Spanish shipping, targeting the Atlantic fleet, which transported silver from the mines in Zacatecas, Mexico, in the bay of Cadiz in the autumn of 1625, and, in support of Huguenot rebels, against the French forces beseiging the fortress of Rhé, an island off La Rochelle on the French coast, in the summer of 1627. Both expeditions proved expensive failures that threatened to bring European warfare to British shores as a series of Franco-Spanish invasion scares swept England, Scotland, and Ireland in the autumn of 1625 and again in 1626–27.

It was during these anxious months of 1626, when the British archipelago waited nervously and expectantly for news of a Spanish invasion, that Milton composed his brief epic, "In quintum Novembris." The poem is a contribution to the commemorative tradition of Gunpower Plot poetry, but also, I propose to demonstrate, a commentary on the dangers and difficulties of English foreign policy at this especially precarious and perilous moment. In her analysis of "Popish-plot thinking," Sharon Achinstein has well remarked that Milton's imagination was caught early by the "religious and dynastic warfare" of Counter-Reformation Europe.[5] By watching Milton "watching Europe, warily, mistrustingly," Achinstein contextualizes the early Latin poems within a longer narrative of Milton's political coming-of-age, concluding with the prose works *Of Reformation* (1641) and *Eikonoklastes* (1649), which rehearse the early evils of Stuart foreign policy and its abandonment, variously attributed to callousness, crypto-Catholicism, and incompetence of the international Protestant church.[6] Taking up Achinstein's insight about the galvanizing influence of European affairs upon Milton's early Latin poetry, I propose we consider English anxiety about Europe as an important motive for Milton's retelling of the Gunpowder Plot in "In quintum Novembris," where the poet adapts the familiar contours of that national story to address the foreign policy dilemmas and choices confronting the nation some two decades later, and at the beginning of another new reign. Certain features of the miniature epic become newly intelligible in the light of this historically specific context and I foreground these in my reading.

But the foreign policy dilemmas Milton is staging in this poem serve a further, still more important, function. It will be the broader purpose of this essay to demonstrate how the Latin political poems that Milton wrote in a short, six-month span in 1626–27, when he was fully preoccupied with European events, prepared him to write the English religious odes just a few years later. In each of these poems, the "Ode on the Morning of Christ's Nativity" (1629), the unfinished "Passion" (ca. 1630), and "Upon the Circumcision" (written sometime between 1629 and 1633), Milton celebrates a feast day in the Christian calendar.⁷ Milton critics have not linked "In quintum Novembris" with this later sequence of devotional feast-day poems. But as we will see, the miniature epic was Milton's first attempt to write a poem commemorating a public religious holiday, albeit one that was narrowly nationalistic, militantly political, and a relatively recent addition to the church's calendar.⁸ As a first attempt or originary moment, "In quintum Novembris" is all the more significant because it thematizes its own change of generic direction: it begins with the heroic material of the epic, and with the foreign policy concerns that epic necessarily entails, only to turn toward and achieve closure through the ritual celebrations of the feast day. It is this turn that offers the strongest hint of the trajectory Milton was to take next in his poetic career.

Fears of Invasion

In the classicizing fiction of "Elegia quarta," it is "vaga Fama" (71), the reliable if errant messenger of bad news, who carries word of the Protestant military collapse in the Holy Roman Empire back to England. But the rapid development of news media, specifically the English-language corantos (letters or papers containing public news) printed in Holland for export to England and the London-printed corantos that quickly followed, saw the wholesale cooptation and commodification of Rumor's one-woman operation. Supplementing as opposed to superseding manuscript newsletters, such as those written by Joseph Mead, Milton's tutor at Christ College, Cambridge, to Sir Martin Stuteville of Dalham, Suffolk, throughout the 1620s, the circulation of foreign news in print meant that events in continental Europe reached a broader (although still elite) section of the English public. As a result, the Thirty Years' War was the first foreign war to become the object of a printed press campaign, uncoordinated and uneven and implicitly anti-Catholic, subjecting Jacobean and later Caroline foreign policy to a limited but nonetheless unprecedented level of public scrutiny.⁹

Ben Jonson's *Staple of News*, performed by the King's Men at Blackfriars and at court during February 1626, satirizes the public appetite for information about the fighting in Europe, attacking the corantos or news-sheets that turned foreign policy into the subject not of informed critical debate but of populist scaremongering, conspiracy theorizing, and errant speculation.[10] In act 3, scene 2, Pennyboy Junior, the hero of the play's prodigal plot, visits the newly established News Office where Cymbal, the Master of the Staple, obliges him with the latest from the Continent, collected and catalogued by religious faction, "Protestant" and "Pontifical," thereby replicating the confessional battle lines of the war itself.[11] The news roundup concludes closer to home, however, when Fitton, Cymbal's sidekick and a liar by name (a "fitton" is an invention or untruth),[12] eagerly retains Pennyboy's attention by not allaying his fears and floats, quite literally, the possibility of a Spanish invasion:

> But what if Spinola have a new project,
> To bring an army over in cork shoes
> And land them here at Harwich? All his horse
> Are shod with cork, and fourscore pieces of ordnance,
> Mounted upon cork carriages, with bladders
> Instead of wheels, to run the passage over
> At a spring tide.   (Jonson, *Staple*, 3.2.86–92)

Fitton's wonderfully thorough account of Spínola's preparations undercuts its own menace, fitting out the imperial troops with the cork-columned shoes or chopines worn by society ladies in Spain and Venice, and, closer to home, by stage players.[13] The prospect of an effeminized Spanish army, horse, men, and heavy artillery, perched precariously on their improvised platform shoes and advancing toward the English coast without getting their feet or ammunition wet, stretches even Pennyboy's credulity—"Is't true?" he asks, to which Fitton responds dryly, "As true as the rest" (3.2.93)—but the reference to Harwich brings the ridiculous disturbingly close to reality. Politically attuned members of Jonson's audience would have immediately recognized Fitton's disembarkation point as the likeliest landing place in the event of an actual Spanish invasion.

The previous autumn had, in fact, been taken up with preparations for just such an eventuality, beginning on September 9, 1625, when the garrison at Harwich was hastily reinforced by some 3,000 men from the Essex Trained Bands amid alarm that the planned departure of the Anglo-Dutch fleet for the Mediterranean would leave the British coast and coastal waters vulnerable to the Spanish squadron stationed in Dunkirk harbor, the so-called "Armada of Flanders." Supplementing the Spanish warships were around 60 smaller vessels or frigates, designed for commerce raiding and owned and crewed by Flemish privateers, more popularly known as "Dunkirkers." On September 18, Robert Rich, the Earl of Warwick, urged the Privy Council to send more ships to guard the Essex coastline from maritime raids, and three days later, on September 21, a warrant "to supply cannon and ammunition necessary for the fortification" of Harwich was rushed through.[14] Fears were raised still further at the end of October when gales, blowing the Spanish-bound fleet off course in the Bay of Biscay, also dispersed the Anglo-Dutch ships that had remained behind to continue the blockade of Dunkirk. Writing to the Duke of Buckingham, Charles I's favorite and Lord Admiral, on October 22, 1625, the Privy Council summed up the potential threat: "Wee doubt not but you have hearde of the great disaster happened in the late storme to some of his Majestie's shipps and manie of those of the United States [of Holland] which lay before the haven of Dunkerke, whereby the Dunkerkers who have a fleete of 22 shipps already fournished and in them 4000 soldiers, as wee are credibly informed, are now at liberty to take their coursse and prosecute their intended dessein.... wee have pregnant reasons which make us doubte that the invasion of Irelande may be aymed at."[15] Writing on October 29, Joseph Mead reports "talk yesterday of some fear of invasion about Yorkshire," and, on November 5, that "a company of Dunkirkers, they say, lie before Scarborough."[16] No landing was to materialize, but Flemish privateers continued to harry and menace the northeast coast of Britain for more than two weeks, attacking the Dutch fishing fleet off the Shetlands, destroying 150 ships, and capturing 1,400 sailors.[17]

Once the English fleet had limped home from Cadiz that winter, with no silver fleet intercepted, no shipping of note destroyed, and no naval base taken, invasion panic only continued to intensify, reaching its highest pitch during the summer of 1626.[18] For Jonson, the panic offered an opportunity for farce, a Spanish invasion that needed no armada. But for Milton, the invasion scare, and the foreign wars of which it was a part, exercised a more profound and consequential hold over his youthful imagination. Before the year was over, he had composed a miniature Latin epic combining the Gunpowder Plot of 1605, when a confederacy of English Catholics conspired to blow up the Houses of Parliament, with the invasion plot of 1625–26, when the Spanish fleet were believed to be conspiring to conquer England from the sea. Through these combined plots, "In quintum Novembris" is able to function both as a contribution to the established tradition of neo-Latin Gunpowder Plot poetry and as a meditation on the same contemporary events that animate Jonson's News Office: the hubris of Charles's maritime ambitions in the Atlantic and Mediterranean, the defensive vulnerabilities exposed by the expedition to Cadiz, and the very real terror not just of Spanish but increasingly of French reprisal and invasion.[19] Milton may well have been motivated to choose the form of the brief epic precisely because it provided him with a generic space in which to formulate his thoughts on these recent foreign policy decisions and, more generally, on the business of war in Europe.

"In quintum Novembris" unifies its two Catholic plotlines — the Gunpowder Plot of 1605 and the invasion plot of 1625–26 — by means of its representation of Satan, who appears in a dream vision to a somnolescent pope midway through the poem. In the course of the dream vision, Satan gleefully explains how blowing up the English Parliament will enable the conquest of England by an invading army from Europe:

> Iamque ad consilium extremis rex magnus ab oris
> Patricios vocat, et procerum de stirpe creatos,
> Grandaevosque patres trabea, canisque verendos;
> Hos tu membratim poteris conspergere in auras,

Atque dare in cineres, nitrati pulveris igne
Aedibus iniecto, qua convenere, sub imis.
....
Perculososque metu subito, casumque stupentes
Invadat vel Gallus atrox, vel saevus Iberus.   (116–21, 125–26)

[And now the great king is summoning patricians from the farthest territories for counsel, and those born in the lineage of the great, and aged fathers venerated for their gown and white hair; these you could spatter piecemeal into the air and turn into ashes with the fire of nitrate powder injected into the depths of the building where they convene.... Either the ferocious Gaul or the savage Iberian will invade them when they are overwhelmed with sudden fear, stunned at the event.]

Milton here proposes his addition to the original Gunpowder Plot story, introducing a satanic invasion plan as the climactic achievement of the plot's successful execution. It is perfectly possible to interpret Milton's intention here as a reassuring one, consigning a present danger to a safely negotiated past. Once housed within this historical surety, however, the threat not only persists but is permitted to escalate. "Vel Gallus atrox, vel saevus Iberus": Satan's chiastic equivalence between the two European powers might suggest disinterest in the geopolitical particulars of his proposed invasion plan were it not for the fact that in the autumn of 1626 England was perilously close to being at war with both of these nations at once.

The breakdown of the Anglo-French alliance had many contributing causes, but the loan of seven English warships to Louis XIII, who used them not against the Spanish but against the French Protestant community of La Rochelle, "woundinge our own Churche with our owne weapons," as Lord Brooke wrote to John Coke on October 12, 1625, was a principal point of contention on the English side.[20] By the time Milton was composing his Gunpowder Plot epic, the slide toward open hostilities appeared unstoppable, despite the return of the English loan ships and the steadfast refusal of Parliament to grant further supply to pay for an expeditionary naval force. The following summer, Buckingham would lead a naval offensive to break the French assault on La Rochelle and liberate the Huguenots, the ill-fated Île de Rhé campaign. Given these developments, Milton's Satan proves himself remarkably well informed about the precariousness of English foreign relations with the two most powerful Catholic nations in Europe.

Written the year after Cadiz, the year before Rhé, "In quintum Novembris" is situated, and self-consciously situates itself, in the context of a divisive polemical debate over English maritime claims at a time when the cost of maintaining a navy capable of defending English sovereignty over the Narrow Seas, still less of challenging the Spanish and French in their own or international waters, was unpopular and fast becoming prohibitive.[21] The poem opens in optimism and triumph with the union of the crowns of England and Scotland under a single monarch in 1603. But with the introduction of an airborne Satan just seven lines in, its focus shifts abruptly from celebrating the achievement of internal union to dramatizing the external forces that threaten the survival of this ancient and now reemergent British realm. Casting Satan as the instigator and flamboyant sponsor of the fighting taking place across the Continent, the poem stages a number of different, conflicting, and competing accounts of the British Isles as at once separate from and inextricably entangled with the affairs of Europe. These competing accounts are articulated through the example of three legendary founders, Aeneas, Albion, and Romulus-Quirinus, each of whom forwards a different model for conducting international relations.

Founding Figures

"In quintum Novembris" begins with a happy ending: the political union of England and Scotland under a single ruler, King James, "pius" (1), like Aeneas, and "pacificus" (5), who has bound—as Milton's syntax also binds—English dominion to the Scottish people: "and now an inviolable treaty brought the English scepter to the Caledonian Scots" (iamque inviolabile foedus / Sceptra

Caledoniis coniunxerat Anglica Scotis) (3–4).[22] No sooner established, this triumphal *telos* starts to unravel as Satan, first identified as "a wandering exile" (vagus exul) (8), and thus as a second, would-be Aeneas, takes to the air in order to survey a wartorn Europe and aggregate his future subjects in what amounts to a census of the damned. The reversion of the Continent from a state of civility to one of bloodshed is represented as Satan's particular achievement—"[He] arms unconquered peoples against one another's vitals, and overturns kingdoms that were flourishing in olive-bearing peace" (Armat et invictas in mutua viscera gentes; / Regnaque olivifera vertit florentia pace) (14–15)—and he desires to draw the newly reunited, Protestant realm of Great Britain into the same impasse of warring states, all unconquerable ("invictas") and therefore all mutually incapable of conquest.[23]

From Satan's synoptic vantage, Great Britain appears as a prelapsarian island, intact, of natural limits and beyond political dissent, being entirely cut off from the vicissitudes of a warring Europe. Milton reinforces the reader's sense of this geographically sanctioned separatism by means of his engagement with the legend of Albion, the giant son of Neptune and ancient king of England. Tracking Satan's flight, the poem approaches the Dover cliffs, the sighting of which recalls an older mythology reaching back to the island's pre-Trojan history: "And now white land with resounding cliffs appears, and territory dear to the god of the sea, to which long ago Neptune's offspring gave his name" (Iamque fluentisonis albentia rupibus arva / Apparent, et terra Deo dilecta marino, / Cui nomen dederat quondam Neptunia proles) (25–27). This tutelary fable appears to confirm a narrative of English exceptionalism, the island as divinely favored and protected. Yet when read a different way, it also sets a somewhat hazardous interventionist precedent. Unnamed within the poem, the mythic name-giver is instead identified patronymically and through the circumstances of his death: "He who after crossing the sea did not hesitate to challenge the fierce son of Amphitryon to furious war before the cruel time of Troy's destruction" (Amphitryoniaden qui non dubitavit atrocem / Aequore tranato furiali poscere bello, / Ante expugnatae crudelia saecula Troiae) (28–30). Albion, so the poem obliges us to remember, was slain in France, having crossed over the English Channel ("aequore tranato") in order to fight on behalf of his brother against Hercules, the son of Jove ("Amphitryoniaden"). A sea giant defeated on land by a land giant, the founder's final campaign establishes a cautionary precedent for English involvement with European land wars, fought by Protestant brothers-in-arms, during the 1620s.[24]

The ambiguity of Albion's example helps to explain, and may indeed motivate, the poem's flight into Elizabethan nostalgia as the predatory sea dogs Francis Drake and Walter Raleigh supply a more recent, triumphal precedent for military adventurism, waged not on land but by sea. In an important twist, however, the cultural memory of these storied triumphs is appropriated by Satan, who arrives in Rome to urge their overdue reprisal. Having flown over the Alps, Satan first alights in Rome atop the citadel of "Mars-born Quirinus" (Marvortigenae...in arce Quirini) (53), a reference to the Sabine god of war, Quirinus, whose name is subsequently adopted by the deified Romulus, the third of Milton's *conditores* or founder figures and whose introduction leads the poem in an unambiguously belligerent direction. Milton's placement is precise: Satan alights on the citadel of Quirinus because he, too, has now become a god of war like Romulus. Moreover, and also like Romulus, Satan is specifically a Roman god of war, revisiting the city so as to inaugurate a new international order, a worldwide Roman *imperium*.

In book 1 of his history of Rome, *Ab urbe condita*, Livy narrates (with suspended skepticism) the testimony of Proculus Julius, a Roman patrician who claims that the divinized Romulus-Quirinus appeared to him the night following Romulus's sudden and suspicious disappearance during a troop muster on the Campus Martius. The god's visitation has a double purpose: to confirm that Romulus's death was an apotheosis or heavenly ascent, and not a political assassination; and to deliver a divinely ordained mandate to the Roman people. In Livy's rendering of this legendary story, the mandate is reported thus: "'Go,' said he, 'and declare to the Romans the will of Heaven that my Rome shall be the capital of the world; so let them cherish the art of war, and let them know and teach their children that no human strength can resist Roman arms'" ("Abi, nuntia," inquit "Romanis, caelestes ita velle ut mea Roma caput orbis terrarum sit; proinde rem militarem colant, sciantque et ita posteris tradant nullas opes humanas armis Romanis resistere posse").[25] In his miniature epic, Milton rewrites this apparition scene to savage and satirical effect, casting Satan in the role of Romulus-Quirinus and the ambushed pope in that of Proculus Julius. To motivate his imperial mandate, Satan looks backward as well as forward, invoking the wreck of the 1588 Armada and the persecution of Catholics under Elizabeth I. But with the pope apparently unwilling to indulge this ethos of retributive resentment, Satan soon resorts to scare tactics to rouse him from his bed. Past horrors cede their priority to future ones, the sacking and occupation of Rome herself:

> Et memor Hesperiae disiectam ulciscere classem,
> Mersaque Iberorum lato vexilla profundo,
> Sanctorumque cruci tot corpora fixa probrosae,
> Thermodoontea nuper regnante puella.
> At tu si tenero mavis torpescere lecto
> Crescentesque negas hosti contundere vires,
> Tyrrhenum implebit numeroso milite Pontum,
> Signaque Aventino ponet fulgentia colle.   (QN, 102–09)

> [Remember and avenge Hesperia's shattered fleet and the banners of the Iberians sunk in the wide ocean, and the bodies of so many saints fixed to the shameful cross while the Thermodontean girl reigned of late. But if you prefer to languish in a soft bed and refuse to quell the enemy's growing strength, he will fill the Tyrrhenian Sea with a great army and plant his gleaming standards on the Aventine hill.]

Satan's resplendent English navy is little more than a warmonger's fiction, as Milton's first audience knew all too well, having lived through the folly and ineptitude of the Cadiz expedition just the previous autumn, an inauspicious anniversary to set against the longstanding one of November 5. Its exaggeration both of England's militancy and of her numerical strength would have resonated more strongly in the autumn of 1626 than at any time since when coastal counties were operating under martial law as unpaid, unfed, and plague-ridden soldiers and sailors deserted en masse, and impressment and the collection of the forced loan to pay for these military expenses continued unabated.[26] Such ongoing concerns sharpen Milton's political satire, which presents a myth of English heroism at once unsustainable and—satanically—self-perpetuating.

It is worth considering carefully, therefore, why it is at this moment, when the poem appears to come up against the responsible limits—both political and poetic—of its own epic fiction-making, that it so abruptly switches its generic allegiance. Satan concludes his speech with an appeal to polytheistic numbers; the pope can rely on the backing not only of contemporary Catholic superpowers, France and Spain, in his reconquest of England, but also of the pagan deities whose feast days Rome continues to celebrate:

> Saecula sic illic tandem Mariana redibunt,
> Tuque in belligeros iterum dominaberis Anglos.
> Et nequid timeas, divos et divasque secundas
> Accipe, quotque tuis celebrantur numina fastis.   (QN, 127–30)
>
> [So at last the Marian ages will return there, and you will again rule over the warlike English. And to keep you from being afraid, know that the gods and goddesses are favorable, all the divinities that are celebrated in your holidays.]

What Satan promises from the Gunpowder Plot is a return to the "saecula...Mariana" or "Marian ages," a compacted, threefold reference to the Roman Catholics' veneration of Mary, to the reign of Mary Tudor (1553–58), and to the seven consulships of Gaius Marius (the first in 107 BCE; the last and by far the bloodiest in 86 BCE), and, thus, a reversion to Catholic rule that is also, since Marius's rise to power anticipated the destruction of the Roman republic, a reversion to imperial tyranny.[27] It is this satanic narrative of return to a lost golden age that is guaranteed the support of the classical gods because it promises the restitution of polytheistic worship, the return of the deities of ancient paganism, to England's shores.

First fighting, and then feasting: Satan's order of priorities fits easily into the poem's enthusiastic performance of a virulent anti-Catholicism with its aggressive conflation of papal and polytheistic forms of idolatrous and sacramental worship. Earlier in the poem, Milton had likened the pope's torch-lit nocturnal procession of the Eucharist through the streets of Rome to the riot and revelry of the bacchanal: "In such a way Bromius wails, and Bromius's company, singing orgiastic songs" (Qualiter exululat Bromius, Bromiique caterva, / Orgia cantantes) (64–65).[28] But Satan goes further, anticipating an actual, as opposed to merely imitative, return to the festal rhythms of the Roman religious calendar and the reinstitution of pagan cultic worship in England. Disclosed belatedly in the final lines of his speech to the pope, but arriving no less prematurely in the middle of the poem, Satan's golden age ending will be at once stolen and canceled out by the poem's actual one, which institutes the single, national, and Protestant holiday at the expense of the multiple pagan holidays over which it triumphs. In so relocating his poem generically, Milton is able to turn first from fighting to *fasti* and then to the *fastus*, the holiday named by its title—"On the Fifth of November"—all along.

Feast Days and Canceled Fictions

Between Satan's plan to restore the pagan gods to their English sites of worship and the poem's triumphal installation of November 5 as the feast day that enacts their definitive banishment stands the prodigious body of Fama, a Virgilian survivor from the poem's first half, who brings word of the Gunpowder conspiracy to England's cities. Located at the boundary of the Christian Occident, the Miltonic House of Fame offers a pastiche of classical representations of the goddess, elaborated in an allegorical set-piece that swells to some 25 lines so as to take up more than a tenth of the poem's total length (QN, 170–94). An agent of misapprehension across literary history, the titaness Fama is now revealed to be the object of an interpretative error of the kind she had herself so often sought to promulgate. Her unbounded, exorbitant description is to be taken, the reader is told only retrospectively, as a form of paying honor, an unlikely song of praise. Turning from third-person characterization to second-person address, the poet apostrophizes the goddess: "But still you have earned praise in our song, Fame, a good thing than which nothing is more true—you are worthy to be sung by us, and there will never be cause to regret have remembered you in such a lengthy song; we English, surely saved through your offices, wandering goddess, give you your due" (Sed tamen a nostro meruisti carmine laudes / Fama, bonum quo non aliud veracius ullum, / Nobis digna carni, nec te memorasse pigebit / Carmine tam longo: servati scilicet Angli / Officiis vaga diva tuis, tibi reddimus aequa) (194–98). In these lines, which justify at length the length of the preceding *hymnos*, we learn that the traditional iconography of Fama has been nationalized to the extent that it must now be read with different assumptions within the national frame. Furthermore, Fame's rehabilitation is heralded by a poetic speaker who has himself been nationalized, entering his fiction not as his singular self but as a collective first-person persona—"in *our* song" (a nostro...carmine); "worthy to be sung *by us*" (nobis digna carni); and, lest we misunderstand the plural referent, "*we English*" (Angli) (italics mine). The poet speaks here as the representative of the nation, sacrificing his poetic autonomy by joining his voice to a national choir. Fame's transformation into an instrument of divine providence, her acceptance of subaltern status within a Christian order, thus coincides with and parallels the poet's own embrace of an undifferentiated Englishness.[29] The song-within-a-song marks the incorporation of the epic singer as surely as it does that of Fama, the unruly voice of the epic tradition.[30]

And yet, when Fama reveals the plot to the English people, first by conjecture and surmise and only then by proclamation, content still to work in the flawed ways of the Jonsonian News Office, her speech induces paralysis—a paralysis suffered universally and protracted, through the catalog of its victims, over several lines: "People were stunned at these reports, young men and girls and weak old men trembled in equal measure, and the sense of great disaster suddenly struck all ages to the heart" (stupuere relatis, / Et pariter iuvenes, pariter tremuere puellae, / Effaetique senes pariter, tantaeque ruinae / Sensus ad aetatem subito penetraverat omnen) (216–19). In what is surely a deliberate echo, Milton's choice of verb "stupeo"—to be stunned, stupefied, brought to a standstill—picks up Satan's earlier prediction that the people would be "struck senseless" (casumque stupentes) (125) by the attack on their Parliament. The intended effect of the Gunpowder Plot has already and inadvertently been realized through Fama's verbal relation. And yet the ideological and symbolic import of this popular paralysis works quite differently from Satan's original expectation. With the repeated adverb "pariter" marking equivalence (in like manner) and simultaneity (at the same time, all at once), Milton levels distinctions between genders and across generations.

Suffering from fear, the British make their nation newly visible: they are, quite literally, frozen into an inclusive and equitable, albeit nonconsensual, unity. Importantly, this is also a unity distinct from other articulations of national identity that the poem has previously delivered. For here the nation is defined neither in dynastic terms, as a sovereign realm, nor in geographical terms, as an island encircled by a protecting and protective sea. Nor is it quite yet defined in religious terms, the exceptional Protestant nation singled out and favored by God.[31] Instead, and at this moment of dramatic suspension, Milton offers a community of citizens brought together through their common, physical apprehension of an outside threat. The nation is to be located in the inert bodies, and thus in the abstracted body, of the British people.

Deprived of rational agency or the capacity for action, this disabled body politic requires God's reanimating intervention, which finally occurs just seven lines shy of the poem's ending:

> Attamen interea populi miserescit ab alto
> Aethereus pater, et crudelibus obsitit ausis
> Papicolum; capti poenas rapantur ad acres;
> At pia thura Deo, et grati solvuntur honores;
> Compita laeta focis genialibus omnia fumant;

>   Turba choros iuvenilis agit: Quintoque Novembris
>   Nulla dies toto occurrit celebratior anno.   (QN, 220–26)

[But in the meantime the heavenly father pities his people from on high, and stopped the papists' cruel venture. Captured, they are hurried off to harsh punishment; but holy incense is offered to God and grateful honors. The happy crossroads all smoke with festive bonfires; a crowd of young people leads the dance: no day in the entire year comes with more celebration than the fifth of November.]

Arguably, the most striking thing about these lines is not the speed with which the business of the Gunpowder Plot is divinely dispatched, but the time it takes for the effects of the people's paralysis to wear off. The execution of justice, devotional offering of incense and paying of homage, and the lighting of bonfires are acts recorded without the people performing them: passive constructions leave grammatical subjects unspecified ("raptantur" [222]; "solvuntur" [223]); it is the crossroads themselves, to whom human joy is attributed, that burn. And when finally the paralysis has—or is—lifted, the people remain undifferentiated, described through simultaneous, synchronous movement. The dancing youths are a collective, "turba...iuvenilis," and their "choros" is as much a rite of foundation as of victory (225), enacting in its returns—the dance was typically choreographed in a round or ring—the calendric returns of the ritual year.

"No day in the entire year comes with more celebration than the fifth of November" (Nulla dies toto occurrit celebratior anno) (226). Here in its final line and with its insistence upon a feast day of singular significance the poem enacts its final concerted movement from *fasti* to the *dies fastus*, from many feast days to one, and from rites of polytheistic to those of monotheistic worship. The satanic narrative of return, which imagined the classical gods and goddesses restored to England and, with them, the restoration of Rome's festival calendar, is here turned against itself. The Gunpowder conspiracy ends in a public scene of worship, a scene of strong Ovidian and cultic associations, as John Hale has importantly pointed out, but one that aggressively rewrites its Ovidian model: the *Libri fastorum*, or, *Fasti*, a poetic record of the etiological and calendric ordering of the Augustan festival year.[32] Put another way, we might say that the devotional template of the feast day poem has first been extrapolated and now finally dissociated from Satan's conception of missionary imperialism with its trajectory from rights of conquest to rites of worship. The result, at the level of the poem's plot, is the release of the British people from the pressures of European confessional warfare into the permanence of political ritual, substituting for the imagined army of epic fiction making the imagined community of devotional celebration, a community brought into being not by derogating the relation between geopolitics and poetics but by staging a more perfect convergence between them.[33]

Yet when no longer read in antagonistic relation to the multiple feast days of the pagan calendar (the *fasti* whose reintroduction Satan imagines himself sponsoring), there is something provocative, even flagrant, about the poem's concluding insistence on the singularity of the fifth of November as the most celebrated of all feast days. Already—and audaciously—Milton has connected the cultic supersession of the pagan gods not to the incarnation of the Son, the linked subjects of the hymn to the newborn Christ that he would write just three years later, but to the divine thwarting of the Gunpowder Plot, an event of narrowly nationalistic significance, albeit one that marks England out for special favor as an elect, and henceforward, inviolable Protestant nation. Yet even this may not fully prepare us for the poem's final declaration, as though in forwarding its liberatory fantasy of national election it is also willing to contemplate the superannuation not just of these pagan holidays, but also of those that traditionally belong to the religious cycle of the Christian year. It is, of course, the case that the Protestant devotional odes Milton was to write four years later commemorate those very holidays that the final line of "In quintum Novembris" excludes from the heights of universal celebration. And it is with this exclusion in mind that I turn now from the

Latin feast day poem to those that would follow in English, positioning the miniature epic as their precursor, although one that demanded both imitation and refutation.

The Poet's Nativity

When he gathered his verses for his 1645 collection of *Poems*, Milton would place his "Ode on the Morning of Christ's Nativity" at the head of the volume, presenting it, as Louis Martz shows, as the auspicious, inaugural work of his career, a "prologue to the rising poet's achievement."[34] In the opening stanzas of "The Passion" and "Upon the Circumcision," Milton had already alerted the reader to his powerful sense of the Nativity ode's absolute and unrivaled priority. Both these devotional odes begin by returning to that earlier occasion when Milton first joined his voice with the angelic choir, as though it were his poem, and not the momentous event of Christian history it commemorates, that supplies the occasion for what he calls in "The Passion" their "latter scenes" (22):

> Erewhile of music, and ethereal mirth,
> Wherewith the stage of air and earth did ring,
> And joyous news of Heav'nly infant's birth,
> My muse with angels did divide to sing.   ("Passion," 1–4)

> Ye flaming Powers and wingèd warriors bright,
> That erst with music, and triumphant song
> First heard by happy watchful shepherds' ear,
> So sweetly sung your joy the clouds along
> Through the soft silence of the list'ning night;
> Now mourn.   ("Circumcision," 1–6)

In each instance, temporal adverbs "Erewhile" and "erst" draw the reader back to the past moment not of Christ's birth, but of its poetic proclamation. In the opening of "The Passion," written in the same verse form as the Nativity ode, the Miltonic speaker claims for his precursor poem the status of holy song, recalling how his muse had accompanied the angelic choir in publishing the "joyous news" of the infant Jesus. In the opening of "Upon the

Circumcision," he addresses these same angelic singers, no longer among their number and now a recipient of their "sweetly sung" effusion of joy and triumph. Here the reader is explicitly recalled to the moment in the Nativity ode when the shepherds are first enraptured by the "music sweet" of the ranked angels who appear in the sky above them ("Nativity," 93). This scene, which takes place at the approach of day, "Or ere the point of dawn," is prolonged over several stanzas, drawing in other listeners, including that wakeful early riser, John Milton ("Nativity," 86). At the end of his sixth elegy, addressed to his friend Charles Diodati, Milton would declare that he wrote the Nativity ode at dawn: "These gifts indeed we have given for Christ's birthday; these the first light brought me at dawn" (Dona quidem dedimus Christi natalibus illa; / Illa sub auroram lux mihi prima tulit) ("Elegia sexta," 87–88). By invoking no achievement prior to itself, the ode is able to preserve this thrilling fiction: that the young poet, himself "a son of dawn" born on a December morning a little over 21 years before, woke early, and, with a sense of occasion uncoerced and entirely sufficient to itself, began to write.[35]

Needless to say, this poetic fantasy of a virgin birth—a fantasy in which critics have eagerly joined their voice to Milton's—exists at the farthest conceptual remove from the deliberate generic plotting of "In quintum Novembris."[36] But I think it should be possible to see how the one helped Milton to arrive at, and to experience the powerful liberation of, the other. For although it presents itself as an absolute point of origin, a beginning gloriously unsullied by false starts and prior efforts, Milton's celebrated ode has its true, formal nativity in his earlier epic poem. The surprising rhetorical turn at the ode's center borrows in its dramatic outlines the proposition and retraction of the satanic fiction forwarded in the feast-day poem he had already fashioned, at the age of 17, to commemorate the fifth of November.

Inscribing into its plot Christianity's supersession of paganism, the Nativity ode asserts the universal narrative of Christian redemption history from the birth of the Messiah to the Passion. Famously, the ode arrives at its articulation of the traditional narrative of Christian history only after it, too, has indulged an extravagant poetic fantasy that has threatened to preempt it. Midway through the poem, the heavenly music of the spheres last heard at the creation of the world joins the "angelic symphony" celebrating the birth of the Christian messiah ("Nativity," 132). The speaker is moved to express the imaginative reach of this song's redemptive power:

> For if such holy song
> Enwrap our fancy long,
>   Time will run back, and fetch the age of gold,
>   . . . .
> And Hell itself will pass away,
> And leave her dolorous mansions to the peering day.
>   . . . .
> And Heav'n as at some festival,
> Will open wide the gates of her high palace hall.
>   (133–35, 139–40, 147–48)

The closing couplets of these stanzas offer contrasting tableaus for this anticipated return to "the age of gold": the vacant, vacated "mansions" of hell abandoned to the curious sunlight; the gates of the "high palace hall" of heaven thrown open to receive the crowd of celebrants. At this culminating moment of the song's imaginative power, Milton compares the entrance of the blessed into the heavenly Jerusalem at the end of time to a "festival," the most glorious, and conclusive, of all imaginable feast days. In the pure heavenly music of this feast of feasts, we recognize the poet's youthful desire, voiced at the end of "In quintum Novembris," for a single feast day to supersede all others. Here, however, in the more mature poem of his twenty-first year, Milton replaces the single feast day of nationalist celebration with a millennial feast day that promises to perform the universal work of redeeming all of fallen humanity.

The earlier Latin Gunpowder Plot epic concludes, we remember, when Milton asserts a nationalist myth of a single feast day over the satanic fantasy of reinstated pagan festivals. But in the "Ode on the Morning of Christ's Nativity," Milton will not permit the idea of a final, culminating feast day to close the poem. Denying the earlier, fanciful desire that the holy angelic song might summon a final feast day at the end of time, Milton will insist instead on a traditional narrative of Christian history:

> But wisest Fate says no,
> This must not yet be so,
>   The babe lies yet in smiling infancy,
> That on the bitter cross
> Must redeem our loss;
>   So both himself and us to glorify.   ("Nativity," 149–54)

In its most painful and charged moment, the Nativity ode commits itself to the theologically privileged narrative of Jesus' life and death on the "bitter cross," moving from there to silence the oracles and to the flight of the pagan gods (173–236). In these moments of correction and purgation, the ode finds itself rewriting, in a different register, the triumphalist political plot of "In quintum Novembris" with its supplanting of Satan's own fantasy for fetching back a lost golden age. At the same time, however, the political plot of "In quintum Novembris" is itself supplanted, or at the least radically deferred, as the nationalist soteriology of eternal earthly reward imagined at the conclusion of the miniature epic comes to be superseded in the more properly religious devotional ode by the temporal scheme of Christian salvation history. Much as the voice of "wisest Fate" must suppress the fancy of Milton's imaginative "holy song," so the Nativity ode must itself suppress the chronological priority and festal fantasy of "In quintum Novembris." Having once detached the poetics from the politics of the feast day, Milton can with confidence assert the religious ode as the *new* first poem.

Queens College, CUNY

Notes

1. John Milton, "Elegia quarta," lines 41–44, in *The Complete Poems and Essential Prose of John Milton*, ed. William Kerrigan,

John Rumrich, and Stephen M. Fallon (New York, 2007). All quotations and English translations of Milton's poetry are taken from this edition, hereafter cited in the text by line numbers. The letter was first published in *Joannis Miltonii, Angli, Epistolarum Familiarium* (London, 1674), 7–9. It is translated—and its misdating to 1625 corrected—in *Complete Prose Works of John Milton*, 8 vols., ed. Don M. Wolfe et al. (New Haven, Conn., 1953–82), 1:311–12; hereafter cited as YP.

2. Geoffrey Parker, *The Thirty Years' War* (New York, 1984), 76–78; Peter H. Wilson, *The Thirty Years War: Europe's Tragedy* (Cambridge, Mass., 2012), 390–91. Anglo-Dutch aid had been agreed upon during negotiations at The Hague in the winter of 1624–25, although the promised subsidies, 30,000 pounds a month from England alone, were paid neither on time nor in full. After its defeat at the Battle of Lutter in August 1626, Christian's retreating army received reinforcement from British recruits under the command of Charles Morgan. Wilson estimates that some 18,700 men, mostly Scottish, but also English and Welsh, enlisted under Morgan's command in Germany between 1627 and 1629 (*The Thirty Years War*, 322).

3. Estelle Haan, "Milton's *Elegia Quarta* and Ovid: Another 'Cross-Comparison,'" *Notes and Queries* 54 (2007): 400–04. *Tristia*, 3.7.1, in *Ovid VI*, trans. Arthur Leslie Walker, rev. G. P. Goold (Cambridge, Mass., 1988).

4. Haan, "*Elegia Quarta* and Ovid," 402. The last of Milton's imperatives—"Segnes rumpe moras" (3)—recalls the end of the proem to Virgil's third *Georgic* when the Virgilian speaker defers the epic project in prospect and recalls himself to the present task: "Meanwhile, haste we to the Dryads' woodlands and untrodden glades, no easy task, Maecenas, that you have laid upon me.... arise then, break with slow delay!" (Interea Dryadum silvas saltusque sequamur / intactos, tua, Maecenas, haud mollia iussa. / ... en age, segnis / rumpe moras) (40–44). The echo is suggestive of Milton's intention to reverse the trajectories of Virgil's proem, from epic to georgic, and from foreign wars to a native landscape, in the outbound journey of his verse epistle toward the central European battlefield. See *Virgil I, Eclogues, Georgics, Aeneid 1–6*, trans. H. Rushton Fairclough, rev. G. P. Goold (Cambridge, Mass., 2000).

5. Sharon Achinstein, "Milton and King Charles," in *The Royal Image: Representations of Charles I*, ed. Thomas N. Corns, 141–61 (Cambridge, 1999), 143.

6. Achinstein, "Milton and King Charles," 146. Like Achinstein, Barbara Lewalski, *The Life of John Milton: A Critical Biography*

(Oxford, 2000), construes the allusions to the Thirty Years' War in the early Latin poems as evidence of Milton's already assimilated hostility toward Caroline foreign and religious policy, passing "oblique judgment on those unheroic English leaders—James I and Charles I—who have kept England from joining the continental Protestants in arms against Rome" (24). Forwarding a very different life narrative for the poet, Thomas Corns, "Milton Biographies for the Current Century," *Milton Quarterly* 41 (2007), 22–31, observes that "there are...surprisingly few references to the Thirty Years' War in Milton, despite it being forever in the public consciousness" (26).

7. For a discussion of the religious odes as "a group, arguably a series" of poems commemorating festivals within the Christian year, see Thomas N. Corns, "'On the Morning of Christ's Nativity,' 'Upon the Circumcision,' and 'The Passion,'" in *A Companion to Milton*, ed. Corns, 215–31 (Oxford, 2001), 216. Nicholas McDowell, "How Laudian Was the Young Milton?," in *Milton Studies*, vol. 52, ed. Laura L. Knoppers, 3–22 (Pittsburgh, 2011), discusses the odes' relation to a Laudian idiom and aesthetic.

8. David Cressy, *Bonfire and Bells: National Memory and the Protestant Calendar in Elizabethan and Stuart England* (Berkeley and Los Angeles, 1998), 141–55, discusses the Gunpowder Plot anniversary as part of a national calendar of Protestant thanksgiving.

9. For the early printed corantos and newsbooks, see Folke Dahl, *A Bibliography of English Corantos and Periodical Newspapers, 1620–1642* (London, 1952); Joad Raymond, *Pamphlets and Pamphleteering in Early Modern Britain* (Cambridge, 2003), 128–38; and Nicholas Brownlees, *The Language of Periodical News in Seventeenth Century England* (Cambridge, 2011). For the reception and readership of military news in particular, see David Randall, *Credibility in Elizabethan and Early Stuart Military News* (London, 2008). Harold Love and Ian Atherton, *Scribal Publication in Seventeenth Century England* (Oxford, 1993), 9–22, survey the manuscript circulation of news; Ian Atherton, "'This Itch Grown a Disease': Manuscript Transmission of News in the Seventeenth Century," in *News, Newspapers and Society in Early Modern England*, ed. Joad Raymond, 39–65 (London, 1999). Joseph Mead's correspondence is held in the British Library: Harleian MS 389, 390; Additional MS 4276, 4254, 4179; selections from his letters appear in *The Court and Times of Charles I*, 2 vols., ed. Thomas Birch (London, 1848). David Randall makes Mead an epitome of the gentry news network in "Joseph Mead, Novellante: News, Sociability, and Credibility in Early Modern England," *Journal of British Studies* 45 (2006): 293–312, while John Rumrich, "Mead and Milton," *Milton*

Quarterly 20 (1986): 136–41, assesses Mead's proximity to and potential influence on Milton.

10. Cogent discussions of Jonson's satirical design include D. F. McKenzie, "The Staple of News and the Late Plays," in *A Celebration of Ben Jonson*, ed. W. Blissett, J. Patrick, and R. W. Van Fossen, 83–128 (Toronto, 1973); Raymond, *Pamphlets and Pamphleteering*, 140–44; and Catherine Rockwood, "'Know Thy Side': Propaganda and Parody in Jonson's *Staple of News*," *ELH* 75 (2008): 135–49.

11. Ben Jonson, *The Staple of News*, ed. Anthony Parr (Manchester, 1986), 1.5.14–15. Subsequent references are to this edition and are cited by act, scene, and line numbers. Timothy J. Burbery, *Milton the Dramatist* (Pittsburgh, 2007), 4–14, conjectures that Milton may have attended a performance of *The Staple of News* during his suspension from Cambridge during the Lent terms of 1626, which coincided with the play's probable run at the Blackfriars Theater, within walking distance of the Milton residence on Bread Street.

12. "Fitten," v., *OED Online*, www.oed.com/view/Entry/70780 (accessed July 18, 2014).

13. "Chopin," n., *OED Online*, www.oed.com/view/Entry/32259 (accessed July 18, 2014); Jonson, *Staple of News*, 3.2.88n; cf. Hamlet's famous greeting to the boy player: "What, my young lady and mistress. By'r Lady, your ladyship is nearer heaven than when I saw you last by the altitude of a chopine" (*Ham.* 2.2.408–10). See *The Norton Shakespeare*, 2nd ed., gen. ed. Stephen Greenblatt (New York, 2008).

14. *Calendar of State Papers, Domestic Series, Of the Reign of Charles I, 1625, 1626* (*CSPD*), ed. John Bruce (London, 1858), 1:108, 119, 128.

15. *Acts of the Privy Council of England* (*APC*), 46 vols., ed. John Roch Dasent, H. C. Maxwell, and J. V. Lyle (London, 1934), 40:213. The council sent letters of similar import to the vice admiral, Sir Henry Palmer; secretary of state, Sir John Coke; lord deputy of Ireland, Henry Cary, Viscount Falkland; the deputy lieutenants of the counties of Kent and Essex; and Sir John Hipsley, lieutenant of Dover Castle.

16. Birch, *Court and Times*, 1:54, 60, 61.

17. Wilson, *Thirty Years War*, 367; R. A. Stradling, *The Armada of Flanders: Spanish Military Policy and European War, 1568–1688* (Cambridge, 1992), 43–45.

18. On June 6, 1626, the Council of War deliberated over a report "of the great preparations of the Spaniards for the invasion of England or Ireland, with 200 ships and 40,000 men" (*CSPD* 1:348). Invasion warnings are also discussed on April 5, April 17, May 16, and May 22 (*CSPD* 1:304, 313, 334, 337). On July 10 the crown issued a proclamation ordering all residents "on the Sea-Coastes, or in any

Ports or Sea-Townes" to return to them, for "if, in these times, when an Invasion is threatened, the Inhabitants...out of an apprehension of danger, should desert the Sea coastes, Ports, or Townes aforesaid...when there is most use of their abiding and commorancy there; those places would be left as prey to the enemies, and they invited to an Invasion" (*Stuart Royal Proclamations*, 2 vols., ed. James F. Larkin [Oxford, 1983], 2:100–01).

19. For Gunpowder Plot poems by Milton's contemporaries and precursors, see Estelle Haan, "Milton's *In Quintum Novembris* and the Anglo-Latin Gunpowder Epic," Part 2, *Humanistica Lovaniensia* 41 (1992): 221–95; part 2, *Humanistica Lovaniensia* 42 (1993): 368–93; J. W. Binns, *Intellectual Culture in Elizabethan and Jacobean England: The Latin Writings of the Age* (Leeds, 1990), 457n31. David Quint, *Epic and Empire: Politics and Generic Form from Virgil to Milton* (Princeton, N.J., 1993), 271–81, traces the influence of Phineas Fletcher's Gunpowder Plot poem, *Locustae*, or *The Apollyonists*—published only in 1627, but perhaps available to Milton in manuscript before that date—on Milton's poetry.

20. Brooke to Coke, Oct. 12, 1625, Melbourne Hall MSS, Bundle 46, qtd. by Thomas Cogswell, "Foreign Policy and Parliament: The Case of La Rochelle, 1625–26," *English Historical Review* 99 (1984): 252.

21. On March 21, 1626, Coke made a financial statement to the Commons that set the expense of guarding the coasts at 10,000 pounds a month; a general survey of the navy reported arrears of 70,000 pounds for wages, supplies, and victuals by the end of the year. Conrad Russell, *Parliaments and English Politics, 1621–1629* (Oxford, 1979), 270; G. E. Alymer, "Attempts at Administrative Reform, 1625–40," *English Historical Review* 72 (1957): 235.

22. For the 1603 regal union of England and Scotland, viewed, at least by its proponents, as a restoration of the British Empire founded by Brutus and subsequently partitioned among his three sons, see David Armitage, *The Ideological Origins of the British Empire* (Cambridge, 2000), 37. Milton is not consistent in his national designations through the epic. "British" and its cognates appear at lines 96 and 202; "English" and its cognates at lines 122, 128, 197, and 211. Paul Stevens, "Milton and National Identity," in *The Oxford Handbook of Milton*, ed. Nigel Smith and Nicholas McDowell, 342–63 (Oxford, 2009), 346–48, explains the inconsistency as the persistence of an "old story" of Britain, inherited from Geoffrey of Monmouth, and, more recently for Milton, from Spenser, within a newer narrative of English nationalism founded upon Reformation history.

23. Charlton T. Lewis and Charles Short, *A Latin Dictionary* (Oxford, 1879), s.v. "invictus" (1): unconquered, unsubdued, not

vanquished; hence, unconquerable, invincible. In *Paradise Lost*, Milton uses the Latin adjective's English derivation to anticipate the military stalemate of the war in heaven as God instructs Gabriel to "lead forth to battle these my sons / Invincible" (*PL* 6.46–47).

24. The beginning of Milton's *History of Britain* reprises this genealogy, appending but also dismissing an alternative feminine derivation from Albina, one of the 50 exiled daughters of Dioclesian: "these *Samotheans* under the reign of *Bardus* were subdu'd by *Albion* a Giant, Son of *Neptune*; who call'd the Iland after his own Name, and rul'd it 44 Years. Till at length passing over into *Gaul*, in aid of his brother *Lestrygon*, against whom *Hercules* was hasting out of *Spain* into *Italy*, he was there slain in fight, and *Bergion* also his Brother" (YP 5:6).

25. See *Ab urbe condita* 1.16.1–8, in *Livy I*, trans. B. O. Foster (Cambridge, Mass., 1939). The competing stories of Romulus's removal from earth (by assassination or by apotheosis) and his posthumous appearance to Proculus Julius are told also by Cicero, *De re publica*, 2.10.20, in *On the Republic, On the Laws*, trans. Clinton W. Keyes (Cambridge, Mass., 1928); by Ovid, *Fasti*, 2.475–532, in *Ovid's Fasti*, trans. James George Fraser (Cambridge, Mass., 1967); and by Plutarch, *Life of Romulus*, 28, in *Plutarch's Lives*, 11 vols., trans. Bernadotte Perrin (Cambridge, Mass., 1967). Alexander Pope refers to the legend in *The Rape of the Lock* as the narrator solemnly confirms the heavenly ascent of Belinda's lock of hair: "But trust the Muse—she saw it upward rise, / Tho' mark'd by none but quick Poetic Eyes: / (So *Rome's* great Founder to the Heav'ns withdrew, / To *Proculus* alone confess'd in view)"; see Alexander Pope, *The Rape of the Lock*, 5.123–26, in *The Poems of Alexander Pope*, vol. 2, *The Rape of the Lock and Other Poems*, ed. Geoffrey Tillotston (London, 1962).

26. *APC*, 41:101, 221, 365; Lindsay Boynton, "Martial Law and the Petition of Right," *English Historical Review* 79 (1964): 261; Michael Oppenheim, "The Royal Navy under Charles I," *English Historical Review* 8 (1893): 486; Stradling, *The Armada of Flanders*, 59; Kevin Sharpe, *The Personal Rule of Charles I* (New Haven, Conn., 1992), 15–23; *Stuart Royal Proclamations*, 2:95–96.

27. Plutarch, *Life of Marius*, 29–30, 43–46, in *Plutarch's Lives*, trans. Bernadotte Perrin, 11 vols. (Cambridge, Mass., 1967)). For the consuls of Sulla and Marius as marking the end of republican freedoms, see also Machiavelli, *Discourses on Livy*, trans. Harvey C. Mansfield and Nathan Tarcov (Chicago, 1998), 1.5, 1.17, 1.28, 1.37.

28. Stella Revard discusses this comparison at greater length in *Milton and the Tangles of Neaera's Hair: The Making of the 1645 Poems* (Columbia, Mo., 1997), 86.

29. Traveling to Geneva in 1639, Milton signs his name "Joannes Miltonius, Anglus." On the title pages of the Latin defenses (1651, 1654) Milton would again identify himself as "Angl[us]," speaking as an Englishman and on behalf of the English people. These marks of national identification are variously discussed by David Loewenstein and Paul Stevens, by Thomas Corns, and by John Kerrigan in their contributions to the important collection of essays, *Early Modern Nationalism and Milton's England*, ed. Loewenstein and Stevens (Toronto, 2008), 3, 214, 242n27. But whether proud or practical, sincere or strategic, they are different in kind and not just by occasion from the plural form "Angli" deployed here.

30. Philip Hardie, *Rumor and Renown: Representations of "Fama" in Western Literature* (Cambridge, 2012), 429–38, locates this episode within a tradition of Christian conversions or revaluations of Fama in Renaissance neoclassical epic.

31. These various articulations of Milton's nationalist imagination are discussed by Loewenstein and Stevens, "Introduction: Milton's Nationalism: Challenges and Questions," in *Early Modern Nationalism*, 3–24.

32. John Hale, *Milton's Cambridge Latin: Performing in the Genres, 1625–1632* (Tempe, Ariz., 2005), 163–84, proposes a precise allusion to Ovid's *Fasti* in the poem's penultimate couplet, which reproduces elements from the first half of Romulus-Quirinus's injunction to Proculus Julius: "bid the pious throng bring incense and propitiate the new Quirinus" (tura ferant placentque novum pia turba Quirinum) (2.507). Writes Hale: "we might even press the parallel, past sound to theme again, and urge that the sounds applied here to Rome's deified founder are transformed into the idea of the event, November 5, as foundational, constitutive for redeemed England" (181).

33. Here I paraphrase the phrase and concept "imagined community" from Benedict Anderson's landmark study, *Imagined Communities: Reflections on the Origins and Spread of Nationalism* (London, 1983).

34. Louis Martz, *Milton: Poet of Exile*, 2nd ed. (New Haven, Conn., 1986), 51.

35. The epithet, "son of dawn," is William Kerrigan's, *The Sacred Complex: The Psychogenesis of "Paradise Lost"* (Cambridge, Mass., 1983), 10.

36. Gordon Teskey begins "Milton's Early English Poems: The Nativity Ode, 'L'Allegro,' 'Il Penseroso,'" in Smith and McDowell, *Oxford Handbook*, by imaginatively invoking this scene of the waiting, wakeful Milton, poised to write "his first work of genius" (66–67).

"On the New Forcers of Conscience" and Milton's Erastianism

Michael Komorowski

In May 1659, John Milton received a letter from his friend Moses Wall, who wrote that he had read and approved of Milton's latest pamphlet, *A Treatise of Civil Power in Ecclesiastical Causes*. But, Wall confessed, he initially worried that Milton had grown too close to the Protectorate, whose increasing authoritarianism had left erstwhile supporters to seek redress in political or military reform or in the assurance that God's final judgment was near. As for himself, Wall took solace in a millenarian confidence. He thoroughly approved of Milton's support for toleration in the pamphlet, but, he writes, "I was uncerten whether yor Relation to the [Protectorate] Court, (though I think a Commonwealth was more friendly to you than a Court) had not clouded yor former Light."[1] Even coming from a friend and even with Wall's assurance that *Of Civil Power* allayed his anxieties about Milton's loyalties, the charge that Milton had sold out his republican ideals for the life of a courtier must have stung badly. Milton's vigorous call in *Of Civil Power* for the separation of church and state as the only means to guarantee religious liberty certainly left no doubts about his credentials as a tolerationist and, in particular, a foe of the Cromwellian state's Erastian control of the church.² But as a recent spate of scholarly work on seventeenth century toleration emphasizes, toleration was more of a strategy for control than a principle.³ Even if liberty of conscience were indeed one of Milton's most cherished principles, its implementation would be subject to the messy process of political compromise and historical contingency. Despite Wall's earnest desire, *Of Civil Power* is a product of its historical moment and not necessarily a reaffirmation of any long-gestating principles of toleration.⁴

Fifteen years earlier, the terrain between church and state looked rather different. By early 1644, big questions had emerged having to do with the transition from an episcopal to a presbyterian church government. Presbyterians in the Westminster Assembly and city divines struggled with Parliament over the next two years to reach a workable solution. For the Presbyterian majority in the Assembly, led by four vocal Scottish commissioners, only a church government separate from the state with the blanket authority to punish sinners and exclude scandalous persons from the sacrament could carry out its godly mission. Parliament expressed trepidation over granting the church power to punish unspecified offenses. At numerous junctures, Parliament demanded a list of offenses that would preclude an individual from receiving the sacrament and proposed various measures to dilute the ministers' power by adding elders and Parliament's own appointees to church government. The Assembly, sometimes aided by London ministers, resisted until a compromise was reached in June 1646 that fixed the Erastian character of church-state relations. In the end, Parliament largely got its way, but not without sparking highly combustible confrontations in print and pulpit.⁵ Milton's famously acerbic view of the Presbyterian position in the controversy, that *"new Presbyter* is but *Old Priest* writ Large," has been read as an attack on hypocritical divines and an endorsement of religious liberty.⁶

It is tempting to read "On the New Forcers of Conscience under the Long Parliament" as an intellectual germ of *Of Civil Power*, as Arthur Barker did more than 70 years ago, or as simply a characteristic Miltonic call for liberty of conscience.⁷ But the poem represents a different project for Milton, and one that has less to do with freedom of conscience as such, however important that may be for Milton, and much more to do with an emerging poetics. The poem exudes a strange hybrid quality, fusing youthful and petulant outrage at indignity with a more mature anxiety about the relationship of poetic utterance to historical event. It is a product of the mid-1640s, when Milton had just published or was just about to publish his very accomplished juvenilia in a handsome, slightly royalist-looking volume and was casting about for a suitable subject for the great English epic he knew he would someday write.

This essay has two aims. First, I would like to offer a new hypothesis regarding the date of the sonnet's composition, and I would like to show that, in the mid-1640s, Milton was sympathetic for both intellectual and practical reasons with the Erastian position that the state ought to hold ultimate authority over the church. Although the increasingly important issue of liberty for dissenting consciences lurked behind the struggles between the Westminster Assembly and Parliament, there was never a clear link between Erastian and pro-tolerationist sympathies. Second, I argue that Milton turned to the sonnet as a discursive form that was uniquely suited for satirizing the Presbyterians in the Assembly and, at the same time, for voicing his unease about the high-handed role he knew Parliament would have to play. Milton's sympathy with the Erastians, and the expression of that sympathy in this sonnet, carried some important implications for his poetics post-1645. In squeezing politics into the not very congenial form of the sonnet, Milton stumbled upon a poetic voice that could represent political energy, if not political ideals, that he used in subsequent political sonnets. In the case of his Erastianism, Milton needed considerable latitude to express his sympathies with this position since it required entrusting Parliament with supreme power over the church while denying that power to Presbyterian ministers because of their tyrannical aims. Poetry gave Milton the freedom that no pamphlet could to voice simultaneous support for and anxiety about the sweeping power with which he would invest the state.

The poetic form those feelings took was novel: Milton chose an ungainly and rare Italian model for "New Forcers." Almost the sole example in English, the *sonetto caudato*, or tailed sonnet, continues past the sestet with two pointed tercets. As with Milton's Dalila, the sting is saved until the end. This sonnet follows in the tradition of Florentine poets Burchiello and Francesco Berni, whose *sonetti caudati* often featured biting invectives against women or the papacy.[8] Milton's generic innovation is to adopt the rarer two-tailed form (Berni's have just one) and to use the tails more explicitly to complicate the satire of the 14-line sonnet proper. In "New Forcers," the tails arrive at what is, in effect, the *volta* of the sonnet. What this formal experimentation allows Milton is clear: he is able to show his anger spilling over the confines of the 14-line container in a visually striking manner. It is less clear that he improves the sonnet by doing so. He is, however, able to probe the state as a category of thought and to show some of the ways that state and church authority penetrate individual subjectivity. The political sonnet becomes for Milton the space not so much for advocating this or that position, but instead for articulating the conflicts and compromises inherent in political activism. The most intellectually productive of those conflicts for Milton occurs at the juncture between politics and poetics. Milton explores the limits of poetry as a rhetorical mode for engaging with contemporary historical drama. Rather than stifle his poetic creativity, this process forces Milton to think about poetry as humanly inspired and to create a hero out of the present, and potentially deeply flawed, Parliament. The poet becomes the contemporary of the actors he describes and participates in both the action of the poem and the act of creation.[9]

Dating the Sonnet

It has been assumed, following David Masson's magisterial Victorian biography, that Milton wrote "New Forcers" in 1646.[10] Masson assigned the poem to the first half of that year on the grounds that the topical references to "shallow *Edwards*" and "Scotch what d' ye call" demonstrate Milton lashing out at critics of his recent divorce tracts. Thomas Edwards had numbered Milton among the ungodly in his sprawling heresiography, *Gangraena*, the first part of which appeared in January 1646.[11] Robert Baillie, who Masson believes to be the "Scotch what d' ye call" of the poem, had been slightly more circumspect in charging Milton with Independency, but had condemned his divorce pamphlets in uncompromising terms.[12] These Presbyterians' attacks provoked Milton to pen a somewhat jejune retort, in Masson's opinion, but one that was entirely defensible given the circumstances:

> Because you have thrown off your Prelate Lord,
>   And with stiff Vowes renounc'd his Liturgie
>   To seise the widdow'd whore Pluralitie
> From them whose sin ye envi'd, not abhorr'd,
> Dare ye for this adjure the Civill Sword
>   To force our Consciences that Christ set free,
>   And ride us with a classic Hierarchy
> Taught ye by mere *A. S.* and *Rotherford?*
> Men whose Life, Learning, Faith and pure intent
>   Would have been held in high esteem with *Paul*
>   Must now be nam'd and printed Hereticks
> By shallow *Edwards* and Scotch what d' ye call:
>   But we do hope to find out all your tricks,
>   Your plots and packings wors than those of *Trent*,
>   That so the Parliament
>   May with their wholesom and preventive Shears
>   Clip your Phylacteries, though bauk your Ears,
>   And succour our just Fears
>   When they shall read this clearly in your charge
>   *New Presbyter* is but *Old Priest* writ Large.
>   ("New Forcers," 1–20)

Later scholars have largely accepted Masson's hypothesis, while adding subtlety to his interpretation of the poem. Milton's major recent biographers have favored a date shortly after Edwards published the first part of *Gangraena*.[13] John Shawcross dated the sonnet to the early months of 1647 by using manuscript evidence and by interpreting topical references.[14] The editors of the variorum edition of Milton's short poems found Shawcross's claims to be too speculative, preferring to date the poem to 1646.[15] More recent editors of Milton's short poems concur, also assigning the poem to 1646.[16]

These dating schemes, however, present a couple of problems. For one, they rely on identifying Edwards's *Gangraena* as the impetus for Milton's poem and on a sharply drawn Presbyterian-Independent dichotomy that Edwards created with *Gangraena* as much as he observed it.[17] For another, they read some of the poem's allusions to contemporary events too narrowly. Milton's reference to the "classic Hierarchy" ("New Forcers," 7), for instance, need not necessarily point to the parliamentary ordinance "For Ordination of Ministers by the Classical Presbyters within their respective bounds" of August 28, 1646. Classes, groups of several parishes following the Scottish model for church governance and the Assembly's preferred administrative unit for the church, had been extensively debated before a proposal was submitted to the Houses in July 1645.[18] As for the insult directed at Edwards, it seems to refer to his *Antapologia* (1644) more than to *Gangraena*, since it was in that former work that Edwards first branded as heretics the "men whose Life, Learning, Faith and pure intent / Would have been held in high esteem with *Paul*" (9–10).[19] These men were almost certainly the five ministers who anonymously published *An Apologeticall Narration* (December 1643 or January 1644), promoting what they called "a *middle way*" of congregational government, "betwixt that which is falsly charged on us, *Brownisme*; and that which is the contention of these times, the *authoritative Presbyteriall Government*."[20] Taking refuge from Laudian persecution, they had led a peripatetic existence in and around the United Provinces before returning to England with the outbreak of civil war. Like Saint Paul, they leveraged the self-denial their exile required as proof that they were indeed servants of Christ. For Edwards, their exile was nothing of the sort, and he savagely attacked them for having fled to places like Hamburg and

Rotterdam, where they ministered to merchants and their monied interests.[21]

It seems likelier that Milton composed his sonnet at a date closer to these attacks. A better estimate of the poem's date would place its composition sometime in the first half of 1645 with a further revision in the closing months of that year. Two references in the sonnet suggest this chronology. First, the somewhat cryptic reference to "*A. S.*" ("New Forcers," 8) has long been assumed to refer to Adam Steuart (also Stewart or Stuart).[22] Steuart had published a number of pamphlets championing the Presbyterian position in 1644, but by the end of that year was in Leiden to take up the chair in philosophy and physics at the university.[23] The last book of his printed in England, *Zerubbabel to Sanballat and Tobiah*, was published by his son David after he had gone to Leiden. The title page of that work bears a date of March 17, 1644/45. Steuart was out of London and out of the public eye after this time.

Second, Milton's revision of line 17 suggests that he may have returned to the poem in late 1645 to correct an outdated and perhaps hastily conceived invective. The canceled version of line 17 in the Trinity manuscript reads, "Cropp ye as close as marginall P—s eares," and refers to the celebrated case of William Prynne and his fellow antiepiscopacy martyrs who had lost their ears (or in Prynne's grisly case, the rest of his ears) in 1637 after attacking Archbishop William Laud and his ecclesiastical hierarchy.[24] Milton retained only the slenderest likeness of the gruesome image by rewriting the line with much less vitriol: "Clip your Phylacteries, though bauk your Ears." It is doubtful that tact played any role here. Milton displays no reservations about naming names elsewhere in the poem. The idiosyncratic Prynne, however, proved a more complex target than the easily caricatured Scottish commissioners. His graphomania and irascibility produced a constant stream of books and with them shifting coalitions of allies and enemies. In 1643, Prynne had published a massive defense of *The Soveraigne Power of Parliaments and Kingdomes*, and he spent much of the rest of the civil war years defending his positions against a multitude of perceived enemies. In the fall of 1644, Prynne wondered how Independents could exempt themselves from secular and ecclesiastical authority by claiming freedom of conscience: "what an *Anarchy* and *Ataxy* this will suddenly introduce, to turn all Kingdomes, Republikes, Nations, Corporations, Churches, Families, and *the World it self, quite upside down,* and ruine them by schisms."[25] In a work published on or near January 2, 1645, Prynne again attacked the "nakednesse, Errors, Over-sights" of Independency.[26] It was for Parliament, not Independent ministers, to reform the church, he proclaimed. Nine months later, though, he had shifted his focus to battle the newest threat to parliamentary authority, attacking the "covetousnesse" of Presbyterian ministers and the ungrounded denunciations of his writings by the Scottish commissioners, particularly George Gillespie.[27] Prynne left little doubt that the Scottish Presbyterians in the Assembly had failed to deliver on their promise to restore orthodoxy to the church.[28] They now posed the real threat to ecclesiastical reform. Baillie anticipated the attack, grousing to his cousin a month earlier that progress in the Assembly was slow since "Mr. Prin and the Erastian lawyers are now our *remora.*"[29]

By October 1645, then, Milton could have sympathized with Prynne's Erastian conviction and his view of the Presbyterian fundamentalists as unyielding obstacles to a church settlement, even while loathing Prynne's pursuit of religious orthodoxy. Prynne simply no longer fit with the company that Milton had named in the preceding lines. Milton accordingly needed to revise the line, and as he did so, he changed its sense dramatically. Parliament will cut the Presbyterians down to size metaphorically, and "bauk" their ears, that is, spare them the literal punishment inflicted on Prynne. With this gesture of magnanimity, though, Milton belittles his adversaries with a pun on "box your ears," implying that they are little more than unruly boys about to receive the schoolmaster's punishment. This implicit call to Parliament to act with fitting restraint signals a change in tone at the end of the poem, and one that would have been appropriate if Milton meant to modulate from his attacks on Presbyterians to a plea for Parliament to act.

This tactical revision may supply another reason to conclude that Milton likely wrote the sonnet in 1645 rather than in 1646. Throughout the poem, the referent of the second person pronouns "ye" and "you" oscillates between the Assembly divines and Parliament. Although it seems that Milton means in the first instance those members of the Westminster Assembly who were sympathetic to the Scottish Presbyterians (as when he refers to plurality, a "sin ye envi'd, not abhorr'd," and continues with the rhetorical question, "Dare ye for this adjure the Civill Sword"?), there is considerable slippage throughout the poem. Milton also glances at Parliament, as in the opening lines, which seem to refer to Parliament's acts of 1643 that abolished episcopacy and convened the Westminster Assembly, as well as to Parliament's abolition of the Book of Common Prayer in 1645. The final lines of the poem, which in an earlier version read, "When you shall read this cleerly in your charge / New Presbyter is but old Priest writt at large," also conflate the members of the Westminster Assembly with members of Parliament. In revising the poem, Milton replaced "you" with "they," making it clearer that Parliament will understand that the pro-Presbyterian members of the Assembly intend to resurrect Laud's odious church government under another name. This ambiguity is revealing. Milton not only castigates those sympathetic to Scotch Presbyterianism in the Assembly, but also boldly calls on Parliament to crush those who challenge its own preeminence. The Assembly has no authority to use "the Civill Sword," but Parliament does. By charging Parliament with the task of interpreting the Assembly's rhetorical shenanigans—"you shall read this"—Milton implies that it has not yet demonstrated that it can read critically. Parliament cannot yet excavate the buried etymology of "priest" in the postclassical Latin word "presbyter."

It would have been odd, then, for Milton to have written the poem any time after the spring of 1646, when Parliament acted much as he had hoped. Under pressure from London ministers, the Assembly petitioned Parliament on March 23, 1646 against the imposition of lay commissioners in church government. Given that the these ministers had seen their own petition asking for the same thing summarily rejected by the Lords less than two weeks earlier, this new appeal was asking a lot. The Assembly then took the audacious step of publishing the petition, much to Parliament's vexation. On April 11, the Commons "did vote the manner of the petition to be a breach of privilege, because [the Assembly] being only called to advise did undertake to prescribe them what they ought to do," according to Parliamentarian officer and Erastian Thomas Juxon.[30] Although it "bore the title of a petition," the House of Commons, in the words of MP Sir John Evelyn, "did observe many things in it hardly consistent with the nature of that title," and dispatched a delegation to scold the Assembly.[31] Nor was that all. By the following week, the Commons had promulgated a declaration reasserting parliamentary supremacy over any church and affirming its commitment to a limited toleration of Independents. Meanwhile, Parliament had split the opposition by reconciling with the London ministers. A thanksgiving service had been held on April 2. The Scottish Presbyterians had been outflanked, and Baillie was left stupefied at what he supposed to be the cowardice of the city divines: "by a few fair words from the Houses, they were made all alse mute as fisch."[32]

Matters had reached a climax and denouement in April 1646 with Parliament's assertion of its supremacy and reconciliation with the city. Tension had been building for months, and everyone could see that the intertwined issues of church government and religious liberty would need to be settled. By June, Presbyterians had managed to claw back some concessions from Parliament primarily due to the strong showing of the Scots army against the king in May. But even with a modified Presbyterian system in place, Parliament reserved final authority in matters of church government and kept the Erastian character of the established church. This apparent victory for Parliament does not definitively exclude the possibility that Milton composed the sonnet in 1646, but the future tense of many of the lines would sit somewhat awkwardly with the circumstances of that year. It seems much more likely that the sonnet was Milton's response to the breakdown among Assembly divines in 1644 on the central issue of church government. Milton draws the battle lines sharply in his poem, but the parties are not Presbyterians and Independents, as they would be for Edwards in 1646, but rather Scottish Presbyterians and their sympathizers on one side and Erastians on the other. The central issue of the poem is the proper scope of state authority, not liberty of conscience, as many have claimed. Erastianism appeals to Milton as the only viable means of safeguarding individual conscience, and he accordingly depicts the struggle as a question for Parliament to resolve. His outline in the poem's codas of the salutary actions that Parliament will take shifts the focus from identifying hypocritical divines to elevating state authority as the final guardian of free conscience. In doing so, Milton makes the state a dynamic character in his poem, forcing him to reappraise the relationship of politics and his poetic expression.

The Invention of the Political Sonnet and Milton's Erastianism

Reading this sonnet as a product of the tension between Parliament and the Assembly in 1644–45 leads to some important implications for Milton's developing conception of state authority. It matters that the poem was likely written in 1645, before Edwards's *Gangraena,* because it shows Milton in the process of dividing the Presbyterian vision from alternative models of church government. He is thinking through the categories of "Presbyterian" and "Independent," not adopting them wholesale from the likes of Edwards. (It is surely significant that the rhetorical structure of so many of the poem's lines groups two individuals or terms with the conjunction "and.") But ultimately, these are not the categories that interest Milton the most. His engagement with the battle lines that were hardening on the confessional map and even with the advocacy of religious liberty as such takes a subordinate position in this sonnet to working out the proper roles of church and state. Here, Milton comes down strongly on the Erastian side. Competing and mutually exclusive claims for state and ecclesiastical authority were at stake in 1645. Though on matters of church governance Milton's heart may have been with the Independents, only the Erastians had enough political clout to leverage the institutions of state in a manner that would protect freedom of conscience. In this landscape, even someone as distasteful to Milton as the hot-tempered Prynne is on the right side of the argument.

Milton's sympathies with the Erastian position become somewhat clearer in the face of the Presbyterian offensive. Edinburgh minister George Gillespie, one of the ablest defenders of Presbyterian church government and foe of religious liberty, took the parallel between religious and civil power to a logical extreme in order to illustrate his case: "If *Liberty of conscience* ought to be granted in matters of Religion, it ought also to be granted in matters Civil and Military. But *Liberty of Conscience* ought not to be granted in matters Civil or Military, as is acknowledged: Therefore neither ought it to be granted in matters of Religion."[33] City divines repeated this call in fast sermons before Parliament. James Nalton, rector of St. Leonard's in Foster Lane, delivered a sober homily before the Commons in which he warned those "that are zealous for vindicating *Civill Liberties*" not to "shrinke and start, and withdraw the shoulder, as being afraid of a Reformation that will be too strict" when it came to church government.[34] For Milton, these arguments fundamentally misunderstood the place of Christian liberty in a free commonwealth. Even if citizens' obedience to the government could be demanded unreservedly (not a point Milton was willing to grant), it does not follow that their consciences could be compelled by an established church. Civil and religious government aimed at different ends: "The Magistrat hath only to deale with the outward part" of humans (YP 1:835), Milton had argued earlier in the decade, while the "other office of preserving in healthful constitution the innerman...[God had granted] to his spiritual deputy the minister of each Congregation" (YP 1:837). Where Gillespie, Nalton, and their sympathizers feared a secularizing impulse behind the push to subordinate the church to Parliament, Milton saw the only viable path for safeguarding individual conscience.

In the sonnet, the lines that most clearly express this sentiment arrive at the beginning of the second quatrain and form a rhetorical question: "Dare ye for this adjure the Civill Sword / To force our Consciences that Christ set free?" ("New Forcers," 5–6). Most editors gloss "adjure" to mean "entreat," thereby suggesting that these lines be read as an endorsement of freedom of conscience *tout court*, since Milton is clearly offended that the Presbyterians in the Assembly would have the audacity to order Parliament to persecute dissenters. The poem, then, can be read as a cry against the Erastian meddling of the state in the church. This verb may be taken more literally, though, since Milton often deployed uncommon Latin terms in their etymological senses.[35] The Presbyterians have drawn close parallels between civil and religious power and are in danger of pledging their loyalties to the methods of civil government rather than to their priestly ministry. They have effectively sworn oaths to (*ad* + *iuro*) the use of violence that is necessary to enforce secular power. The Assembly divines wanted Parliament to grant them leave to erect the form of church government that they believed to be godly and the right to punish all who dissented. The Presbyterian ministers have sought power that does not rightfully belong to them, and only Parliament can halt this dangerous arrogation of authority.

Milton needs to be more clearly identified as an Erastian in the middle years of the 1640s, and probably a moderately enthusiastic one, who saw the position as something more than a simple *mariage de convenance*. Despite his suspicion of the state's power to coerce, Milton perceived that Parliament was the only body with the authority to establish and regulate church government. As all sides in this battle understood, the question of church government entangled participants in the vexed issue of toleration. Erastians were not united on this score, and indeed the label encompassed a motley assemblage of individuals from the erudite and brusque John Selden to the eccentric Prynne. Some were Presbyterian; others leaned toward the Independents, and they accordingly espoused different visions for what the church ought to look like and whether toleration had any place. Many were lawyer MPs, such as Prynne, Selden, Simonds D'Ewes, and Bulstrode Whitelocke. They agreed that Scripture established the civil magistrate as a religious authority but split on the increasingly crucial issue of toleration. Prynne and D'Ewes were against; Whitelocke and Selden for. There is no reason why Milton, traditionally regarded as a party of one on issues of religious freedom, could not have numbered himself among this diverse company.[36]

In the Assembly, the principal Erastians were John Lightfoot, an accomplished Hebraist, and Thomas Coleman, rector of St. Peter Cornhill in London. Both expressed reservations about Independency, but when Coleman preached a fast sermon before the Commons on July 30, 1645, laying out the case for a limited sphere of ecclesiastical government, he deeply offended his Presbyterian brethren. "A Christian Magistrate, as a Christian Magistrate, is a Governour in the Church," Coleman asserted, because "Christ hath placed Governments in his Church, 1 *Cor.* 12.28. Of other Governments, besides Magistracie, I find no institution, of them I doe, *Rom.* 13.1, 2."[37] Although he was careful to articulate his case as tactfully as he could, Coleman was clear that he could find no basis *iure divino* for the Presbyterian form of church government favored by the Scottish commissioners.

Baillie knew that Coleman's sermon had fallen on receptive ears: "The most part of the House of Commons, especiallie the lawyers, whereof they are many, and divers of them very able men, are either half or whole Erastians." He put a sharper point on the argument than Coleman had been willing to in his sermon: it was a call "exhorting them to keep all the Church-government in their own hand, and to give churchmen none of it."[38] But it was Baillie's colleague Gillespie who produced the most effective response. In his sermon before the Lords four weeks later, he bluntly summarized the position he opposed: "Mens Consciences may be compelled for the good of the State, but not for the glory of God. We must not suffer the State to sink; but if Religion sink, we cannot help it. This is the plain English of it."[39] Gillespie went on to publish three pamphlets against Coleman and the Erastian position between August and the following January and to write a compendium of these arguments by the following August.[40]

It may, indeed, have been Gillespie at whom Milton directed his dismissive epithet, "Scotch what d' ye call" ("New Forcers," 12). Following Masson, most commentators have assumed that Milton meant Baillie, but the phrase would seem to imply either the bearer of an outlandish surname or someone very obscure. Baillie fit neither category. As the most prominent of the Scottish Presbyterians in London, with the possible exception of Samuel Rutherford, already mentioned in the poem, Baillie furnished a highly visible target for his enemies. Gillespie, too, was prominent, but Milton had already mocked his surname in one of his sonnets on *Tetrachordon* (a name "harder Sirs then.../...Galasp?") and may be doing so again here. Another candidate may be Alexander Forbes, identified by Thomason as the author of a hostile response to *An Apologeticall Narration*, and about whom nothing else is known.[41] At any rate, Milton blots this individual's name from the record, as he later seems to call upon Parliament to do.

It may have particularly irked Milton that the Independent ministers had been "nam'd and printed Hereticks" ("New Forcers," 11). The solution, in what are the most strongly Erastian lines of the poem, will require that Parliament "with their wholesom and preventive Shears / Clip [their] Phylacteries" (16–17). This term from Matthew 23:5 for the small boxes containing a scroll inscribed with the Mosaic law and worn by Jews during morning prayer recalls Jesus' denunciation of the scribes and Pharisees.[42] The word had been used by the Presbyterian ministers writing under the corporate name Smectymnuus to refer to those who justified episcopal hierarchy based on the spurious postscripts to 2 Timothy and Titus, which named the addressees of these letters as bishops. According to Smectymnuus, "our Episcopall men of late in newer impressions [of the Bible] have inlarged their Phylacteries" by having the postscripts printed with the same size type as the rest of the epistles, "that the simple might beleeve they are Canonicall Scripture."[43] The enemies of Independency have denounced its ministers not only from the pulpit, Milton suggests in his sonnet, but also in printed books that have enlarged their authority and, by doing so, copied the tactics of the prelates they once opposed. Milton may be thinking back to the Smectymnuus controversy in the final line of the poem as he inveighs against the Presbyterians' outsized claims for authority. They are the new Laudians literally "writ Large" whose arrogation of power rests on foundations as weak as the typographical hijinks of earlier generations of bishops. Now is the time for Parliament to strip away their pretensions to authority and reassert itself as the final arbiter of church government.

Milton's argument for protecting free conscience requires that Parliament rule supreme in matters of both state and religion. His call for parliamentary suppression of religious ministry is a radical step and one that demonstrates just how desperate the situation had become by the mid-1640s. For the sake of freedom of conscience, Milton is willing to deny opponents of religious liberty the means of institutionalizing their beliefs, a position to which he will return at moments of crisis throughout his life.[44] By exhorting Parliament to shear off the "Phylacteries" of his opponents, Milton proposes a bold solution to the problem he had identified in *Areopagitica* of "our inquisiturient Bishops, and the attendant minorities their Chaplains," who had imitated the worst practices of the Inquisition in censoring the English press (YP 2:507). He had fingered the vocal Presbyterians in the Assembly as the new Laudians, "who but of late were little better then silenc't from preaching, shall come now to silence us from reading, except what they please, it cannot be guest what is intended by som but a second tyranny over learning" (YP 2:539). Anticipating the final line of "New Forcers," Milton concludes in *Areopagitica* that the Presbyterians' actions "will soon put it out of controversie that Bishops and Presbyters are the same to us both name and thing" (ibid.). Milton had, of course, defended Smectymnuus and Presbyterians in 1641–42, but even in *Of Reformation* (1641) and especially in *The Reason of Church-Government* (1642), Milton's anti-Constantinian argument against episcopal power leaves far more room for individual and congregational authority than most Presbyterians were comfortable granting. After two years of the Westminster Assembly, Milton's Erastianism does not necessarily demonstrate his greater faith in what civil government could accomplish, but rather his conviction about what it had to do. Erastianism is the most viable option along the political spectrum that Milton sees in 1645 rather than a fully elaborated theoretical principle.

For this reason, his strong call to Parliament cannot overcome his trepidation that it might not be up to the task of putting the Presbyterians in their place. That anxiety is first reflected in the striking rhyme of "Trent" ("New Forcers," 14) with "Parliament" (15) that occupies the charged space between the sonnet proper and the coda. By carrying the rhyme across the line- and genre-break, Milton adds a second *volta* to the poem (following closely on the heels of "But" in line 13) and powerfully signals that the poetic speaker is moving from attack to proposed solution. And yet the juxtaposition of the Council of Trent, origin of the Counter-Reformation, with the contemporary Long Parliament is odd. By linking the words with a rhyme, Milton appreciates the disturbing irony of his position. Granting Parliament the power to punish hardliners does entail risks, most obviously that Parliament itself will direct its persecutory zeal against the Presbyterians.

Milton's knowledge of the Council of Trent, like any English Protestant's, would have come from Paolo Sarpi's subversive *Historia del Concilio tridentino*, first printed in England in 1619 and translated into English the following year. Milton read this work carefully, taking down 13 excerpts in his commonplace book in the 1640s.[45] Sarpi, that "great unmasker of the *Trentine* Councel" (YP 2:501), had argued that the body was packed with pro-papal agents and excluded reformers. The Holy See had set out to centralize and buttress its power, and the Council's verdicts were therefore foregone conclusions. This charge supplied Sarpi with the evidence he needed to invest the secular magistrate with ultimate authority.[46] Milton draws the obvious analogy between Trent and the Westminster Assembly at line 14, though since it was Parliament that had appointed the Assembly some of the blame for its performance inevitably falls on the superior authority. Parliament, in the contemptuous estimation of the Scottish Presbyterians, was itself packed with "lawyers...making it their work to spoile our Presbyterie, not so much upon conscience, as upon fear that the Presbyterie spoile their mercat, and take up the most of the countrey-pleas without law." They left it to their stooge in the Assembly, Coleman, "a professed Erastian; a man reasonably learned, but stupid and inconsiderate, half a pleasant, and of small estimation," or in the derisive words of Gillespie, a mere "Parliament parasite," to voice their interests.[47] Milton does seem to be sensitive to these charges—his recent appeals to Parliament on the questions of divorce and prepublication censorship would have taught him a lesson in political frustration—and he conveys that sensitivity by showing how easily power can oppress.

The "Trent" and "Parliament" rhyme unlocks a register of meaning that runs throughout the poem. Rhyme words are constantly juxtaposed ironically: the *b* rhyme, for instance, neatly demonstrates the mutation of the Presbyterian mindset. Although the ministers may have held the best of intentions when they terminated the old Laudian liturgy, they have become corrupted by the possibility of plurality and, to protect their newfound wealth, must consolidate their power in a repressive hierarchy. Later in the sonnet, the pairing of "Paul" and "Scotch what d' ye call" emphasizes just how far apart Presbyterian visions of church government are from apostolic practice. Presbyterian ministers have been called to the priesthood by the lure of power and wealth; their vocation contrasts immediately with the calling of Paul to preach the Gospel. This rhyme interlocks with another that turns on the same principle. Readers are meant to understand that the word "Hereticks" is but an epithet that brands the opposition as illegitimate. It is simply one of the "tricks" of the Presbyterians, a neat summary of a point that Milton argues at greater length in *Areopagitica* and will later generalize in *Of Civil Power*.[48]

With this technique, Milton superimposes an ironic counterpoint over the explicit and usually straightforward meaning of the lines of verse. This pattern reaches its fullest potential in the sonnet's tails as Milton overlays the two parts of the poem's conclusion with a rhyme that links them. The accumulated energy of Milton's attack is compressed into three lines ending with the words "Shears," "Ears," and "Fears." With the first two of these words Milton echoed a particularly significant passage in *Lycidas:*

> But the fair Guerdon when we hope to find,
> And think to burst out into sudden blaze,
> Comes the blind *Fury* with th' abhorred shears,
> And slits the thin-spun life. But not the praise,
> *Phœbus* repli'd, and touch'd my trembling ears.
>
> (*Lycidas* 73–77)

Ears, the organs of poetic inspiration, become the primary sites of mental and spiritual renewal in both poems.[49] At a moment of vocational crisis in *Lycidas*, Phoebus Apollo redirects the young bard toward a humbler, but more profound, poetic mission whose value is known perhaps only to God. In retrospect, that mission could include, as Milton describes it in the headnote to *Lycidas* that he wrote for the 1645 edition, prophesying "the ruine of our corrupted Clergy then in their height." In the revised version of "New Forcers," Milton grants his enemies a single reprieve from his verbal onslaught in the final lines of the poem. For a moment, it seems as though accommodation may be possible even with Presbyterian zealots. Parliament will preserve their ears, as if they, too, might be converted and hear the voice of reason. But the half-line ending in "Fears" completes the triplet and returns the poem to its previous theme.

In the mid-1640s, Milton seems to have reflected on his vocation, both past and future, and concluded that politics had forced his poetry to respond. While "New Forcers" draws boundaries between legitimate and illegitimate exercise of authority, between individual conscience and outward obedience, and between criticism and libel, it ultimately collapses those distinctions. This collapse is unavoidable for Milton, since by calling on Parliament to tame clerical power he aligns himself with the Erastian position that the church ought to be subject to the state's authority. There is simply no way to guarantee that Parliament will not itself follow the Assembly's easy slippage from legitimate exercise of authority to tyranny. Parliament, as the people's representative, would seem to be a better protector of individual conscience, although Milton does not make that argument explicitly in the sonnet. Indeed, argumentation cannot be Milton's primary reason for writing the poem, despite what appears on its surface to be a philippic. The sonnet was not printed until 1673, long after the crisis, when Milton collected a number of his unpublished poems to be included with a reissue of his 1645 collection. Milton's purpose in writing "New Forcers" is surely not to name and print heretics, as his opponents have done, but to probe the outer boundaries of his poetic voice.

His exploration of that voice in one of his first overtly political poems leads to a number of implications for Milton's poetic practice. Implicitly, the sonnet asks how far a poem can represent a contemporary political subject and still remain a poem.[50] As it happened, the political sonnet would be the principal (and with psalm translations, almost the only) form of Milton's poetic expression during the period 1645–58, if we can believe Edward Philips's assertion via John Aubrey that he began *Paradise Lost* "about 2 yeares before the king came-in."[51] These years were ones of major life changes for Milton, including the births of his children, the deaths of his father and two wives, blindness, and an increasingly burdensome workload. (By 1656, a blind Milton was left responsible for the bulk of the Protectorate's international correspondence, provoking the Swedish ambassador to grumble about the backlog because no one in the English foreign office could "write a decent line of Latin" except for Milton.)[52] It is not surprising that Milton's time for poetry was limited and what he did write took on the themes and even the rhetorical characteristics of his formal occupation.

But what Milton stumbled upon while writing "New Forcers" was not simply an outlet in verse for political frustration. One of the effects of turning toward poetry during this crisis was to prod Milton to reevaluate some of the youthful themes contained in the volume of poems he was preparing for the press in 1645. *Comus* offered one model for thinking through the challenges youthful idealism faced in a hostile world. But if heaven did not stoop to help feeble virtue, humans and their institutions would have to do it.[53] The next phase of Milton's career explores the possibilities and the dangers of this endeavor. He transforms the state into no less than a spiritual force that protects virtuous action even as his poems delay any final resolution. There is always more to be done, as at the end of his sonnet to Cromwell, in which Milton entreats him to "helpe us to save free Conscience from the paw / Of hireling wolves whose Gospell is their maw" (Sonnet 16, 13–14). The heroes of "New Forcers" and the political sonnets that would follow move in the twilight space just beyond temporal constraints. They are both timeless, romantic representations of political power, exempla of classical martial prowess (Cromwell and Fairfax) or of Roman senatorial eloquence (Vane), and they are also contemporary, and therefore corruptible, humans. They exist at the meeting point of poetry and history, on the cusp of what Sidney might call the point at which the author needs to decide whether he affirmeth nothing or something.

In "New Forcers," Milton is exploring the possibility of having it both ways. The state fascinates him because it seems to be an exception to every other human institution. It is charged, in Milton's estimation, not only with guaranteeing the civil order but also with protecting the freedom of all citizens so that they can best cultivate the "innerman." As such, it is special, set apart from every other human institution.[54] It does not merely discharge secular power since by delimiting clerical authority it effectively subordinates the church to the civil magistrate. Like God, the state is supreme and immortal, but unlike him, it is mutable. By the late 1650s, Milton would observe the English state's fragility firsthand as the Protectorate crumbled after Cromwell's death. The state may be immortal, but it needed to be represented under the guise of a hero. That hero must be exceptional, but the very fact that the state depended on such a representation rendered it unstable. In "New Forcers," the exceptional heroes who endeavored to reinstill godliness in the English church have themselves lost that exceptionality and become utterly conventional copies of Laud. Milton's relentless logic, though, forces him to think obliquely about what could happen if Parliament lost its exceptionality in a similar manner.

"New Forcers," as a highly compressed rhetorical space even for a poem that spills past its generic boundaries, provides Milton the opportunity to do so. It is through the rhetorical and generic innovation of this poem that Milton probes his concern about Parliament's exercise of supreme power. (As we have seen, an early draft that called for Parliament to cut off the Presbyterians' ears, just as Laud had ordered done to Prynne, had to be emended.) Parliament is not nor can it ever be exactly like the godlike force that Milton imagines. This central problem of politics becomes a problem of poetic form that Milton chooses to address by means of the unconventional tailed sonnet. The tails, in particular, are revealing. Parliament both wields the shears of state and heals the ears of self-aggrandizing ministers with a regenerative touch. It combines the roles of the Fury (or the Fate) and Apollo in *Lycidas*. The state exists both at a specific moment in history as it intervenes in the lives of its citizens and throughout history as an ageless presence.

The state, in Milton's imagination, is both an artifact, a creation of human rhetoric, and the creator of the conditions under which that rhetoric can exist. It is thus entirely appropriate that the subject of poetry should be taken from secular history, although the focus in "New Forcers" on immediate causes rather than ultimate ones may explain the occasionally clumsy results. The unoriginal repetition of "whore" (3) and "abhorr'd" (4), for instance, or the inability to stay within the confines of the genre may be symptoms of this poem's uncertainty about how, exactly, politics is best represented in verse. The representation of Erastianism posed a further difficulty, since the position of an Erastian who promoted religious liberty would have seemed at times out of place among the likes of Prynne. Milton's sonnet wrestles with this inherent problem that constantly threatened to pull its logic apart. How can state control of the church ever truly guarantee freedom for dissenting consciences when those who would invoke the state do so in order to promote orthodoxy?

"New Forcers" is not the first poem in which Milton confronts the conflict between history and poetry, but it does seem to be the first in which Milton wonders whether the ends of poetry are subordinate to those of history.[55] At the conclusion of *Lycidas*, the bard can be assured that he can go "to morrow to fresh Woods, and Pastures new" (193), having overcome (or repressed?) his earlier trepidation at the failure of the muse of epic poetry, Calliope, to save her son Orpheus. The revivifying power of poetry makes *Lycidas* a poem of constant renewal. Neither the intervention of the "dread voice" (132) with its indictment of the corrupt clergy nor the fact that Lycidas's physical body cannot be found dilutes the efficacy of verse. But as Milton explores the dangerous symmetry between divine power and state power in "New Forcers," it becomes harder to locate the restorative function of verse. The dread voice now speaks for the entirety of the poem, and there can be no call for the muse to return. The moment of poetry is long, while historical particularity is short. Celebrating the state as a hero is one way to attempt to collapse the distance, but as Milton makes Parliament synonymous with the everlasting state, he joins the work of the poet to that of the civil magistrate. By the end of the poem, the pronouns almost unconsciously reflect this change: "we do hope" (13); "our just Fears" (18). The balancing act in this poem is a delicate one, but ultimately the poetic voice is merged with that of the political rhetorician.

Milton's original motive in writing "New Forcers" may have been to see how well poetry was up to the task of defending freedom of conscience, but at least by the time he had begun to revise it he had found perhaps a more interesting reason for writing. Poetry is the ideal space for Milton to assert a position and to deconstruct it at the same time. By making the contemporary state speak in the voice of the poet and as an adversary of the Presbyterians, he effectively removes the state's exceptionality. Milton merely asserts that Parliament is currently stronger than the Assembly of Divines, and with that assertion he finds a place for poetry in understanding the nature of state power. Poetry, too, is produced by historical event. It can be a medium to think through the categories that bind and divide a society, although that thought process ultimately results in Milton needing to take a side in a political conflict rather than claim a poet's prerogative to remain beyond it. His sonnet exemplifies the poetics of tactics rather than a more "Miltonic" poetics of principle. "New Forcers," while clearly a satirical production that shares much with Milton's two sonnets on *Tetrachordon*, is also the first of his bold political sonnets to attempt to find a proper voice for representing heroism and state authority in nonpanegyric verse. In 1645, Milton found himself attracted to the Erastians in Parliament and at the same time keenly aware of the delicacy of his argument. In pamphlet warfare, Milton nearly always runs for the moral high ground. But when there was none to be had, when he simply felt compelled to assert the overriding power of Parliament to dominate his foes, he explored the possibilities of Erastianism, an Erastianism that, it became clear to him, could only be expressed poetically.

Yale University

Notes

I wish to thank David Quint, John Rogers, the members of the Pomerium Working Group at Yale University, attendees of the 2013 Conference on John Milton at Murfreesboro, Tennessee, and an anonymous reader for *Milton Studies* for their incisive and generous criticism of this essay.

1. Letter 31, Moses Wall to Milton, in *Complete Prose Works of John Milton*, 8 vols., ed. Don M. Wolfe et al. (New Haven, Conn., 1953–82), 7:510. All citations from Milton's prose are from this edition, hereafter cited in the text as YP. The letter is dated May 26, 1659, but may have been written in March.

2. On the relationship of church and state under the Protectorate, see Blair Worden, "Toleration and the Cromwellian Protectorate," in *Persecution and Toleration: Papers Read at the Twenty-Second Summer Meeting and the Twenty-Third Winter Meeting of the Ecclesiastical History Society*, ed. W. J. Sheils, 199–233 (Oxford, 1984), repr. in Blair Worden, *God's Instruments: Political Conduct in the England of Oliver Cromwell* (Oxford, 2012), 63–90.

3. See, for instance, Tom Webster, *Godly Clergy in Early Stuart England: The Caroline Puritan Movement, c. 1620–1643* (Cambridge, 1997), 333–38; Gary S. De Krey, *London and the Restoration, 1659–1683* (Cambridge, 2005); John Coffey, *John Goodwin and the Puritan Revolution: Religion and Intellectual Change in Seventeenth-Century England* (Woodbridge, 2006); and Alexandra Walsham,

Charitable Hatred: Tolerance and Intolerance in England, 1500–1700 (Manchester, 2006). For the European context, see Benjamin J. Kaplan, *Divided by Faith: Religious Conflict and the Practice of Toleration in Early Modern Europe* (Cambridge, Mass., 2007). The last decades of the seventeenth century were something of a turning point, led by writers in the United Provinces and Locke in England. See John Marshall, *John Locke, Toleration and Early Enlightenment Culture: Religious Toleration and Arguments for Religious Toleration in Early Modern and Early Enlightenment Europe* (Cambridge, 2006).

4. On Wall's career and his relationship with Milton, see Noel Malcolm, "Moses Wall: Millenarian, Tolerationist, and Friend of Milton," *Seventeenth Century* 27 (2012): 25–53.

5. For accounts of these conflicts, see Murray Tolmie, *The Triumph of the Saints: The Separate Churches of London, 1616–1649* (Cambridge, 1977), 85–143; George Yule, *Puritans in Politics: The Religious Legislation of the Long Parliament, 1640–1647* ([Appleford], 1981), esp. 132–207; Keith Lindley, *Popular Politics and Religion in Civil War London* (Aldershot, 1997); and Ann Hughes, *"Gangraena" and the Struggle for the English Revolution* (Oxford, 2004).

6. John Milton, "On the New Forcers of Conscience under the Long Parliament," line 20, in *The Complete Works of John Milton*, vol. 3, *The Shorter Poems*, ed. Barbara Kiefer Lewalski and Estelle Haan (Oxford, 2012). All citations from Milton's short poems are from this volume, hereafter cited in the text. Janel Mueller, "The Mastery of Decorum: Politics as Poetry in Milton's Sonnets," *Critical Inquiry* 13 (1987), argues that "Milton accords total priority to freedom of conscience in matters of religion throughout this sonnet" (496), while Barbara Kiefer Lewalski, *The Life of John Milton: A Critical Biography*, rev. ed. (2000; repr., Oxford, 2003), asserts that "Milton takes on the role of spokesman...for the Independent tolerationist cause" in this poem (205). While Milton clearly disapproves in the poem of the forcing of consciences, he subordinates that position to the need for an Erastian church settlement. Much less plausible, for reasons I explain below, is Anna K. Nardo's argument in *Milton's Sonnets and the Ideal Community* (Lincoln, Neb., 1979), that the sonnet advocates "the separation of church and state" (9).

7. See Arthur E. Barker, *Milton and the Puritan Dilemma, 1641–1660* (Toronto, 1942), 220–59, esp. 236–59. Recent works that focus on Milton and toleration include Sharon Achinstein, *Literature and Dissent in Milton's England* (Cambridge, 2003); *Milton and Toleration*, ed. Sharon Achinstein and Elizabeth Sauer (Oxford, 2007); Phillip J. Donnelly, *Milton's Scriptural Reasoning: Narrative and Protestant Toleration* (Cambridge, 2009); Catherine Gimelli Martin, *Milton*

among the Puritans: The Case for Historical Revisionism (Burlington, Vt., 2010), esp. 305–17; and Angela Balla, "Wars of Evidence and Religious Toleration in Milton's *Samson Agonistes*," *Milton Quarterly* 46 (2012): 65–85.

8. For an overview of Berni's development of this genre, see Guillaume Bernardi, "Le sonnet bernesque," in *Le Sonnet à la Renaissance: des origines au XVIIe siècle,* ed. Yvonne Bellenger (Paris, 1988), 195–204. Jean Dubu, "Le *sonetto caudato* de Michel-Ange à Milton," in Bellenger, *Le Sonnet à la Renaissance*, 111–18, offers some correspondences between Milton's "New Forcers" and a *sonetto caudato* of Michelangelo.

9. This argument shares some of the features of the thesis of Gordon Teskey's *Delirious Milton: The Fate of the Poet in Modernity* (Cambridge, Mass., 2006), though, as I argue, Milton's participation in the act of creation occurs not only or perhaps even principally in an aesthetic dimension, but in a profoundly historical one as well.

10. David Masson, *The Life of John Milton: Narrated in Connexion with the Political, Ecclesiastical, and Literary History of His Time,* 7 vols. (London, 1859–94), 3:466–71.

11. Thomas Edwards, *Gangraena; or, A Catalogue and Discovery of Many of the Errours, Heresies, Blasphemies and Pernicious Practices of the Sectaries of This Time* (London, 1646), 34, and *The Second Part of Gangraena; or, A Fresh and Further Discovery of the Errors, Heresies, Blasphemies, and Dangerous Proceedings of the Sectaries of This Time* (London, 1646), 9.

12. Robert Baylie, *A Dissuasive from the Errours of the Time* (London, 1645), 116.

13. William Riley Parker, *Milton: A Biography*, 2 vols., 2nd ed., ed. Gordon Campbell (1968; repr., Oxford, 1996), 1:301–02, 2:928n33; Gordon Campbell, *A Milton Chronology* (Basingstoke, 1997), 86; Lewalski, *Life of Milton*, 205–06; and Gordon Campbell and Thomas N. Corns, *John Milton: Life, Work, and Thought* (Oxford, 2008), 168.

14. John T. Shawcross, "Of Chronology and the Dates of Milton's Translation from Horace and the *New Forcers of Conscience*," *SEL* 3 (1963): 77–84. Shawcross builds on James Holly Hanford, "The Arrangement and Dates of Milton's Sonnets," *Modern Philology* 18 (1921): 475–83, who speculatively dated "New Forcers" to the summer of 1646. There is, however, a note in the Trinity manuscript in Milton's hand stating that "New Forcers" should come after his sonnet, "A book was writ," suggesting, according to Parker's reasoning, that it comes before his sonnet to Henry Lawes, dated February 9, 1646. See Parker, *Milton: A Biography*, 2:928n33. The manuscript evi-

dence seems to me to be ambiguous and not strong enough to provide a reasonable guess at a precise date.

15. *A Variorum Commentary on the Poems of John Milton*, vol. 2, *The Minor English Poems*, ed. A. S. P. Woodhouse and Douglas Bush (New York, 1972), 2:509.

16. John Milton, *Complete Shorter Poems*, 2nd ed., ed. John Carey (London, 1997), 298–300; *The Complete Poetry and Essential Prose of John Milton*, ed. William Kerrigan, John Rumrich, and Stephen M. Fallon, 163–65 (New York, 2007); Lewalski and Haan, *Complete Works*, 3:505; John Milton, *Complete Shorter Poems*, ed. Stella P. Revard (Chichester, 2009), 314, which dates the poem ca. 1646–47; and *Milton's Selected Poetry and Prose: Authoritative Texts, Biblical Sources, Criticism*, ed. Jason P. Rosenblatt (New York, 2011), 75.

17. On Edwards's construction of this dichotomy, see Hughes's masterful account, *"Gangraena" and the Struggle*.

18. See *The Minutes and Papers of the Westminster Assembly, 1643–1652*, 5 vols., ed. Chad Van Dixhoorn (Oxford, 2012), 2:493–517, 664–80; 3:51–87, 274–78, 421–25, 558–59, 603, 616–27; 5:193–97, 210–11, and Robert S. Paul, *The Assembly of the Lord: Politics and Religion in the Westminster Assembly and the "Grand Debate"* (Edinburgh, 1985), 249–313, 478.

19. The reference to *Antapologia* rather than to *Gangraena* was first proposed by Thomas Warton in his 1785 edition of Milton's poems. See John Milton, *Poems upon Several Occasions, English, Italian, and Latin, with Translations*, ed. Thomas Warton (London, 1785), 328n. I am also in agreement (below) with Warton's guess that "Scotch what d' ye call" could refer to George Gillespie.

20. Thomas Goodwin, Philip Nye, Sidrach Simpson, Jeremiah Burroughs, and William Bridge, *An Apologeticall Narration, Humbly Submitted to the Honourable Houses of Parliament* (London, 1643), 24.

21. See, for instance, Thomas Edwards, *Antapologia; or, A Full Answer to the Apologeticall Narration* (London, 1644), 191.

22. Why Milton used initials here when the surname "Steuart" would appear to scan as two syllables is not clear. The argument that Milton only knew him by these initials is unconvincing. David Loewenstein, "The War against Heresy in Milton's England," in *Milton Studies*, vol. 47, ed. Albert C. Labriola, 185–218 (Pittsburgh, 2008), points out that these initials allow Milton a pun on "mere ass." Could "A. S." be an amanuensis's error for "A. H."? A reference to Alexander Henderson, who preached before Parliament and served as one of the

four Scottish commissioners in the Assembly, would in some ways fit better in this poem. In this case, substituting his initials for his trisyllabic surname would allow the line to scan.

23. *Album studiosorum Academiae Lugduno Batavae* MDLXXV–MDCCCLXXV, ed. Guilielmus du Rieu (The Hague, 1875), xlii. Steuart was hired to replace Franciscus du Ban, who had died in 1643.

24. The Trinity manuscript version of the poem is transcribed in Lewalski and Haan, *Complete Works*, 3:571. On another possible motivation for revising this line, see Donald C. Dorian, "'On the New Forcers of Conscience,' Line 17," *Modern Language Notes* 56 (1941): 62–64, who argues that Milton suggests that the Presbyterian clergy should consider themselves fortunate if they are not ejected from ministry since Levites needed to be free from physical deformities.

25. William Prynne, *Independency Examined, Unmasked, Refuted, by Twelve New Particular Interrogatories* (London, 1644), 6. Thomason dated his copy September 26.

26. William Prynne, *Truth Triumphing over Falshood, Antiquity over Novelty* (London, 1645), sig. [A5]r. The date is Thomason's.

27. William Prynne, *A Vindication of Foure Serious Questions of Grand Importance* (London, 1645), 10 (mispaginated as p. 2). Thomason dated his copy October 3.

28. On Prynne's changing views on the Scottish Presbyterians, see William M. Lamont, *Marginal Prynne, 1600–1669* (London, 1963), 149–74, who argues that Prynne had become disgusted with them by 1645 for failing to bring about the moral reform they had promised.

29. Letter to William Spang, Sept. 5, 1645, in *The Letters and Journals of Robert Baillie, A.M.*, 3 vols., ed. David Laing (Edinburgh, 1841), 2:315.

30. *The Journal of Thomas Juxon, 1644–1647*, ed. Keith Lindley and David Scott (Cambridge, 1999), 113–14.

31. Van Dixhoorn, *Minutes and Papers*, 4:85.

32. Letter for Scotland, Apr. 24, [1646], in Baillie, *Letters*, 2:366. Narrative accounts of these months can be found in Mark A. Kishlansky, *The Rise of the New Model Army* (Cambridge, 1979), 76–102; Robert Brenner, *Merchants and Revolution: Commercial Change, Political Conflict, and London's Overseas Traders, 1550–1653* (Cambridge, 1993), 473–75; and Hughes, *"Gangraena" and the Struggle*, 343–47. For the individuals behind the petitions, see Michael Mahony, "Presbyterianism in the City of London, 1645–1647," *Historical Journal* 22 (1979): 93–114. For the Assembly debates relating to these events and the petition, see Van Dixhoorn, *Minutes and Papers*, 4:22–29, 54–55, 82–97; 5:300–02.

33. George Gillespie, *A Sermon Preached before the Right Honourable the House of Lords...upon the 27th of August, 1645* (London, 1645), 16.

34. James Nalton, *Delay of Reformation Provoking Gods Further Indignation* (London, 1646), 38.

35. In using "adjure" in a sense very close to the Latin, Milton is not out of step with the English usage of his contemporaries. Although in some contexts in the 1640s "adjure" clearly means "to entreat" or "to command" (as when Milton uses the word in *The Reason of Church-Government* [YP 1:847]), a more literal meaning was also common. See, for instance, I. B., *An English Expositor: Teaching the Interpretation of the Hardest Words Used in Our Language* (London, 1641), s.v. "adjure," which is defined as follows: "To binde by oath: to make one to sweare"; and the paraphrase of Song of Solomon 2:7 in John Cotton, *A Brief Exposition of the Whole Book of Canticles, or, Song of Solomon* (London, 1642): "I adjure you, that is, I cause you to sweare by the Roes, and by the Hinds of the field, not by them as the persons thou art to sweare by, but by those for whose sake, and by whose means they are to take themselves bound as by a solemne oath" (59).

36. Sharon Achinstein, "John Milton and the Communities of Resistance, 1641–42," in *Writing and Religion in England, 1558–1689: Studies in Community-Making and Cultural Memory*, ed. Roger D. Sell and Anthony W. Johnson (Farnham, 2009), 289–304, argues convincingly that Milton did not clearly display loyalties to specific religious communities in the early 1640s, partly because of his "pastoral minimalism" (299) and partly because Presbyterians and Independents were generally unwilling to draw sharp distinctions between themselves in print on issues of toleration and church government. By the middle of the decade, the landscape was becoming quickly polarized.

37. Thomas Coleman, *Hopes Deferred and Dashed* (London, 1645), 27.

38. Public letter, [1645], in Baillie, *Letters*, 2:307, 2:306.

39. Gillespie, *Sermon*, 15.

40. The three pamphlets are *A Brotherly Examination of Some Passages of Mr Colemans Late Printed Sermon* (London, 1645), printed with Gillespie's sermon of August 27, 1645; *Nihil respondes; or, A Discovery of the Extream Unsatisfactorinesse of Master Colemans Peece* (London, 1645); and *Male audis; or, An Answer to Mr. Coleman His Male dicis* (London, 1646). The compendium is *Aarons Rod Blossoming; or, The Divine Ordinance of Church-Government*

Vindicated (London, 1646). Gillespie's legacy in the Presbyterian church is largely tied to his anti-Erastian publications. A transcription of his epitaph in a collection of biographical memoranda assembled by Bishop White Kennett records that "Erastum germinante aaronis virga castigavit" (he rebuked Erastus with *Aaron's Rod Blossoming*). See BL Landsdowne MS 985, f. 10v., and *Works of Mr. George Gillespie*, 2 vols. (vols. 1–2 of *The Presbyterian's Armoury*), ed. W. M. Hetherington (Edinburgh, 1846), 1:xxxii.

41. [Alexander Forbes], *An Anatomy of Independency* (London, 1644). Patrick Forbes, a controversialist known to Baillie, has also been proposed as the author of this tract. See Keith L. Sprunger, *Dutch Puritanism: A History of English and Scottish Churches of the Netherlands in the Sixteenth and Seventeenth Centuries* (Leiden, 1982), 344n113.

42. For Milton's engagement in this sonnet, sometimes tinged with anti-Judaism, with the Hebrew Bible and with England's status as a second Israel, see Achsah Guibbory, "Israel and English Protestant Nationalism: 'Fast Sermons' during the English Revolution," in *Early Modern Nationalism and Milton's England*, ed. David Loewenstein and Paul Stevens (Toronto, 2008), 115–38.

43. *An Answer to a Booke Entituled An Humble Remonstrance* (London, 1641), 61. Simonds D'Ewes delivered a speech to Parliament on June 11, 1641, in which he argued that the postscripts were much later additions. See Simonds D'Ewes, *The Greeke Postscripts of the Epistles to Timothy and Titus Cleared in Parliament. And an Occasionall Speech Touching the Bill of Acapitation, or Poll-money* ([London], 1641). Milton had argued in 1641 that neither Timothy nor Titus was a bishop but, rather, "either an *Apostle*, or an *Apostles* extraordinary Vice-gerent, not confin'd to the charge of any place" (*Animadversions upon the Remonstrants Defence, against Smectymnuus* [YP 1:711]). He makes the same argument in *Of Prelatical Episcopacy* (see YP 1:625–26, 630–33). The Calvinist argument that the words *presbyteros* and *episkopos* are used interchangeably in the New Testament was common in Presbyterian apologies of the period. See, for example, [Robert Baillie], *Prelacie Is Miserie; or, The Suppressing of Prelaticall Government* (N.p., 1641 [1642]), 9 (mispaginated as p. 5).

44. See, for instance, the positions Milton will later stake out on the Irish (*Observations upon the Articles of Peace*), royalists (*The Readie and Easie Way to Establish a Free Commonwealth*), and Catholics (*Of True Religion*).

45. On the presence of Sarpi in the Commonplace Book, see Nigel Smith, "Milton and the Index," in *Of Paradise and Light: Essays on*

Henry Vaughan and John Milton in Honor of Alan Rudrum, ed. Donald R. Dickson and Holly Faith Nelson (Newark, Del., 2004), 101–22; and Thomas Fulton, *Historical Milton: Manuscript, Print, and Political Culture in Revolutionary England* (Amherst, Mass., 2010), 79–80. On Sarpi's *Historia,* see Frances A. Yates, "Paolo Sarpi's 'History of the Council of Trent,'" *Journal of the Warburg and Courtauld Institutes* 7 (1944): 123–43; and William J. Bouwsma, *Venice and the Defense of Republican Liberty: Renaissance Values in the Age of the Counter Reformation* (Berkeley and Los Angeles, 1968), 556–623.

46. For Sarpi's views on the relationship of ecclesiastical and secular power, see Clemente Maria Francescon, *Chiesa e stato nei consulti di fra Paolo Sarpi* (Vicenza, 1942); Gaetano Cozzi, *Paolo Sarpi tra Venezia e l'Europa* (Turin, 1979); David Wootton, *Paolo Sarpi: Between Renaissance and Enlightenment* (Cambridge, 1983); Corrado Pin, "'Qui si vive, con esempi, non con ragione': Paolo Sarpi e la committenza di Stato nel dopo-Interdetto," in *Ripensando Paolo Sarpi: atti del convegno internazionale di studi nel 450° anniversario della nascita di Paolo Sarpi,* ed. Pin, 343–94 (Venice, 2006); and *Paolo Sarpi: politique et religion en Europe,* ed. Marie Viallon (Paris, 2010).

47. Baillie, *Letters,* 2:360; and Gillespie, *Male audis,* sig. A3v.

48. For *Areopagitica,* see YP 2:543–45, and for *A Treatise of Civil Power,* see YP 7:247–55. For an overview of Milton's use of this term throughout his career, see Janel Mueller, "Milton on Heresy," in *Milton and Heresy,* ed. Stephen B. Dobranski and John P. Rumrich, 21–38 (Cambridge, 1998).

49. John Leonard, "'Trembling Ears': The Historical Moment of 'Lycidas,'" *Journal of Medieval and Renaissance Studies* 21 (1991): 59–81, argues that this passage alludes to the public disfigurement of Prynne and his fellow antiepiscopacy pamphleteers who lost their ears in 1637. An argument has also been made that these passages allude specifically to Henry Burton, who lost his ears with Prynne in 1637. See Geoffrey M. Ridden, "Henry Burton and a Possible Source for Milton's 'Lycidas' and 'On the New Forcers of Conscience,'" *Notes and Queries* 31 (1984): 319–20. Stella P. Revard, "'Lycidas,'" in *A Companion to Milton,* ed. Thomas N. Corns, 246–60 (Oxford, 2001) esp. 254–55, argues against this narrow reading, though she perhaps goes too far in discounting the link between these passages in *Lycidas* and "New Forcers." This passage does not have to be interpreted so narrowly in order to see the correspondences between *Lycidas* and "New Forcers," especially since Milton had added the anticlerical headnote to the former poem in 1645.

50. Janel Mueller, "The Mastery of Decorum," esp. 497, argues convincingly that seven sonnets that Milton wrote in the decade 1642–52 ask this question and ultimately revise an Aristotelian poetics that subordinates poetry to history and philosophy. For Mueller, "New Forcers" is a successful political poem because it manages to speak about a historical particularity as it also expounds general truths of political philosophy.

51. John Aubrey, *"Brief Lives," Chiefly of Contemporaries, Set Down by John Aubrey, between the Years 1669 and 1696*, ed. Andrew Clark, 2 vols. (Oxford, 1898), 2:69.

52. Quoted in Martin Dzelzainis, "Juvenal, Charles X Gustavus and Milton's Letter to Richard Jones," *Seventeenth Century* 9 (1994), 28.

53. Critics have noted that Milton characterizes the Presbyterians as sexual aggressors in general (they attempt "to seise the widdow'd whore Pluralitie" ["New Forcers," 3]) and of the purity of conscience specifically (they attempt "to force our Consciences" [6] and "ride us" [7]). On the innuendo in the poem, see Nardo, *Milton's Sonnets*, 105–06; and Mueller, "Mastery of Decorum,". 495.

54. Although this argument shares some terms with Carl Schmitt's definition of sovereignty as the unique ability to declare an exception, my argument here is closer to Hobbes's point that sovereignty is unitary and cannot be divided. It is therefore exceptional in this sense. On this issue, Milton and Hobbes may not be as far apart as is commonly thought. See Christopher N. Warren, "When Self-Preservation Bids: Approaching Milton, Hobbes, and Dissent," *English Literary Renaissance* 37 (2007): 118–50, for some correspondences between the two on the question of toleration. On the state of exception, see Carl Schmitt, *Political Theology: Four Chapters on the Concept of Sovereignty* (1922), trans. George Schwab (Chicago, 2005), 5; and Giorgio Agamben's elaboration, *State of Exception*, trans. Kevin Attell (Chicago, 2005).

55. Readings of Milton's sonnets as a body of work that probes the interaction of literature and history include Mary Ann Radzinowicz, *Toward "Samson Agonistes"* (Princeton, N.J., 1978); Nardo, *Milton's Sonnets*; and Annabel Patterson, *Early Modern Liberalism* (Cambridge, 1997), 62–89.

INDEX

abstinence. *See* chastity
Ab urbe condita (Livy), 218–19, 234n25
Achinstein, Sharon, 210
Act of Indemnity and Oblivion, 181, 182, 184, 185
Acts of Grace, 180–81, 184–85. *See also* pardon
Adam: introduction of, 92; knowledge and, 56, 61, 63, 72, 77–78; labor and, 104–05, 107; as natural theologian, 61; pardon of, 178, 179, 189–92, 194–96, 197–99; reason of, 62–63, 70; science and, 64–65, 72–74; supplication and, 126–29, 130–33; and temptation of Eve, 102–04; tending and, 93–95. *See also Paradise Lost* (Milton)
Addison, Joseph, 149, 153
Ad Patrem (Milton), 157
Advancement of Learning, The (Bacon), 66, 82n38
Aeneid (Virgil), 116–17
agriculture, 92, 93
Akenside, Mark, 150
Anatomy of Melancholy, The (Burton), 17, 40
Andrewes, Lancelot, 209
animals, 64, 82n35
Antapologia (Edwards), 242, 263n19
Antidote against Atheism, An (More), 61–62, 64
Apologeticall Narration, An (anon.), 242, 251
Appletree, Thomas, 203n9
Areopagitica (Milton), 252, 254
Aristotle, 81n27, 144n31
Arne, Thomas Augustine, 152–53, 163
Aspden, Suzanne, 153
assizes, 189–90, 205n47
astrology, 7–8, 9, 12
"astro-theology," 59
attendre, 91
Aubrey, John, 256

Auden, W. H., vii–viii, xin1
Augustine, 179

Bacon, Anthony, 205n42
Bacon, Francis, 54, 60, 82n38; on assizes, 190, 205n47; God in, 66–67, 73; humility in, 66; pride in, 55
Baillie, Robert, 241, 250, 251
Barrough, Philip, 18, 25
Barrow, Samuel, 149
Baxter, Richard, 56, 57, 64, 65; animals in, 82n35; on education, 80n16; love in, 76, 77; Milton vs., 80n12
Bentley, Richard, 58–59, 68, 81n22, 83n31
Berni, Francesco, 240
Blessington, Francis, 116, 117
Bloody Code, 178
Book of Common Prayer, 245
Boyle, Robert, 56, 59, 65
Boyle Lectures, 58, 71
Bradwell, Stephen, 22, 25, 27
Breasted, Barbara, 6, 7
Bridgewater, Earl of, 6
Bright, Timothy, 20
Brill, Sara, 118
Broaddus, James, 28–29
Brome, Richard, 17, 40
Brown, Cedric, 39
Burchiello, 240
Burney, Charles, 152, 153
Burrow, Colin, 138
Burton, Henry, 267n49
Burton, Robert, 17, 19, 23–25, 30, 35–37
Bye Plot, 192

Calvin, John, 179
Calvinism, 209
Cambridge Platonism, 54, 61–62, 71, 74
caritas, 78
Castlehaven scandal, 6

269

270 Index

Castro, Roderigo à, 29
Catholicism, 35–36
ceremonial devotion, 179–80
Chamberlain, John, 197
Charles I, King of England, 182, 187, 188, 209, 214, 231n6
Charles II, King of England, 181, 184
chastity: in *The Doctrine and Discipline of Divorce*, 19; in *A Maske Presented at Ludlow Castle*, 24, 25, 37; of nuns, 35–36; paralysis in, 23; and suffocation of the mother, 4
chastity diseases: in Burton, 23; examples of, 5; in Jorden, 23–24; in *A Maske Presented at Ludlow Castle*, 22–26; Protestantism and, 35–36; symptoms in, 23. *See also* suffocation of the mother
Chaucer, Geoffrey, 150, 169
Christian Directory, A (Baxter), 57
Christian IV, King of Denmark, 208, 230n2
Claudian, 103
Coke, Edward, 201n6
Coke, John, 215, 233n21
Cole, Abdiah, 35
Coleman, Thomas, 250, 254
colere, in Virgil, 91
collective pardon, 180–81. *See also* pardon
Collins, William, 150
Compleat Midwifes Practice, The, 21, 32, 34
Comus (Arne), 152–53, 163, 171n14
Comus (Milton). *See A Maske Presented at Ludlow Castle*
"contend," 97–98
convulsions, 18–19
Cooper, Thomas, 91
Cornhill, Peter, 250
coronation pardons, 183–84. *See also* pardon(s)
Cortesi, Giovanni Battista, 30–31
Cosby, Arnold, 191
cosmology, 59–61
Council of Trent, 253
Counter-Reformation, 210
Cranfield, Lionel, 197, 199
Creaser, John, 6
Cromwell, Oliver, 257
Crooke, Helkiah, 17, 25, 30
Crotty, Kevin, 121
Crucifixion, 138
Cudworth, Ralph, 58, 75
Culpeper, Nicholas, 35
Culverwell, Nathaniel, 71, 73, 83n48
cura, in Virgil, 91
curare, in Virgil, 91
Cutler, Gervase, 16

Dalton, John, 163
Darwin, Charles, 81n29
Davis, Zemon, 193
De anima (Aristotle), 81n27
debt, 180–81
De conceptu et generatione hominis (Rüff), 32
De doctrina Christiana (Milton), 125
De praxi medica (Zacuto), 30
De raptu Proserpinae (Claudian), 103
Derham, William, 59
Descartes, René, 75
destruction, 97–98
devotion, 179–80
D'Ewes, Simonds, 250, 266n43
Dictionarium etymologicum Latinum (Holyoake), 99–100
Discoverie of Witchcraft (Scot), 20
divorce pamphlets, 241
Doctrine and Discipline of Divorce, The (Milton), 19, 36, 189, 190
Domesticall Duties (Gouge), 36
Donnelly, Phillip, 67
Drake, Francis, 218
Dryden, John, 149
Duran, Angelica, 81n23, 81n26
DuRocher, Richard, 93

Ecclesiastes, 65–66
education, 80n16
Edward Augustus, Duke of Albany and York, 147
Edwards, Karen, 68
Edwards, Thomas, 241–43, 247
Egerton, Alice, 5–6; birthdate of, 44n19; convulsions in, 18–19; and *A Maske Presented at Ludlow Castle*, 6–11, 41–42; under Napier's care, 9–16
Egerton, Frances, 16, 22
Egerton, John, 39, 41
Egerton, Magdalen, 7–8, 10–11, 13–16, 44n19
Eikon Basilike (Charles I), 182, 187
Eikonoklastes (Milton): foreign policy and, 210; pardon in, 178, 182, 187; submission in, 114; supplication in, 116
Elegant and Learned Discourse on the Light of Nature, An (Culverwell), 71
"Elegia quarta" (Milton), 207–10, 211, 230n4
Elegies (Jackson), 154–56, 157–58, 160–61, 169
Eliot, T. S., 84n53
Elizabeth I, Queen of England, 180, 194, 196, 203n9
empiricism, 84n56
Empson, William, 103, 113, 140n1, 145n36
Erastianism: of Milton, 247–58; Presbyterians and, 244–45; and separation of church and state, 237–38, 246, 249–50

Evans, J. Martin, 199
Eve: call for separation by, 95; introduction of, 92; labor and, 92–95; as natural theologian, 61; pardon of, 178, 179, 189–92, 194–96, 197–99; science and, 64–65; supplication and, 126–30, 132–33; temptation of, 99–104; tending and, 92–95. *See also Paradise Lost* (Milton)
Evelyn, John, 246
existence, 62
Expert Midwife (Rüff), 32, 34
eye, 81n29

Fairer, David, 150
Faithfull Shepheardesse (Fletcher), 40
Fall, the: action and, 99; agriculture and, 93; in Culverwell, 71; georgic mode and, 101–04, 105–06; intention and, 99; knowledge and, 71–72; labor and, 92, 93, 104–05, 110n36; in More, omission of, 71; natural theology and, 70–71; pardon and, 177–78; reason and, 61–62, 70; separation and, 90; Son and, 96; and temptation of Eve, 99–104
feast days, 211, 221–26, 231n7
"female seed," 4, 25
Fish, Stanley, 68, 82n39
Flannagan, Roy, 62
Fletcher, John, 17, 24, 40
Folly of Atheism, The (Bentley), 58, 68, 71, 83n41
Forbes, Alexander, 251
Forbes, Patrick, 266n41
Ford, John, 24, 40, 47n67, 52n129
foreign policy: in *Eikonoklastes*, 210; in "In quintum Novembris," 218–20; in *Of Reformation*, 210; in Thirty Years' War, 209–10, 213–14, 230n2, 232n18
Forestus, Petrus. *See* van Foreest, Pieter
forfeiture, pardon and, 198–99
Four Ages, The; Together with Essays on Various Subjects (Jackson), 172n23
Fowler, Alastair, 90, 129
France, 150, 183, 215–16
Frye, Roland Mushat, 102

Gadesden, William, 10
Gangraena (Edwards), 241, 242, 247, 263n19
General History of Music (Burney), 152
Genesis, book of, 93
George III, King of England, 147
georgic: accounts of use of, 89–90; didactic strain of, 92; the Fall and, 101–04, 105–06; Satan and, 97–98, 100–01, 107n2; "tend" and, 90–91, 92, 97; in Virgil, 90–91. *See also* modes, literary

Georgics (Virgil), 90–91, 109n22, 116, 144n34
Gerard, John, 105–06
Gillespie, George, 244, 248, 250–51, 254
Gillies, John, 60
glory, 82n32
Glover, Mary, 17, 22, 25
God: in Bacon, 66–67, 73; in Baxter, 57; in Bentley, 58–59; in "In quintum Novembris," 223–24; and knowledge, 63; knowledge of, 57; love and, 84n59; natural theology and, 55–56; nature and, 66–67; pardon and, 179, 185, 186–87, 191–92; in Ray, 66–67; reason and, 67–68; Son and, 136–37, 138–39; supplication and, 133, 134–40; truth and, 61
Goodman, Kevis, 92
Gouge, William, 36, 37
Gould, John, 142n15
Gowing, Laura, 31
grace, 70, 179, 185, 187
"Grateful Tribute, The" (Underwood), 148
Gray, Thomas, 150
Green, Monica, 33
greensickness, 5. *See also* chastity diseases
Guibbory, Achsah, 179–80, 191
gunpowder, 97
Gunpowder Plot, 210, 214–15, 223–24, 228–29, 233n19

Haan, Estelle, 208
Hale, John, 224–25, 235n32
Hall, John, 18–19, 34, 38, 180
Hamilton, Newburgh, 153
Handel, George Frideric, 152, 153
Harada, Jun, 143n27
Harley, David, 33
Hay, Douglas, 193–94
Hebrews, book of, 195
Henderson, Alexander, 263n22
Henry VII, King of England, 180
Herball (Gerard), 105–06
Herbert of Cherbury, 84n56
heroism, 116–17, 120
Hesiod, 90, 103, 104
hierarchy, 123, 125–26, 138, 144n33
Historia del Concilio tridentino (Sarpi), 253
historicity, 114, 141n2, 141n5
History of Britain, The (Milton), 189, 234n24
Hobbes, Thomas, 54, 268n54
Hogarth, William, 169
Holyoake, Francis, 100
Homer, 103, 116, 118–21, 129, 131
homicide, 185–86, 191
Hooker, Richard, 186
humility, 66, 71

humour, 25–29, 32
hysteria, 18

idolatry, 122, 123, 221
Iliad (Homer), 103, 116, 119–20, 121, 131
imago dei, 56–57
incisions, therapeutic, 8
Independents, 241, 242, 244, 246–51, 265n36
inequality, supplication and, 117–19
"In Memory of W. B. Yeats" (Auden), vii–viii, xin1
"In quintum Novembris" (Milton), 209; feast days and, 224–26; foreign policy in, 218–20; God in, 223–24; Satan in, 214–16, 217–21, 223, 225, 229; significance of, 211; Thirty Years' War and, 214–16
intention, 98–99, 109n22
"issues" (therapeutic incisions), 8

Jackson, William: in literary criticism, 150–51; on Milton, 151–52, 161–62; music and, 153–59; nationalism and, 159–60. *See also Lycidas* (Jackson)
James I, King of England, 183, 192, 197, 231n6
Jerusalem Delivered (Tasso), 151
Johnson, Anthony W., 265n36
Johnson, Samuel, 173n23
Johnson, Thomas, 27, 30
Jonson, Ben, 212–13
Jorden, Edward, 12, 17, 22, 23–24, 25, 30, 44n20
Juxon, Thomas, 246

Keats, John, 149
Kendrick, Christopher, 6
King, Edward, 148, 170n3
King, Helen, 31
kneeling, 123–25, 193
knowledge: Adam and, 56, 61, 63, 72, 77–78; in Bacon, 66; in Baxter, 76; creation and, 56; the Fall and, 71–72; of God, 57; God and, 63; love and, 76; in *Paradise Lost*, 63, 66
Knowledge and Love Compared (Baxter), 76

labor: Adam and, 104–05, 107; creation and, 97–98; in critical discussions, 90; destruction and, 97–98; Eve and, 92–95; the Fall and, 92, 93, 104–05, 110n36; in Hesiod, 104; "performance principle" and, 92; separation and, 89–90; tending and, 91–95; tragedy and, 106–07
Lambarde, William, 181
land forfeiture, 198–99
Laud, William, 243, 245, 258
Laudian, 37, 180, 242–43, 252, 254
Lawes, Henry, 39
leaching, 8

learning, 57, 66
"lees," 20–21
Lemnius, Levinus, 24
Leonard, John, 267n49
Lewalski, Barbara, 90, 102, 230n6, 261n6
light, in natural theology, 72
Lightfoot, John, 250
Linley, Elizabeth Ann, 161
Linley, Thomas, 155, 158, 161
Linley, Thomas (the younger), 161
Livy, 218–19, 234n25
Loewenstein, David, 114, 145n36
Louis XIII (King of France), 215
love, 76, 77, 84n59, 105
Lovers Melancholy, The (Ford), 24, 40, 47n67, 52n129
Low, Anthony, 107n2
Lucan, 142n9
Lycidas (Jackson): in Bath, 147–48, 153–54; debut of, 147; libretto of, 154, 172n16; Milton's version vs., 165–68; music of, 161; nationalism and, 149–53; swain in, 163–66, 168–69; targets of, 169–70
Lycidas (Milton), viii; Jackson's version vs., 165–68; Edward King and, 148, 170n3; "New Forcers" and, 254–55; poetry and, 258–59

MacDonald, Michael, 12
madrigals, 157, 158
Mandelbrote, Scott, 79n6, 81n17
Martz, Louis, 226
Mary Magdalene, 129
Maske Presented at Ludlow Castle, A (Milton): and chastity, 22–26, 37; Egerton and, 6–11, 41–42; in Jackson, 151; medical references in, 19, 21–22, 25; paralysis in, 20–21, 22; suffocation of the mother in, 4, 24–29; witchcraft in, 20–21; womb imagery in, 24–25
Masson, David, 240, 251
masturbation, 3, 4–5; medical ethics of, as treatment, 30–39; in medical literature, 30–31
materialism, 54
Matrimoniall Honour (Rogers), 37
Matthew, book of, 251
Maus, Katherine Eisaman, 24
McColley, Diane, 94
McGrady, Richard, 152, 155, 158
Mead, Joseph, 211, 213
measurement, 67
media, 211–12
medicine: astrology and, 7–8, 9, 12; masturbation in, 30–31; midwifery and, 33; relationships in, 7, 33; witchcraft and, 12

melancholy: in Egerton sisters, 14; menstruation and, 21; suffocation of the mother and, 19–20; witchcraft and, 20
menstruation: melancholy and, 21; in midwifery literature, 21; suffocation of the mother and, 4, 18, 19, 20, 21
Merchant of Venice, The (Shakespeare), 192
mercy, 178, 187. *See also* pardon(s)
Middlesex, Earl of. *See* Cranfield, Lionel
"midwife's cure." *See* masturbation
Midwives Book (Sharp), 18
Milton, John: arrest of, 181; and *Comus*, 163; Jackson on, 151–52, 161–62; as natural theologian, 54–58; as neglected genius, 162–63; pardon of, 179, 180–83, 200; poetry and, 149–50
Milton, John (works). *See individual works*
monarchy, 178, 201n6
Monthly Review, 147, 148, 172n16
More, Henry, 58, 61–63, 64, 67; Aristotle vs., 81n27; glory in, 82n32; omission of the Fall in, 71
Morgan, Charles, 230n2
"mother-fits," 9, 10, 13, 28, 35
Mountjoy, Lord, 193, 196
Mueller, Janel, 267n50
murder, 185–86, 191
music: Jackson and, 153–59; nationalism and, 152–54, 159–60; trends in, 156

Nalton, James, 248
Napier, Richard, 6, 7–16, 21
Napier, Richard (nephew), 16
nationalism: Jackson and, 159–60; music and, 152–54, 159–60; poetry and, 150–52
natural theology: in Bacon, 55; in Baxter, 56; in Boyle, 56; creation and, 56–57; defined, 54; empiricism and, 84n56; eye in, 81n29; the Fall and, 70–71; God and, 55–56; light in, 72; in Milton, 56–57; Milton in, 54–58; in More, 62–63; in *Paradise Lost*, 63; *Paradise Lost* and, 58–61; reason and, 67–78; science and, 54–56; theocentric vs. anthropocentric, 64
Neely, Carol Thomas, 23
"New Forcers" (Milton). *See* "On the New Forcers of Conscience under the Long Parliament" (Milton)
Newgate prison, 180
"New Science," 54
Newton, Isaac, 59, 81n22
Newton, Thomas, 103
Noli me tangere, 129
Northern Lasse, The (Brome), 17, 40–41
nuns, 35–36

Observations on the Present State of Music, in London (Jackson), 158, 160, 165, 172n15
Observations upon the Articles of Peace (Milton), 178, 187, 188
Observationum et curationum medicinalium libri (van Foreest), 3, 25, 34
"Ode on the Morning of Christ's Nativity" (Milton), 210–11, 226–29
Odyssey (Homer), 118–19, 129
Of Civil Power (Milton), 237–39, 254
Of Education (Milton), 57
Of Reformation (Milton), 124, 210, 252
On Christian Doctrine (Milton), 54, 56–57
O'Neill, Hugh, 193, 196
"On Genius" (Jackson), 161–62
"On Rhyme" (Jackson), 172n23
"On Taste" (Jackson), 151
"On the New Forcers of Conscience under the Long Parliament" (Milton): *Of Civil Power* and, 238–39; dating of, 240–47, 262n14; Edwards and, 241–43; and Erastianism, 249–50; Gillespie and, 250–51; *Lycidas* and, 254–55; Prynne and, 243–44; and separation of church and state, 249–50, 257–58; Steuart and, 243, 263n22; as tailed sonnet, 240
Ovid, 208, 225

Pandaemonium, 97
Pandora, 103, 104
Paradise Lost (Milton): Bentley and, 58–59; contract for, 173n33; cosmology and, 59–61; as deliberately misreadable, 141n7; devotion in, 179–80; as encyclopedia of literary modes, 90; in Jackson, 151; knowledge in, 63, 66; natural theology and, 58–61; pardon in, 177–79, 187–89; reason and, 61–63, 65–66, 67–78; science and, 63–64, 65, 76–77; supplication in, 113–14, 121–40; temptation of Eve in, 99–104; tragic mode in, 90. *See also* Adam; Eve; Satan
paralysis: in chastity diseases, 23; in *A Maske Presented at Ludlow Castle*, 20–21, 22; suffocation of the mother and, 18–19, 22–23, 38
pardon(s): in seventeenth century, 178–79; of Adam and Eve, 178, 179, 189–92, 194–96, 197–99; assizes and, 189–90, 205n47; authority of king to, 178, 201n6; collective, 180–81; coronation, 183–84; the Fall and, 177–78; forfeiture in, 198–99; God and, 179, 185, 186–87, 191–92; individual, 180, 192–99; intercessors in, 193–95; location of, 179,

202n9; in Milton, 187–89; of Milton, 179, 180–83, 200; motive and, 185–86; as political, 187–88; of Satan, 178, 179, 183–87, 192–93, 196–98, 199–200; in Shakespeare, 192; Son and, 177–78, 189–90, 191–92, 198; special, 180, 192–99; as spectacle, 192; submission and, 193–94; transportation (legal punishment) and, 199–200
Paré, Ambroise, 25, 27, 28, 29, 30
Passion, 138
"Passion, The" (Milton), 145n39, 211, 226
Patterson, Annabel, 89, 116
Paul, 54, 179
Pelling, Margaret, 33
Percy, Henry, 194
"performance principle," 92
Pharsalia (Lucan), 142n9
Philip II, King of England, 204n42
Phillips, Edward, 181, 256
physician-patient relationships, 7, 33
pity, 120–21, 126–27, 138
Platonism, 54, 61–62, 71, 74
Poems (Milton), 207–08
poetry: history and, 258–59; Jackson on, 151–52, 172n23; Milton and, 149–50; nationalism and, 150; supplication and, 116–17, 120–21
poison, 28–29
political favor-seeking, 116
pomander, 13
Pope, Alexander, 150, 234n25
Practice of Physick (Rivière), 28, 35
prayer, 116, 117
Presbyterians, 238–39, 242–55, 268n53
pride, 55
Primrose, James, 29
Principles and Duties of Natural Religion (Wilkins), 71
prison, 180
Protestantism, 35–36, 208, 209, 225
providence, 95–96
Prynne, William, 243–44, 250, 267n49
Psalm 14, 71
Purcell, Henry, 152, 156

Rajan, Balachandra, 57
Raleigh, Walter, 218
Ray, John, 57, 58, 65–67, 80n15, 81n29
Readie and Easie Way, The (Milton), 114
reason: of Adam, 62–63, 70; "fallen," 67–78; the Fall and, 61–62, 70; God and, 67–68; in More, 62–63; natural theology and, 54, 67–78; *Paradise Lost* and, 61–63, 65–66, 67–78, 71–72; passion and, 144n31; Satan and, 68; science and, 65–66

Reason of Church-Government, The (Milton), 149, 252
Reasons of the Christian Religion (Baxter), 56, 57, 64
redemption, 227–28
Reformation, 210
religious odes, 210–11, 231n7
Restoration, 179, 181
retained seed, 3, 19, 20, 28
Revard, Carter, 149
Revard, Stella, 120
rhyme, 157, 172n23, 254
Rich, Robert, 213
Richard III (Shakespeare), 99
Richardson, Jonathan, 181
Ricks, Christopher, 141n7
ritual, 179–80
Rivière, Lazare, 28, 35
Rogers, Daniel, 37
Rome, 218–19, 234n25
Romulus, 218, 234n25
Rosamond (Addison), 153
Rowe, Nicholas, 147
Rowland, William, 35
Royal Society, 55, 61, 71, 81n26; motto of, 74
Rüff, Edward, 32
Rumrich, John Peter, 80n12

Saint Augustine, 179
St. Mary Magdalene (Titian), 129
Saint Paul, 54, 179
Salmasius, Claudius, 169
Samson Agonistes (Milton), 81n29, 153, 172n14
Sarpi, Paolo, 253
Satan: georgic mode and, 97–98, 100–01, 107n2; as historical figure, 114; historicity of, 114, 141n2, 141n5; in "In quintum Novembris," 214–16, 217–21, 223, 225, 229; opening speech of, 113–14; pardon of, 178, 179, 183–84, 185, 186–87, 192–93, 196–98, 199–200; reason and, 68; Son and, 123, 124–25; supplication and, 113–15, 122–27, 133–34, 136–37; temptation of Eve by, 99–104; tending and, 91, 95–97, 99. *See also Paradise Lost* (Milton)
"Satan controversy," 141n2
scent therapy, 9–10, 13, 44n21
Schleiner, Winfried, 28–29, 30, 34
Schmitt, Carl, 268n54
science: Adam and, 64–65, 72–74; in Baxter, 56; in Boyle, 56; Milton in, 53–54; natural theology and, 54–56; *Paradise Lost* and, 63–64, 65, 76–77; pride and, 55; reason and, 65–66

Scodel, Joshua, 106
Scot, Reginald, 20, 21
Scotland, 216–17, 233n22, 244. *See also* Presbyterians
scrofula, 8, 10
Secret Miracles of Nature (Lemnius), 24
seed: "female," 4; as poison, 28–29; retained, 3, 19, 20, 28; semen as, 18; suffocation of the mother and, 18
Selden, John, 249, 250
semen, 18, 28, 29
Sennert, Daniel, 34
separation, 89–90, 95
Shafto, Michael, 194
Shakespeare, William: Jackson on, 151; *Merchant of Venice, The*, 192; nationalism and, 150; pardons in, 192; *Richard III*, 99; *Tempest, The*, 192; *Two Noble Kinsmen*, 17, 24, 40–41
Sharp, Jane, 18
Shawcross, John, 242
Shelley, Percy, 149
sigils, 13
Simmons, Samuel, 173n33
Skinner, Cyriack, 182, 203n18
Smectymnuus, 251–52
Sokol, B. J., 21, 24
Somerset, Earl of, 197
Son: the Fall and, 96, 177–78; God and, 136–39; pardon and, 177–78, 189–90, 191–92, 198; sacrifice of, 134–35, 144n28; Satan and, 123, 124–25; supplication of, 134–36, 139–40
sonetto caudato, 240
Soveraigne Power of Parliaments and Kingdomes, The (Prynne), 243
sovereignty, 268n54
Spain, 153
Spectator (Addison), 149
Spenser, Edmund, 150, 169
spontaneous generation, 68
Staple of News (Jonson), 212–13
Steuart, Adam, 243, 263n22
Strier, Richard, 144n33
Stubbe, Henry, 53
Stuteville, Martin, 211
submission: in *Eikonoklastes*, 114; pardon and, 193–94; supplication and, 123–25
suffocation of the mother: chastity and, 4; Egerton sisters and, 6–16; humour and, 25–29; in Jorden, 17, 44n20; in *A Maske Presented at Ludlow Castle*, 4, 24–29; masturbation as therapy for, 3, 4–5, 30–39; in medical literature, 3, 17, 35; melancholy and, 19–20; menstruation and, 4, 18, 19, 20, 21; origin of term, 9; paralysis in, 18–19, 22–23, 38; scent therapy for, 13; "seed" and, 18; symptoms of, 18–19; treatments for, 8–12; witchcraft and, 4, 6, 11–14, 16, 17–18, 19, 20–22. *See also* chastity diseases
superstition, 68
supplication: communication and, 115–16; creation and, 135; etymology of, 117; favor-seeking and, 116; God and, 133, 134–40; heroism and, 116–17, 120; hierarchy and, 123, 125–26; in Homer, 116, 118–21, 129, 131; idolatry and, 122; inequality and, 117–19; interaction and, 116, 117–19; kneeling and, 123–25; meaning of, 114–15; in *Paradise Lost*, 113–14, 121–40; pity and, 120–21; "poetics" of, 116–17; poetry and, 120–21; political, 116; prayer and, 116, 117; reciprocity and, 117–19, 127; Satan and, 113–14, 122–27, 133–34, 136–37; of Son, 134, 135–36, 139–40; in Virgil, 116–17
Survey of the Wisdom of God in Creation, A (Wesley), 58
Svendsen, Kester, 53, 54, 63–64

tailed sonnet, 240
Tamerlane (Rowe), 147
Tasso, Torquato, 151
teleology, 68
Tempest, The (Shakespeare), 192
"tempt," 99–100
temptation, 99–104
tendere, 91
"tend/tending": Adam and, 93–95; agriculture and, 92; Eve and, 92–95; georgic mode and, 90–91, 92, 97; as keyword, 91; labor and, 91–95; overview of use of, 89; and Satan, 91, 95–97, 99; semantics of, 91; and temptation of Eve, 99–104; in Virgil, 90–91
Tenure of Kings and Magistrates, The (Milton), 180
therapeutic incisions, 8
Thesaurus linguae Romanae & Brittanicae (Cooper), 91
Thirty Letters on Various Subjects (Jackson), 151, 161–62
Thirty Years' War: background of, 209; fears over, 211–14; foreign policy and, 209–10, 213–14, 230n2, 232n18; France in, 215–16; "In quintum Novembris" and, 214–16; in Milton's poetry, 209, 231n6; press and, 211–12; Spanish invasion and, 209–10, 212–14; *Staple of News* (Jonson) and, 212–13

Tillyard, E. M. W., 170n3
Tilmouth, Christopher, 144n31
Titian, 129
tragedy, 90
transportation (legal punishment), 199–200
Tristia (Ovid), 208
Twelve Songs (Jackson), 155, 159, 160–61
Two Noble Kinsmen, The (Fletcher & Shakespeare), 17, 24, 40–41
Tyringham, Anne, 10
Tyrone, Earl of. *See* O'Neill, Hugh

Underwood, Thomas, 148
"Upon the Circumcision" (Milton), 211, 226–27
Usefulness of Philosophy (Boyle), 56

van Foreest, Pieter, 3, 18, 25, 34
vapors, 18, 20
Vaughan, William, 20
venomous matter, 27–28
Virgil: *Georgics*, 90–91, 109n22, 110n36, 116, 144n34; Milton as, 151

Wall, Moses, 237, 238
Warton, Joseph, 150
Warton, Thomas, 150

Warwick, Earl of. *See* Rich, Robert
Weber, William, 152
Wesley, John, 58
Westminster Assembly, 245, 252
Whiston, William, 59
Whitelocke, Bulstrode, 250
Wilkins, John, 71
Winter, James, 33
Wisdom of God Manifested in the Works of Creation, The (Ray), 58, 66, 80n15
witchcraft: in *A Maske Presented at Ludlow Castle*, 20–21; medicine and, 12; melancholy and, 20; Napier and, 12; suffocation of the mother and, 4, 6, 11–14, 16, 17–18, 19, 20–22
womb imagery, 24–25
women, as patients, 33
"women's melancholy," 5, 23. *See also* chastity diseases; melancholy
Works and Days (Hesiod), 103

Yeats, William Butler, vii–viii
Young, Thomas, 207–08, 209

Zacuto Lusitano, Abraham, 30
Zerubbabel to Sanballat and Tobiah (Steuart), 243